FOX MATCH

Guide to

Commercial Fisheries

Contents

FOX MATCH GUIDE TO COMMERCIAL FISHERIES

First Published in 2006 by Fox International,
Fowler Road, Hainault Business Park,
Hainault, Essex. IG6 3UT.
United Kingdom

TEL. +44 (0) 208 559 8500
FAX: +44(0) 208 501 1655
E Mail: info@foxint.com
Web: www.foxint.com

ISBN: 0-9549238-4-7

Writing and Additional Photography by Tom Legge.

Designed and produced by the Creative Team at Fox International.

Introduction Bob Nudd

I don't think it's overstating the case to say that I and indeed most others who work in the angling industry owe our current positions to Commercial Stillwaters. They are the single most important reason why the sport is thriving.

If you turn the clock back 15 years, angling was slumping in popularity as once-productive rivers went into decline. Young blood was not coming into the sport in anything like former levels, due in part to the abundance of other modern attractions including TVs and computers, and also increased fears for their safety.

The main reason why commercial fisheries have proved so popular is the fact that they offer plenty of bites from hard fighting fish. But the surroundings also play a part. They're safe and secure - you know you car won't be broken into, and parents have peace of mind when they can drop their children off for the day. Plus there's cafes and toilets, a godsend for the ladies in our sport.

Ironically, many natural waters are now enjoying a comeback in terms of their stock levels. But commercials will remain first choice for the majority, and despite my well-known love of roach fishing I still tend to fish them at least twice a week - mainly in midweek series.

Barford Lakes near Norwich and Cross Drove near Lakenheath are my two current favourites, and there's a whole host more within half an hour's drive of my home in the Cambridgeshire Fens. But it wasn't always that way. In the mid-80s, I used to have to drive all the way to Willow Park near Aldershot to take part in a 'commercial' match. It was a real novelty back then to fish for tench and carp in matches, but I loved it and so did many others. Now we really are spoiled for choice.

Going back even further to the late 70s, when I lived in Essex, I used to love fishing Layer Pits near Colchester. Although this was and still is a club water rather than a commercial fishery, many of the modern day carp fishing techniques such as long range waggler and buoyant hook baits (we used to use Sugar Puffs sometimes!) were first developed here.

Today, there's a host of tackle specially designed for the rigours of hard fighting carp. Float and feeder rods have been beefed up accordingly, but the pole is the main weapon. You need a good strong pole, and can get them at surprisingly low prices, plus with as many top kits as you can afford to fit with different strengths and types of elastics. Although I work for

a different tackle company, I know the kit you'll see used within these pages will do the job. But above all, you need to remember that the best tackle in the world won't catch the fish for you.

Above all, it's how you feed and where you fish that brings success - on commercials or natural venues alike. I wish I had £1 for every pole cup or pot that's been sold. What an invention! Any angler really should learn to use these precision feeding devices to their best ability. Also, consider the weather and where the fish are likely to be feeding. Shallow or in deeper water? If you're not catching, ring the changes until you do.

One important piece of advice I'd give to any newcomer, especially on the match front, is to stick with fishing one or two venues until you know them really well. You can reach a point where you can beat other good anglers faster on commercial fisheries than on other types of water in my experience, and that can give you to confidence to branch out further afield afterwards.

When I was asked to provide the foreword to this book, I was delighted to accept. I've known the main contributor - Mark Pollard - for more than 20 years since we both worked for the late Terry Freeman at Browning. We did some of our early angling videos together, and straight away I could see that this young man was a class act.

It's hard to sum up what makes somebody really good at angling, but in Mark's case speed plus attention to detail are major factors. He made his name on canals, but he's such a fast learner and so adaptable so it's no surprise that he's had a lot of commercial fishery success - not to mention rivers - in recent times. Nowadays, he's a vital part of the Fox Match headquarters team and my captain at Van den Eynde Essex County. I'm surprised he's never achieved full England international honours. His sheer consistency across a variety of venues certainly suggests he'd be up to the task.

"One important piece of advice I'd give to any newcomer, especially on the match front, is to stick with fishing one or two venues until you know them really well"

I also know Derek Willan, who has also had a lot of input to the book, quite well from fishing festivals over in Ireland. Like most of the North West anglers he's very good on leger techniques, having grown up fishing for bream on natural lakes and dams. But if you check the match results in Angling Times these days you'll see Derek and his Manchester pals' names in the frame on commercial stillwaters in both the North West and North East. They've had to adapt in order to keep fishing big matches, and being good anglers they've learned the game fast.

Although we live in an era of fast moving information, via the internet, DVDs and multiple TV channels, books will never die. I love reading, whether it's the weekly or monthly angling magazines or books such as this one.

One thing's for sure - if this book manages to capture even a fraction of Mark Pollard and Derek Willan's combined angling knowledge, as I'm sure it will, then it's something you'll want to pick up and use as reference time and time again. Happy reading and Tight Lines!

Bob Nudd
Four times World Freshwater Angling Champion

Chapter 1

baits

Selecting the right baits to get the best from a visit to a Commercial Fishery can sometimes be the easiest angling decision you'll ever make. At other times it can be one of the hardest!

Let us explain. At certain times of year, notably in late spring and summer when the carp are feeding vigorously in warm water, you can catch them on just about any bait under the sun.

But in the hardest mid-winter conditions, only two or three baits are likely to tempt a bite while others which worked really well just a couple of months earlier will be ignored.

This latter situation can make deciding what to take in winter – typically maggots, sweetcorn, perhaps bread or, where permitted, bloodworm and joker – very straightforward. Ironically, given their free-feeding nature, it's those summer fish which you'll have to deliberate longer and harder about if you wish to be size-specific in what you catch.

"The knack is to understand which bait will have a slight edge in it's effectiveness over others"

You'd more than likely get bites on the following list of baits: pellets, paste, luncheon meat, cat food, Chum Mixers, sweetcorn, maggots, casters, hemp seed, chopped worms, mini boilies…we could continue, but we're sure you get the picture.

Nobody in their right mind would attempt to take all of the above baits, especially when you consider how many different sizes and types there are of pellets alone. You'd need a crane to lift your carryall and cool bag in and out of the car boot!

What's more, you will always need to check whether your chosen baits are permitted at a fishery. If you're visiting a water for the first time, make this your No.1 task on arrival.

Also, find out what methods are likely to score. There's no point turning up with corn if you're expecting to fish the feeder, for example. Flavours and colourings are becoming hugely popular, and whilst we won't go into these in too much detail they can certainly give you an edge on hard fished waters.

From a competitive angler's perspective, the knack is to understand which bait will have a slight edge in its effectiveness over the others. And this knowledge will certainly also bring benefits to the general pleasure angler.

For instance, at a lot of venues chopped worm will outfish everything else at certain times of the year. But three weeks earlier meat may have been boss, and before that paste could have been catching larger and more fish than anything.

Every venue is different in how its residents respond to different baits at different times of year. Being a regular at one particular water or complex, plus developing good relationships with other regulars plus the bailiffs and management, is the best way to stay in touch. Being prepared is a big part of success in any sport, and that also means having an alternative on standby in case your first choice bait and tactic fails to produce for whatever reason.

A cooler bag is an invaluable aid for keeping bait in top conditions in extremely warm weather.

However, there's no need to feel lost if you're new to this game or if your time is limited to just occasional visits. For there are basic ground rules on when and how to use all the different baits which work on Commercial Fisheries, which we'll look at in this chapter. You can take them on board for your future fishing sessions, ensuring you turn up with the right baits for the task in hand instead of a bewildering array for unnecessary expense.

Talking of expense, there's no point in shelling out hard earned cash on an array of top quality baits only for them to quickly deteriorate in condition due to extreme weather conditions such as searing summer sunshine or winter frosts. A thermally insulated cooler bag is one of the best tackle investments you can make, particularly for summer, regardless of the baits you take.

Small bottles filled with water then frozen make great cooler blocks. As they thaw out you can drink the contents.

Let's look now at the main baits to use at Commercial Fisheries, together with some tips on their preparation and presentation.

Flavours and colourings have been used with great success by Specimen anglers for the last two decades.

Probably the most widely used of the 'live' natural baits, maggots can catch absolutely every species of fish. They are one of the easiest and most effective baits to use, but as with everything there are rights and wrongs along the way.

POLLY'S COMMENT

Always try to buy the freshest maggots possible. A fresh maggot will be plump, lively and carry a clearly visible dark 'feed spot' towards the front of its body

The larvae of the common house fly, maggots are sold by the pint (or 'measure' if European Community trading legislation is strictly observed) at all high street tackle shops plus many fishery shops. A 'measure', which happily happens to exactly fill a pint glass, typically costs around £3.

Maggots are naturally off-white but can be dyed various colours. Mass bred at bait farms for supply to tackle shops, you can opt for a single colour or a mixed batch. Red is by far the most popular colour, followed by natural white, pink (often called 'fluoro' or 'disco') then bronze. Yellow is less readily available, and although a typical 'pint of mixed' contains a smattering of blue maggots, we have yet to hear of anyone who reports great success using this latter colour.

"Be assured, fish can show distinct colour preferences on different days"

As with many baits, it's good to have a selection of colours. Be assured, fish can show distinct colour preferences on different days. A typical maggot order for a winter stillwater session would be a pint of reds with perhaps a few whites and fluoros mixed in. You can then experiment with the different shades, or 'cocktails' involving different colours on the same hook, to see which draws the best response.

During summer, loose feeding larger amounts of maggots – up to a gallon (eight pints/measures) – can be a devastatingly effective, albeit rather expensive, way to catch lots of fish. But three pints is normally ample, and as with all baits some fisheries apply limits so you must check first.

If fishing range allows you can loose feed maggots by hand, but for longer distances you'll need a catapult. The process of catapulting maggots in large quantities is widely known as 'spraying' – not to be confused with spraying on a flavouring.

A relatively small and delicate bait, maggots are best presented either as singles, doubles and occasionally triples on hooks in the size 14 to 22 range. Mark Pollard favours Fox Match Series 2 Barbless spade end hooks for this bait, ranging from a size 22 Fine Wire version for single maggot in winter, through the Standard type in sizes 20, then 18 and 16 for double maggot, through to a size 14 for triple maggot. If larger than average carp are the target he may opt for an Extra Strong version of this hook, or occasionally a Series 6 Barbless Carp Feeder or a Series 7 Carbon Carp pattern.

Fox Match Series 2 Barbless is favoured by Mark Pollard

Always try to buy the freshest maggots possible. A fresh maggot will be plump, lively and carry a clearly visible dark 'feed spot' towards the front of its body – the pointed end. This is evidence of recent removal from whatever type of meat they've been munching at the bait farm.

Striking up a good relationship with your tackle dealer is always a wise move, especially so when it comes to learning which day of the week they take delivery of a fresh batch of maggots. Buy yours on or shortly after this day rather than just before it, unless you plan to turn them for casters. Older bait is better for this.

Always store your maggots in a bait box, bowl or tray with ample capacity. Keep them dry by dusting on a generous portion of maize meal or, as shown later, a fine flavoured groundbait such as Carp Dust. Crowding will cause them to sweat, exuding a nasty ammonia substance which is repulsive to fish and humans alike!

Adding a handful of maize stops Maggots from sweating and keeps them in tip-top condition.

Store your maggots in a cool fridge with the lid of your bait box off. An escape-proof box with a top lip is handy in case of fridge failure. If you don't have access to a fridge, a cool garage or shed floor is a short-term storage solution during colder months. But if you have no fridge and it's a hot summer's day, you're always best off buying them on the morning of a session. To do otherwise spells disaster!

As already mentioned, an insulated cool bag is vital for transporting maggots – plus many other baits - to the fishery. In summer it's an absolute must. Maggot riddles are another must-have item, enabling you to remove dead skins, casters plus unwanted maize meal or sawdust before you start.

Talking of dead maggots, these can be a superb hook bait in situations where you don't want to attract small fish or to run the risk of them burrowing out of sight into silt. Incidentally, some tackle dealers sell off old maggots cheap as 'feeder bait'. This can be a good way to reduce the cost of a session, and the fact that old maggots tend to be less active than fresh ones is a benefit when laying down a bed of feed – particularly over silty bottoms for this very reason.

There's several ways to kill maggots, and the whole preparation and presentation process is outlined in detail in this book's Feeder Fishing section.

Another brilliant method, dealt with in the Float Fishing section, is 'Stickymag'. As the name implies, it involved sticking maggots together into balls which can be fired out to distances way beyond normal loose feeding range.

In summary, although maggots lack the sheer convenience of tinned and packaged baits, you'd be wise to learn and master their many uses if you're to get the best from Commercial Fisheries.

Pinkies

Around half the size of the standard maggot, pinkies are the larvae of the greenbottle fly and have only a very limited role on commercial fisheries. In winter, when bites are hard to come by on larger baits, a single or double pinkie lowered carefully into a swim with minimal freebies sprinkled around it via a small pot can sometimes tempt a lethargic and otherwise uninterested carp or skimmer bream into feeding.

As with maggots, numerous colours are available but when it comes to pinkies it's fluorescents which are by far the most popular.

Price-wise, pinkies are similar to maggots but they are a lot easier to store in decent condition. Indeed, a half-pint/measure will last several weekends if stored in a cool bait fridge or on a garage or shed floor. Just an occasional riddle is required to remove the skins of dead ones.

The chrysalis stage of the maggot, before it turns into a fly, is known as a caster. A caster undergoes various colour changes, the shell starting out a pale cream when the maggot first ceases moving. It moves through a pale tan to a deeper reddish colour, eventually reaching a chestnut brown which is most anglers' preferred stage to feed and fish the bait. Left to go further still, a caster's shell will go very dark brown – almost black – at which point it will float.

Selling from between £3.10 to £3.40 a pint/measure in the tackle shops, the extra cost over and above maggots reflects the fact that you can never get a pint of casters from a pint of maggots. During the process, known as 'turning', old maggots – which should be natural whites rather than dyed – are regularly placed on top of large bait riddles. Those not ready to turn wriggle through, while the inert casters remain on top to be picked off. The process is repeated every two to three hours, but there is a percentage which die or become misshapen and therefore undesirable as bait.

A fantastic bait which will catch as many species as maggots, casters are supplied in airtight plastic bags but are best transferred to bait boxes as soon as possible after buying them, to avoid 'fridge burn'. This is the name given to a discolouration of their outer shell caused by it resting against

polythene when stored in a fridge. Ensure your bait boxes have tight fitting lids and perhaps add a sheet of folded, slightly damp newspaper between the lid and the casters. This slows down their metamorphosis and keeps them as 'sinkers'.

On commercials there's normally no need to 'bury' the hook. When using single caster simply nick it on a size 18 or 20 maggot-style.

For double baits, use a bigger Series 2 such as a 14 or 16.

But remember that casters are living creatures, and thus require more care than a truly inert bait like a pellet or a seed. If you can, open the bait box lid at regular intervals for ten minutes or so to allow an exchange of air, thus allowing the casters to 'breathe'.

Once you get to the bank, cover the casters in water to keep them fresh. However, it's a good idea to have some darker and crispier-shelled casters for the hook as they tend to counterbalance its extra weight. So make sure you keep a decent handful out of water, either resting on your bait tray or in a separate small bait tub, to achieve this. As they day progresses you'll notice them becoming darker.

You can hook casters in several ways, the traditional means being to bury the hook entirely within the chrysalis by carefully threading it in. A good tip here is to use a darker and therefore more buoyant caster to disguise the added weight of the hook, ensuring your bait falls at as close a rate as possible to the loose feed. But carp and tench, especially in summer, not generally as fussy as roach and chub when it comes to this. Several casters nicked onto a larger hook, maggot-style, are often all you need.

When it comes to hook selection, Series 2 Standard Barbless Spade Ends are ideal for casters – a size 20 for single, stepping up to sizes 14 and 16 for double caster.

POLLY'S COMMENT

When hooking double caster a good trick is to hook one through the top and the other through the bottom as the bait may seem to sit more naturally on the hook.

There are occasions when different shades of casters bring more bites than others, but again this relates mainly to roach fishing. In commercial carp terms there are two main considerations – whether you want to catch fish below or on the surface. If the latter is desirable, floating (ie. very dark) casters will work well – either loose fed or fired out in balls of soft groundbait to explode on impact. If you want lots of dark casters, do not add a layer of polythene or a plastic bag to the bait box when storing.

But on most occasions casters are used to attract a mixed catch, either by forming a sizeable bait carpet on the deck or a regular curtain of loose feed in the upper layers – often in conjunction with chopped worms, our next bait topic…

CARING FOR CASTERS

Despite their inert appearance, casters are as much of a 'live' bait as maggots and worms. To ensure they stay in perfect nick between purchase and arrival at the fishery, follow these steps.

Transfer your casters from the plastic bag they come in from your tackle shop into a bait box with a tight fitting lid. Aim to fill the box as near to the top as possible or add damp newspaper to fill any void.

Place a plastic food bag, folded over if necessary, on top of the casters. Its outer edges should extend beyond the bait box's four sides, so that when you snap the lid it traps the bag securely in place keeping the casters extra airtight.

Remove from the fridge on the morning of your fishing session. At your swim, remove the plastic bag and cover the casters in water. You'll notice that some will float.

Pour off the excess water, retaining the floaters for hook baits if they're a decent size and a nice symmetrical shape. Discard any mis-shapen ones. Retain just enough water to keep the remaining bulk of casters wet at the surface.

Worms are one of the most effective Commercial stillwater baits, and yet another which will tempt a wide variety of species according to the type and size used, the pattern of feeding and the time of year.

They can be sub-divided into three distinct categories – dendrobaenas, lobworms and redworms. Of these, the first is by far the widest used and most effective on Commercials. That said, lobworms remain a big fish bait par excellence and even the smallest redworms have their uses, most usually in winter conditions.

Dendrobaenas, or dendras as they're commonly nicknamed, are a hardy breed of worm which isn't native to the UK. Imported mainly from Canada where they are bred for the angling market, they're usually sold over here by the kilo, half-kilo or 'match pack' frequently graded into large, medium and small sacks or packs. Typical costs for a kilo are £16, with a £5 match pack normally containing enough worms for a session. Buying in bulk is obviously the cheaper option, and provided you keep them cool they will last well. A fridge is essential in summer, although cold outbuilding will suffice in winter.

POLLY'S COMMENT

A size 14 or 16 Fox Match Series 2 Barbless is my choice for small segments of dendrobaenas up in the water, or larger pieces on the bottom.

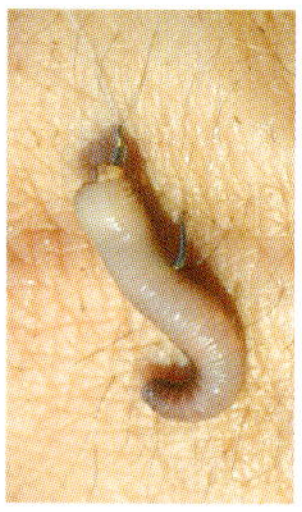

Although every type of worm will tempt occasional bites when used either as a solo hook bait or with a few broken pieces lobbed in as loose feed, you really need to feed chopped worms quite aggressively to get the best from the bait.

Dendras are ideal for chopping, either in a separate bait tub or your pole pot, before accurately depositing into your swim. It's common to add a generous portion of casters plus, on occasions, chopped maggots and sweetcorn. Bait droppers can also be used to deliver chopped-worm-based feed to the deck.

> **"As a general rule, broken pieces of worm on a hook, do better than whole worms "**

We'll talk more about chopped worm presentations in the various tactical chapters, especially on the pole, but as a general rule you'll do better using broken pieces of worm than whole worms on the hook. Try half a lobworm on as large a hook as fishery rules permit to tempt a real biggie. Mark Pollard recommends a size 12 Fox Match Series 2 eyed Extra Strong for this.

For small segments of dendrobaenas up in the water or larger pieces on the bottom, a size 14 or 16 Standard Series 2 Barbless is his choice. On occasions when skimmer bream are feeding well, he'll drop to a smaller worm on a size 18 or even a 20 to hit more bites.

Nine times out of ten these offerings, and any in between on the size scale, will outfish a whole worm whose fish-attracting juices remain largely locked up inside rather than seeping out into the surrounding water.

Lobworms are an excellent bait for sorting out the bigger fish in natural venues, and the same can apply to Commercials. Double-figure carp, big tench, perch and chub all find them hard to resist at times. Early or late in the day are good times to target these fish. You can either collect your own lobs from lawns or grass verges by torchlight on damp nights, or buy them from tackle shops or specialist suppliers.

A large tub containing around 50 lobs typically sells for around £6.50, while smaller tubs or 'match packs' range from £2.50 to £5.

Redworms are sometimes sold in small tubs at tackle shops, but more typically you'll have to collect your own from manure heaps on farms or at riding stables. Be sure to gain permission first. They're an excellent bait for bream, perch and quality roach. Indeed, a tiny redworm is one of the best 'get out of jail' baits going when it comes to winkling out a few tiny perch, as many team match anglers will testify.

Hooking Worms

Anglers often get confused about the best way to hook a worm, so we've come up with a few useful pointers for the next time you try the bait.

With big baits like lobworms, break the worm in half and hook the tail end - that's the flatter part - by going in through the broken part. Try to thread part of the worm up the hook shank before coming out the side, which also applies when hooking larger pieces of dendrabaena.

In the pole section, you'll get to see the best ways to hook small, caster-sized pieces of chopped worm. These are a superbly robust hook bait with which you can often catch several fish on the same piece. As a general rule, you use dendra heads when fishing up in the water and tails when fishing further down on the bottom. It's an easy one to remember. Redworms are generally nicked whole, often towards one end, as their lively movement is a big part of their attraction.

PREPARING YOUR CHOP AND CASTER FEED

If you're going to fish worms, you'll need to master the correct feeding techniques. But first of all it's vital to keep this fragile bait in top condition before you reach the banks. Whether you buy worms in bulk or in smaller amounts, you'll notice they come supplied in white tubs, pots or sacks. This is to reflect the sun, which can quickly cause them to shrivel up and die. Rather than fridging them up, storing them in a constant temperature such as a shaded garage floor between trips will ensure they last longer – especially in summer where the sudden drop in temperature when placing them in a fridge is too much of a shock to their system. For perfect chopped worm feed, follow this procedure as recommended by top North West angler Derek Willan.

1

Remove a handful of worms from the sack or tub and place in a square bait tub in readiness for chopping up. You can either buy double or triple bladed worm scissors, or use a pair of large kitchen scissors in tandem.

2

Many anglers wash the soil off their worms by dunking them in the margins on a riddle, but all they are doing is removing an excellent medium for soaking up and retaining the fish-attracting juices. Leave it in!

3

Keep on chopping until the worms are mainly in tiny pieces, with just a few larger chunks. You want your hook bait, which will generally be a bigger piece, to stand out in the area. As well as showing comparative sizes between whole and chopped worm feed, note the difference in soil colours.

4

Casters are an excellent addition to chopped worm feed, and they too benefit from a quick treatment from the scissors to release some of their inner juices which Derek also believes to be highly attractive to fish of all kinds.

DOUBLE LEAM

Leam is a fine continental soil which binds superbly but has no feed value. This makes it ideal for delivering jokers straight to the bottom of your swim in winter, without risking overfilling the fish. But first, you'll need to blend two types of leam.

1

Damp brown leam (the bag) provides weight whilst dry grey leam - marketed as Krystonite in shaker dispensers - helps it to break up fast on the bottom.

2

Start by pouring damp leam onto a riddle to catch the lumps, then break these down and push through the mesh by hand.

3

Carefully shake on a dusting of grey leam then mix together and spray with water from an atomiser to dampen further.

4

Now add your joker, stirring it in well to distribute evenly. Be sure to check first whether the fishery stipulate a limit on amounts, which is often the case in matches.

5

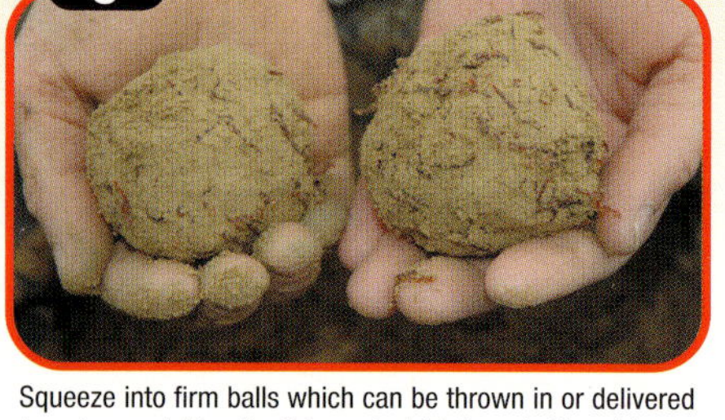

Squeeze into firm balls which can be thrown in or delivered via pole cup, taking the jokers straight down but breaking up fast for an instantly attractive bed of bait.

Although more associated with canal fishing and the continental match scene, a handful of (dare we say enlightened?) commercial fisheries allow the use of these two delicate baits during the winter months. Their reputation as something which can tempt a bite when all others fail in the coldest conditions is well deserved.

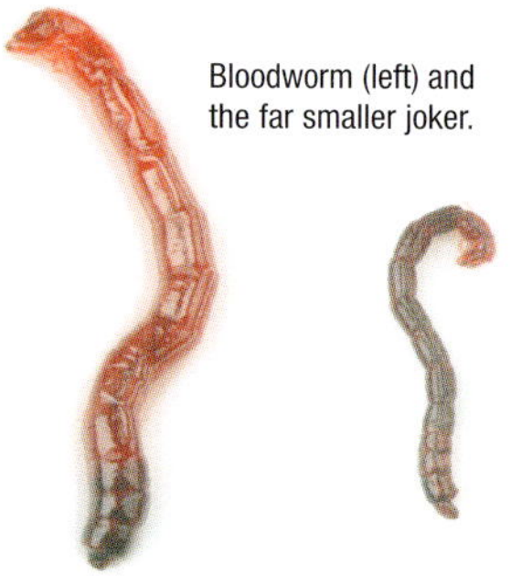

Bloodworm (left) and the far smaller joker.

During the long, cold and dark months of winter, carp are less likely to feed as consistently and tend also to be shoaled up tighter, leaving some pegs 'solid' but a great many almost barren.

Some Commercial venues found dwindling attendances were the upshot, and so the concept of 'Silver Fish Matches' was born. This is where the use of Bloodworm and Joker came to the fore in Commercial Fishery terms, as these baits will be readily taken by most species even in the coldest of water temperatures. Unless you are fishing in December, January and February, they aren't really something you'll need to consider.

Bloodworm are mosquito larvae, typically 3cm long and bright red with a darker greenish section at the head end. Found naturally in all waters, they are collected by bait breeders – usually in Europe – for import and sale in 'hooker packs' of around 250 grams, wrapped in slightly dampened newspaper, for around £3.

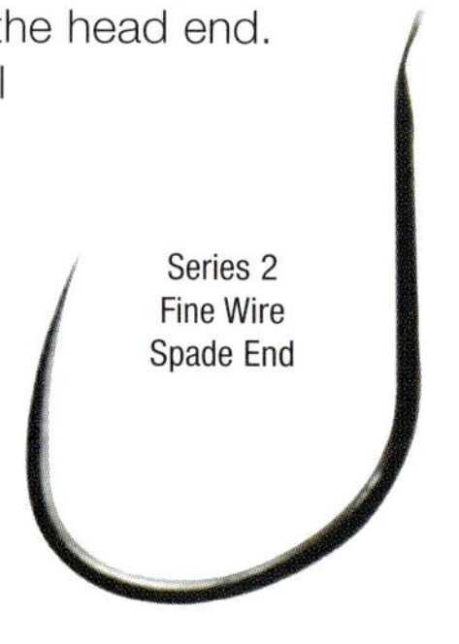

Series 2 Fine Wire Spade End

Jokers are the much smaller larvae of the midge. Again, they are present in many waters but tend to thrive best in semi-polluted streams or shallow lagoons, as found at some sewage treatment works. Almost exclusively imported from the continent, especially eastern Europe where polluted waters have not yet been cleaned up to the same extent as in the UK, they are generally sold by the kilo – again in damp newspaper 'wraps' at around £16. Due to their cost, most shops do not stock the bait routinely so orders should be placed a week before you fish with them.

A darker red colour than bloodworm, jokers can be frozen then reused to create an inert feed bed, although most anglers prefer fresh live joker. Although jokers are sometimes used as hook baits on canals, it's almost exclusively a feed bait on Commercials with the larger bloodworms used on the hook. Check out the picture sequence on the left to learn how to prepare jokers for feeding using the tried and trusted 'double leam' method.

One very important reason why jokers are so attractive to fish is that once immersed in water, they tend to 'dance' around up to four inches off bottom, producing an active bed of feed which attracts fish from a wide area.

It almost goes without saying that small, ultra sharp, fine wire hooks are best to present delicate bloodworm baits – often in bunches of two, three or four. When targeting silver fish, Mark Pollard favours a size 22 or 24 Fox Match MP1 Barbless Spade End hook, but when F1s and larger skimmers are likely he'll switch to the stronger Fine Wire Series 2 in size 21 or 22.

Traditional species such as roach, perch and skimmers are normally first to respond to the bait, but that's not to say you can't catch heavier species on them.

MP1 Silver Fish Hook

Although widely regarded as a niche bait of use only to match anglers, the further spread of F1 common-crucian carp hybrids across the nation's fisheries may yet persuade more venues and anglers – including pleasure anglers – to give them a go. F1s will feed in the very coldest conditions, and bloodworm over a small ball of leamed-up joker is one of the very best ways to put a catch together.

Although the prices may seem expensive, you can store joker for reasonable periods in trays on your garage floor. Simply return the bait to a water-filled tray after a trip, passing them through a squatt riddle to remove the dead, then switch them to another tray with just enough water to cover them. This resembles a tray of jam! Before your next trip, return the batch to newspaper. Bloodworm are hardier and can survive a week or more in their damp paper wrap in the fridge.

POLLY'S COMMENT

Keep bloodworms covered in water while fishing. A white bait box speeds the hooking process.

POLLY'S COMMENT

Always ensure your hooked pellet sinks by dropping it into the margins before shipping out and discovering your float won't sit right in the water.

The undisputed No.1 Commercial Fishery bait, pellets are loved by fishery managers because they provide pure nutrition and by anglers because they catch fish and come in a compact, long lasting, easy storage format.

There are so many different types, sizes, colours and flavours of pellet that they deserve what amounts to a mini chapter of their own within this Baits section. But firstly, a brief history lesson on how this brilliant bait burst onto the scene in the mid-1980s.

How It All Started

As more and more Commercial fisheries were dreamed up and created, the landowners and entrepreneurs behind these projects – many of them farmers with little or no prior angling or fisheries experience - sensibly sought professional advice from fishery consultants or the fish breeders from whom they sourced their stocks. The advice from these scientifically qualified sages was to keep their fish well fed with pellets.

However, back then the only type of pellet produced in large enough quantities to make them financially viable on a large scale was trout pellets. After all, there'd been a large UK commercial stillwater trout fishery industry since the early 1970s. Therefore it was trout pellets which were first bagged up for sale to the angling public by forward thinking fisheries and tackle shops, to be enthusiastically embraced by their growing band of customers.

By the early 1990s, new scientific research (plus greater awareness of existing work) indicated that the high oil content of trout pellets was not necessarily desirable for maximum growth potential of carp and other coarse species.

> **"There is an array of options including a host of bait company-branded coarse pellets"**

Indeed, some felt that when fed in large amounts, they could actually risk harming the carp's internal organs. The upshot was the emergence of coarse pellets, a lower oil content version with reduced fishmeal and increased vegetable content.

The Current Choice

Nowadays, there's an array of options including the dark and ultra-oily halibut pellets, a host of bait company-branded coarse pellets in various shades and colours with additives drawn from the specimen carp arena including Betaine, Green Lipped Mussel and Corn Steep Liquor. There's floaters, sinkers, expanders, Jelly Pellets. There's hemp pellets, bloodworm pellets…and still good old trout pellets on the market.

> **"The fresher the better is a wise bait mantra to follow in all your fishing"**

The fact that high oil content pellets are still widely used at many Commercial coarse fisheries indicates that those fears about fish health were perhaps largely unfounded.

However, while some fishery owners are happy for any type of pellet to be used, others insist on the use of 'fishery own' pellets – bought on site – as a safeguard to control what goes into their water.

In some cases they also impose limits on amounts, so it's essential for any angler to check the rules before fishing as they will vary from venue to venue. Some anglers view an insistence on 'fishery own' pellets as being nothing more than a money-spinning exercise which prevents them from gaining an edge by using a certain type they favour. The only answer if you feel this way is to vote with your feet and fish elsewhere.

All this can be rather baffling to even expert anglers. Our aim is to demystify the muddied waters by stating the types Mark Pollard and his extensive network of contacts like to use, plus how to prepare and present them for various different tactical approaches.

Price-wise, pellets tend to sell for between £2.35 per 800 grams to a kilo for the cheaper Expander type through to around £3 for the oilier marine/halibut types. Once opened, the pellets have an almost indefinite shelf life provided they are kept dry, but as with most baits the top anglers prefer to use an opened bag up within a couple of weeks at the most. The fresher the better is a wise bait mantra to follow in all your fishing.

If, like many anglers, you find the sheer variety of types and sizes of pellets bewildering, then we guarantee that the following advice will remove all the doubts and improve your results dramatically.

Like all successful anglers, Mark Pollard knows that confusion and doubt lead to disappointing results. So whether you're a pleasure angler or a match angler, you'll appreciate knowing that he places his faith in just a few types of pellet – each well proven to work for specific jobs. And over the next four pages, Mark reveals exactly what he uses for the many and various angling situations you'll encounter, starting with hook pellets.

Create a fish-attracting noise by throwing pellets down hard onto the water.

EXPANDER PELLETS

As their name suggests, Expander Pellets grow in size once water is added to them. Straight from the bag they are rock hard, unhookable and will float, rendering them useless for all bar surface fishing applications.

But when combined with water in the correct manner - shown in the picture sequence on the right - they can be transformed into a lovely spongy textured bait which is easy to hook, seeps fish-attracting oils and is simplicity itself to use on the pole. Expanders in their basic form are best used when fishing at full depth or just off bottom.

There are various types and sizes of Expander pellets available, but 3mm and 6mm tend to be the most common. Mark Pollard favours the Van den Eynde RS Elite brand, followed by Ringers original version (or Ringers Cold Water in winter). But it's worth preparing both types for a session to see whether the fish show a preference for one or the other.

3mm and 6mm tends to be the most popular sizes for Expander Pellets

To prepare a batch of Expander pellets, you'll require a Pellet Pump. These come in various sizes and are a vital piece of kit if you want to fish expanders properly to maximise your catches.

Pellet pumps work on the vacuum principle, which means expelling all air from within the pellets. It's this air, trapped between the fibres, which makes them float. Replace it with water and they sink. A simple principle, but brilliantly effective as the many massive catches taken on pumped expanders every year at waters across the UK proves!

POLLY'S COMMENT

Always remember to hook a pellet 'across the grain', ie. through the middle, so that the shank of the hook grips the fibres which run from one end to the other.

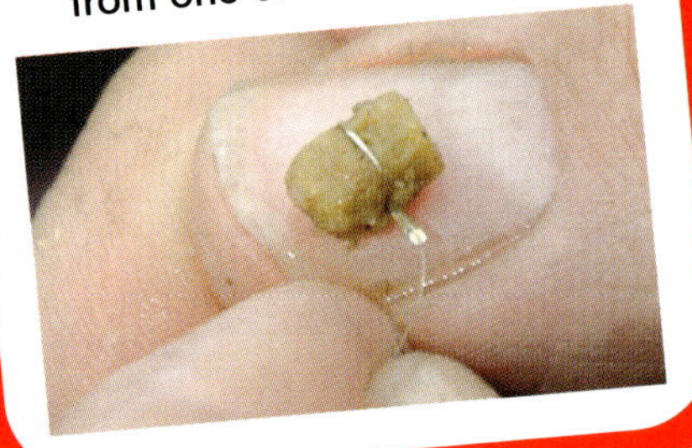

PREPARING EXPANDERS HERE'S HOW...

1

Tip your required amount of dry Expanders into a pellet pump.

2

Add approximately twice as much water as pellets. If you wish, you can also add liquid flavourings at this stage .

3

Secure the lid and pump out the air for about 30 seconds.

4 Remove the pump and gently squeeze the rubber aperture at the top of the pump to release the air with an audible whoosh.

5 As the air passes out of the tub the pellets will start to sink.....

6 ....until most of the pellets have come to rest on the bottom of the container.

7 Do not drain off the remaining water. Instead, pour it into a bait box with the Expanders and leave it for an hour.

8 After an hour the Expanders will have soaked up the excess water and be a perfect texture, sinking slowly and attractively through the water.

JELLY PELLETS

'Jellies', as they are commonly known, normally come into play when you want to fish pellets on either a float or feeder rig rather than the pole. That said, they work on the pole too. Making Jelly Pellets is relatively straight forward, but pre-prepared Jelly Pellets are also available commercially, such as the Van den Eynde range of Jellets or Mainline soft hooker pellets (shown below).

As the name suggests, Gelatine is used to firm up the pellet's texture. Although most anglers prefer to use unflavoured sachets of Gelatine, flavoured childrens' dessert jellies (or jelly blocks) such as strawberry and pineapple can be used. In the sequence shown below we have used 6mm Elite Expander Pellets and strawberry jelly crystals to create a sweet scented soft hookable bait.

HERE'S HOW MARK MAKES UP A BATCH OF JELLY PELLETS.

1 Melt the sachet of gelatine in boiling water, stirring to create a smooth solution, then leave for five minutes to cool slightly.

2 Add your Expander pellets to the container before pouring in the jelly/water solution.

3 Ensure there is enough solution to cover the pellets and allow for their expansion.

4 Pump as normal then release the air.

5 Pour all of the contents, including all the solution, into a bait box and leave for a couple of minutes to cool.

6 Transfer the contents into a plastic bag and distribute them evenly so they're fairly flat. Turn occasionally, then store in the fridge overnight.

Armed with a far clearer understanding of what types of pellet to use for different types of hook bait presentation, we'll move on now to feed pellets.

Feed Pellets

Here the choice gets slightly easier. For 99 per cent of Commercial Fishery situations a simple, good quality specifically developed pellet, such as Van den Eynde Fishmeal Carp Stimm will do the job. This particular pellet comes in three sizes – micro, 3.5mm and 8mm. For most commercials the smaller sizes are the best to use as feed but when fishing up in the water it is worth carrying some of the bigger sizes to use on the hook in conjunction with a Pellet Band.

On most occasions it is a good idea to wet the pellets with a modest amount of water prior to fishing – but not too much as this can make them go a bit on the mushy side. The idea is just to encourage the fish-attracting oils contained within to start seeping out as soon as they enter the swim.

Occasionally – most notably during summer when fishing up in the water or at close range – it is better to leave them dry. When fish are more active it is possible to attract the carp through the noise of a load of freebies going into the swim as much as through their taste. Hard pellets make more noise on impact with the water's surface than those which have been moistened.

> **"Summer carp view the familiar noise of bait hitting water as a dinner gong, so make sure you bang that gong nice and loud!"**

One good tip at close range is to really rain them down from a decent height, raising your arm high and throwing them down around your float with a strong downward thrust.

You will also need to consider how you introduce your feed pellets – whether by a cup-style device attached to your pole, by hand, by catapult or by swimfeeder. We'll show you some pellet tricks for both float and feeder tactics in subsequent chapters, but for now we'll cover the preferred methods for when you are pole fishing.

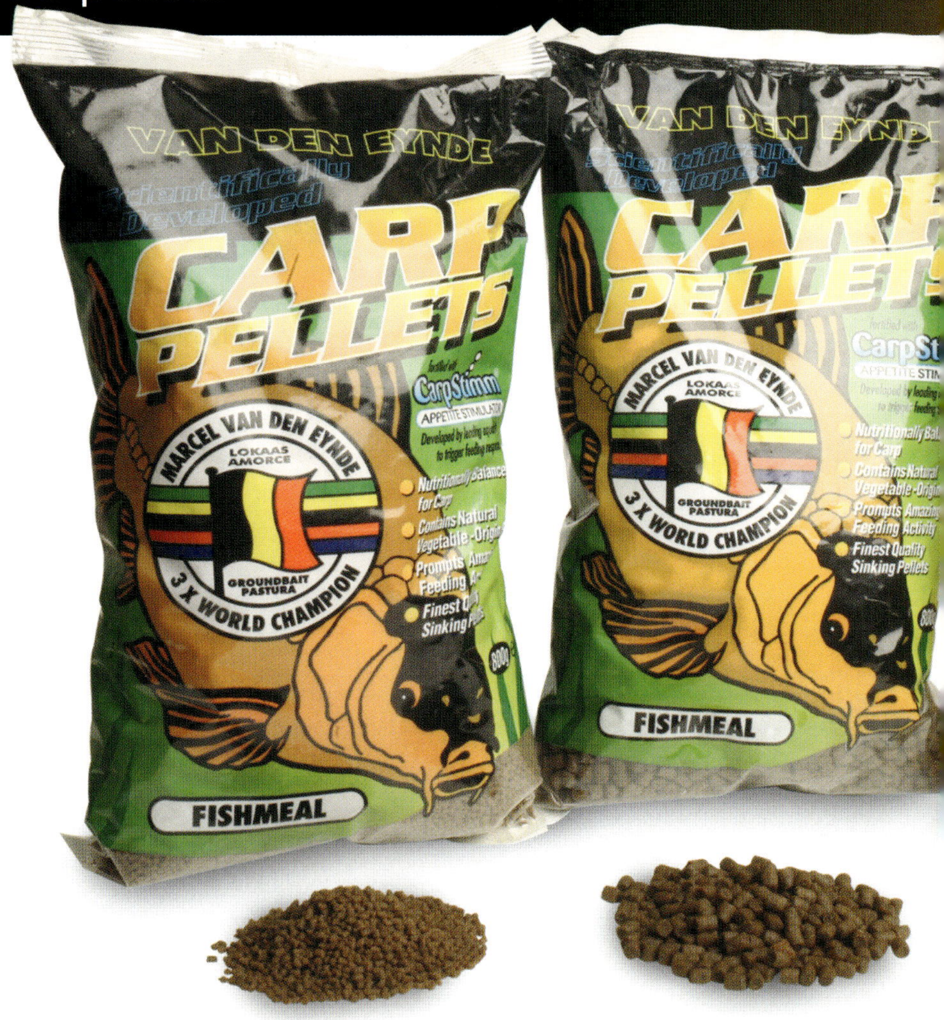

Micro Pellets

Ideal for creating maximum attraction with minimal risk of overfeeding the fish, Micros are a good ploy in spring, autumn and through winter when the fish are less active.

Being so small limits the feeding of micro pellets by hand to margin swims only. At catapult distance, they tend to get blown over too wide an area by any wind, and a small bubble of air will often form against them on impact which will hold them up for a while, drifting them away from your target area before it bursts and allows the pellet to start sinking. Therefore nine times out of ten, a Toss Pot is the best way to introduce Micro Pellet into the swim.

3.5mm Pellets

Being larger and heavier, the 3.5mm pellets are ideal for most summer fishing. Like Micros, they can be fed via pole cup or a smaller Toss Pot, especially at the start of a session to introduce a decent bed of bait in one or more chosen spots.

However, these larger pellets also lend themselves to accurate feeding by hand at ranges up to around six or seven metres, plus of course in margin swims, and then by catapult when fishing further out.

Remember, summer carp view the familiar noise of bait hitting water as a dinner gong, so make sure you bang that gong nice and loud!

8mm Pellets

The larger 8mm pellets aren't as versatile due to their size and increased food content. It is always worth carrying some big pellets for using banded on the hook but they should very rarely be used as feed.

One exception is in the height of summer when fishing the margins and big fish and large weights are expected. The fishes' increased metabolism and competition for food means more bait can be used as there is little fear of over-feeding the fish.

If using a bigger pellet on the hook, it is also worth adding a few bigger pellets to your feed so as not to arouse suspicion.

BANDED PELLETS

When fishing up in the water during the warm summer months, carp often charge around a swim in a feeding frenzy. This can result in a lot of false bites as well as true ones, and if you're using Expander pellets on the hook then you'll inevitably strike the pellet off on many occasions. To avoid wasted time shipping in, rebaiting then shipping back out you need something which will stay on the hook far better.

Enter Banded Pellets! Banded Pellets is the term which covers the use of hard sinking pellets attached via the use of a small circular rubber bait band, which grips the bait tightly against the hook. Pellets for banding need to be the 3.5mm and 8mm sizes. Fox Match Pellet Bands come in three sizes, small, medium and large. These translucent rubber hoops have a small protruding section to slip your hook through to keep them on.

METHOD 1

Mark prefers to fit the pellet to the band before hooking. This is faster than trying to fit a fresh pellet to an already-hooked band. A banded pellet will inevitably come adrift on occasions in the course of striking and playing fish. Pre-banding a dozen or so pellets of various sizes in advance is time well spent. Simply slip off the empty band and re-hook another ready-loaded one. Always position the pellet on the bend rather than the shank of the hook.

METHOD 2

1

Tie a small loop and attach the hook to the line using a knotless knot. Attach a bait band to the loop by threading it back on itself.

2

Drill a hole through the pellet using a 1mm Pellet drill. You can do this with twenty five or so pellets the night before.

3

Using a paste stop needle, pull the band through the pellet. There's no need to use a hair stop the pellet will swell up and is secure.

Mark Sawyer of European Groundbaits

In a bid to discover more about just what goes into the pellets we fish with, we asked baits guru Mark Sawyer of European Groundbaits if he'd spill the beans - or at least some of them. Mark, Commercial Manager of the firm whose brands include Van den Eynde and Bait Tech, has been involved in pellet research and development for more than a decade. And his revelations make fascinating reading.

> "The basic ingredients of any pellet are fish meal, carbon and fibre, ash and fish oils are added to form the pellet shape"

"It is the general belief that pellets have advanced considerably since they were first used on commercial fisheries as both a feed and hook bait. However, it would be more true to say that as anglers our knowledge of the pellet as a bait and feed has advanced more than the actual make up and basic ingredients used in the formulation of the pellet itself.

To understand 'the pellet' it is necessary to look at the fish feed industry as this is where the first pellets actually came from in the first instance.

Here's a fact which may make you pause and think about the scale of this industry compared to ours. Even though pellets are used on commercial fisheries the length and breadth of the country, the UK angling bait market is only responsible for around 2% of the fish feeds industry's output. It's a fact that even today, the majority of pellets are generally produced solely for the fish farming community, whether it's Trout, Salmon or Carp they are farming.

So What Goes Into A Pellet?

The very basic ingredients of any pellet are fish meal, carbon and fibre, ash and fish oils that are added to the pellets after the extrusion process that forms the pellet's shape. The differing protein levels, whether high or low, are derived mainly from the amount of fish meal contained within the recipe of any given pellet. This protein level depends upon the pellet's original purpose.

Halibut pellets, as the name suggests, were developed specifically for feeding farmed Halibut. The Halibut is a huge flat-fish that needs high protein levels to sustain its growth. Therefore Halibut's have some of the highest protein levels of any pellets which also means they are the darkest 'natural' pellets, natural meaning undyed in this instance.

When anglers first started realising the potential of pellets on Commercial fisheries, the only pellets available for purchase where those developed for the farming community. All these pellets had been designed with high oil and fishmeal content to precipitate the growth of the farmed fish. All good news, surely? Well, not entirely when you consider that we don't fish for salmon, trout and halibut in Commercial Fisheries. Instead we fish for carp and other cyprinid species, and hence we now have specifically designed 'coarse pellets' or 'carp pellets' at our disposal as well as the darker, oilier types.

Why Use Coarse Pellets?

There is little if any proof that high oil content pellets such as trout, salmon and halibut pellets affect the well being of cyprinid fish, such as carp, in the short term at any rate. However, if carp are fed exclusively on high oil pellets for a prolonged period, this scenario could lead to a rapid growth and weight gain which could, possibly, cause the fish to produce excess fat that may in the future lead to vital organ failure. However, as already stated, there is little documented evidence of this. But enough concerns were voiced in the mid to late 1990s to force the bait trade into investigating alternatives.

So, as pellets gained almost exponentially in popularity during this period, companies such as Van den Eynde worked with pellet manufacturers to produce low oil coarse pellets which are considered to be more fishery friendly and healthier for the carp's overall dietary needs.

Compressed Or Extruded?

There are two main manufactured types of pellet: the extruded pellet and the compressed pellet. The latter comes in more of a cylindrical stick shape and has uneven broken ends while the former is harder and more uniform.

Compressed pellets tend to break down much quicker once in water than the (standard) extruded type pellet, taking around 5-10 mins depending on water temperature and which pellets are used. As well as coming in basic fish meal flavour, compressed pellets

Compressed pellets include hemp and CSL types

ANGLING PELLET BREAKDOWN

COMMERCIAL PELLET BREAKDOWN

are also available as a hemp or a CSL pellet. This is also the type of pellet where the basic recipe and diet can be adjusted to create a differing taste, smell, or colour. Being less aerodynamically shaped than extruded pellets, they are harder to feed accurately via catapult.

The majority of Commercial pellets are extruded

Most extruded pellets that are sold as a flavoured and coloured pellet, are in most cases originated from a low oil standard coarse feed pellet that has been tumbled in a solution of colour and flavour before being left to stand and dry. The only extruded pellets that have both flavour and colour cooked in are, to the best of my knowledge, Van den Eynde's Strawberry pellet. The temperatures used on the extruding machines are so high that they evaporate all but the most specialised of flavours and colours before the process is finished.

Breakdown Times And Colours

The breakdown times of the extruded varieties of pellet varies enormously from type to type. However, in my experience, the lower the oil content the faster the breakdown time. I've found around 30 to 40 minutes to be the quickest. The process will be quicker during periods of high water temperatures, and obviously slower in cold water. The easiest way to distinguish a low oil extruded pellet from a high oil extruded pellet is in the colour. As a rule, pellets with low oil content are always paler than the darker high oil equivalents. Based on the knowledge I've imparted about lighter coloured pellets invariably being the low oil coarse variety, you can continue using these with confidence into the colder months. However, as with any type of fishing, in the winter the fish don't require nearly as much feed so introduce loose offerings sparesly or only when a fish has been caught.

What Does The Future Hold?

In recent years, a substance called Betaine has been used as an additive to many pellets. Betaine is a synthetic substance which acts synergistically as a feeding stimulant and a digestion aid to fish and improves the efficiency with which their enzymes can break down food into smaller particles to be absorbed more easily.

Continued investment in Research and Development by the manufacturers and scientists means pellets will continue to subtly evolve with time. New products are coming onto the market all the time. As anglers' knowledge of the bait also continues to grow, one thing is for certain - this will bring improved results.

Anglers have used various types of paste, most involving bread or cheese, to catch fish for centuries. But in modern Commercial Fishery terms, just about all pastes are of the fishmeal variety, formed from either finely ground pellets or groundbaits.

When paste first came on the Commercial scene it was synonymous with pellets, but nowadays the two are generally fished in very different styles. Paste is widely regarded as a big fish bait to be used at close quarters, along reeded margins and under landing stages, but there's far more to it than just that. We'll show you some hot tips in the Pole chapter.

Some bait companies produce tubs of ready-made paste in various flavours, although these tend to contain preservatives to lengthen the paste's shelf-life. And preservatives are something many top anglers go to great lengths to avoid.

It is far better to create your own paste - preferably from the pellets you are going to be feeding. The result is the bed of smaller pellets which are used as loose feed act as an attractant, drawing the fish in to the area and stimulating them into feeding. Once feeding the carp come across a globule of paste; identical in flavour, but softer, larger and more pungent than the free offerings. What carp could resist such a delicacy? Very few is the answer!

MAKING PASTE

Making fresh paste is a relatively simple process. To do so you will need the following ingredients. Half a bag of pellets or a bag of fishmeal-based groundbait. A little water - preferably rain water or lake water rather than tap water.

1

Pour the powdered pellets into a clean bait tub.

2

Pour in water until the pellets are covered by about 3mm.

3

Leave the pellets for about 25 minutes. During this time they should absorb all the water

4

Stir well with your fingertips. It should now be possible to knead the dampened pellets into a soft ball of paste. If the mixture is too dry add a little more water.

5

Transfer the ball of paste to a plastic bag and store overnight in the fridge. At this stage, the paste can also be split and stored in the freezer.

A good alternative to making youre own paste is one of the bags of paste powder such as Ringers Bag-Up. These even have a dotted line on the packet which is a water fill level, which removes the guesswork about how much to add.

Top paste anglers insist that the correct consistency is such that you should retrieve an empty hook each time. In effect, you're simply presenting a slightly stiffened nugget of groundbait on the hook.

> **"A Paste Stop can be tied to the end of a hair rig to give better grip when casting the bait any distance"**

An extremely useful aid to paste fishing is the Paste Stop, a device which can be tied to the end of a hair rig to give better grip when casting the bait any distance, or when shipping it out on the pole. Another is to use a Mega Toss Pot or Sprinkle Pot to slip your paste-baited hook into. When shipping out long distances, this keeps the paste out of the water so it doesn't fall off. Once you reach the desired spot, turn your pole 180 degrees to release the rig from the bait arm.

If you prefer to use tubs of paste or bags of powder to the soaked pellets method, these mostly retail for around £2.99.

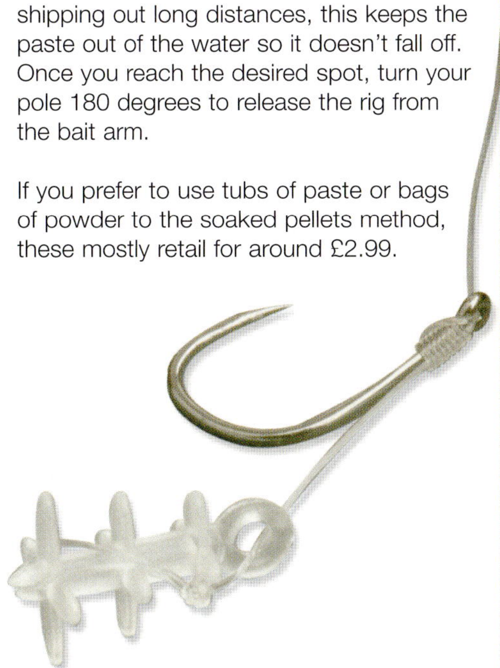

Best hook patterns and sizes are the Fox Match Series 2 Extra Strong Barbless in size 12 and 14. Mark tends to fish fairly generous sized lumps of paste around the size of a ten pence piece, so there's no need for small hooks.

There are various Powdered Pastes which are a good alternative if you don't have the time to make your own from soaked pellets.

PASTE COIL RIGGING

In addition to the paste coil, you will need a baiting needle and a size 12 or 14 hook tied with a knotless and 10mm hair.

1

Thread the paste coil onto the Baiting Needle.

2

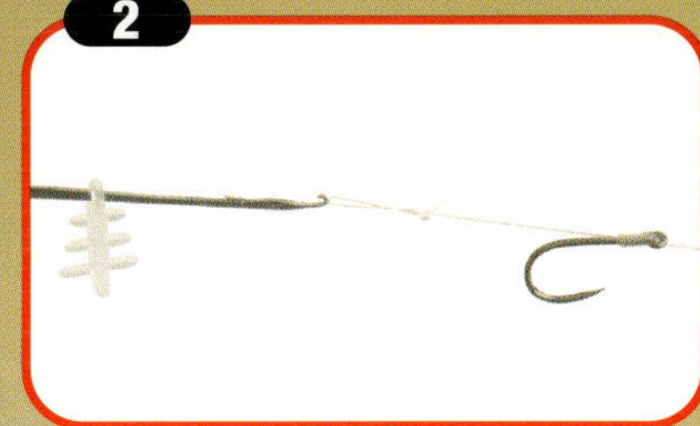

Place the loop over the hook in the hair over the end of the splicing needle.

3

Thread the coil onto the hair.

4

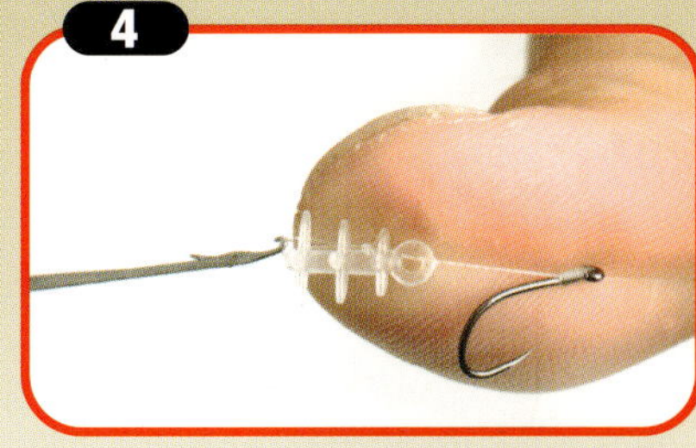

Using the baiting needle, thread the loop over the slot at the back of the coil.

5

It is then simply a case of moulding the paste around the coil, creating the perfect hair-rigged bait.

The 'golden grains' have long been a pleasure angler's favourite, straight from the can off the local supermarket, corner shop or cash-and-carry depot's shelves.

Some bait companies also offer tinned corn, often with a difference such as an added flavouring. Vanilla, strawberry, tutti-frutti, maple, scopex, and even curried versions are available. These often come in alternative colours - red, orange and, occasionally, black. There's even a new Green Lipped Mussel flavoured sweetcorn, in a colour scheme which matches its name, just out in the Van den Eynde range. It's widely believed in the world of specimen angling that fish can wise up to certain colours of corn, so it can pay to ring the changes if your catches aren't matching expectations. You may just find that the fish are wary of traditional yellow corn!

"Corn comes into its own in the winter months when it tends to be more selective as to the size of fish it attracts."

Generally speaking, corn comes into its own more in the winter months when it tends to be more selective as to the size of fish it attracts. Even 3oz rudd and roach, which are ten-a-penny in many Commercials during summer, can wolf down a grain. And because it's so highly visible, the chance of getting it down to the deck past hordes of these can make it a no-win summer option.

In the depths of winter when lethargic fish are unwilling to eat much, loose feeding whole grains risks overfilling them before they've had the chance to take your hook bait. Some anglers get round this by chopping up their corn into smaller particles, or even liquidising it into a mushy cupping feed nicknamed 'liquid gold'. Both these are excellent dodges, well worth a try in the colder months ahead but best avoided in summer as they pull too many small silver fish into your swim.

Depending on size and brand, a standard tin of sweetcorn costs around 30-50p at the supermarket, while the bait company versions are more typically in the £1.50 to £1.65 range.

Coloured sweetcorn can work well on pressured waters.

A versatile bait, corn can be nicked onto hooks as small as a size 20 or several grains can be impaled on much larger hooks. Hair rigging also comes into play when legering. Mark Pollard likes a size 14 Fox Match Series 7 Carbon Carp hook for double corn on the pole in summer. At the opposite extreme in colder weather, when searching around a swim on the waggler, he'll drop to a size 18 or occasionally size 20 Series 2 Spade End Standard wire model. An Eyed Barbless Series 2 is used on the tip when hair rigging one or two grains, typically a size 18.

Finely chopped or liquidised corn is a great winter feed.

HOOKING CORN

There are three preferred ways of hooking a grain of corn:

1 Take the hook in and back out of the outer skin towards one corner of the rounded end, when you need to cast or ship out any distance.

2 For closer range, take the hook through the narrow open end and back out the skin.

This is how to hook a grain of sweetcorn when you are casting out any distance on a float, bomb or feeder rig.

And this is the best way on the pole or at closer range on running line gear, coming in through the soft open end for a fast strike.

HAIR RIGGING

The third method of hooking corn can also be used with almost any bait and is becoming increasingly popular on commercials the length and breadth of the country. Step forward the Hair Rig. Since it was invented by carp angler Len Middleton in the early 80's, it is probably fair to say: "The Hair Rig changed the face of modern carp fishing".

Hair rigging separates the bait from the hook, allowing the bait a greater degree of movement and to behave more naturally like the free offerings surrounding it. When a fish tries to eject the bait, the Hair rig allows a distinct separation and the hook falls downwards into the bottom lip.

Tying a hair rig is relatively straight-forward if it is done with an eyed hook in the correct manner. The sequence on the right shows how to do this.

If you're hair rigging corn, the hair stop should come to rest against either the rounded end or the side. Fox produce a range of stops and the ideal one for corn is the Fox Corn Stop. When hair rigging all of the smaller match baits, it is best to use a fine baiting needle rather than one with a thicker metal shaft.

Try hair rigging a single grain of sweetcorn length-ways, the hair stop resting against the rounded end

Double sweetcorn on the hair is best mounted back-to-back through the broad flat sides.

KNOTLESS KNOT!

1

Begin by tying a small figure of eight loop in the end of your chosen hook length line.

2

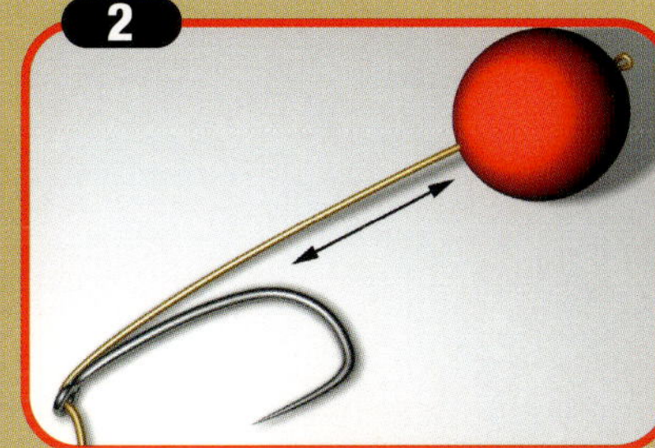

Cut the line to the desired length, ensuring you leave sufficient space between hook bend and bait once it's pulled through the loop.

3

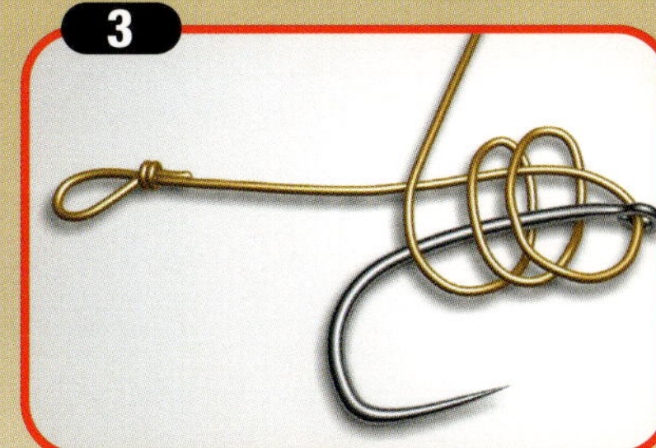

Passing the line through the top of the hook eye and out the bottom, begin looping it back up the shank and over the section that will form your hair rig.

4

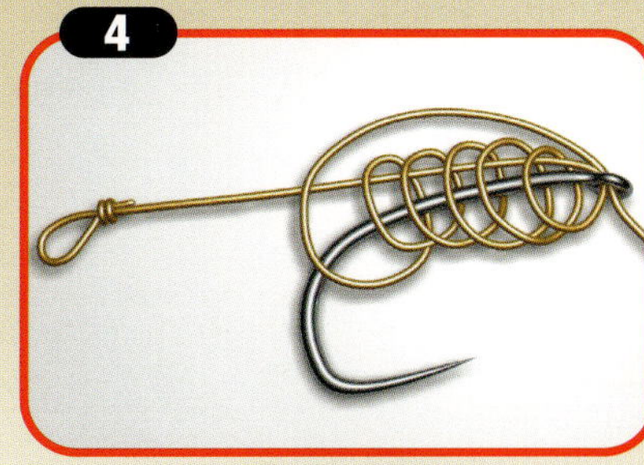

After a minimum of six turns, bring the top end of your hook length back up to the hook's eye and pass down through a second time.

5

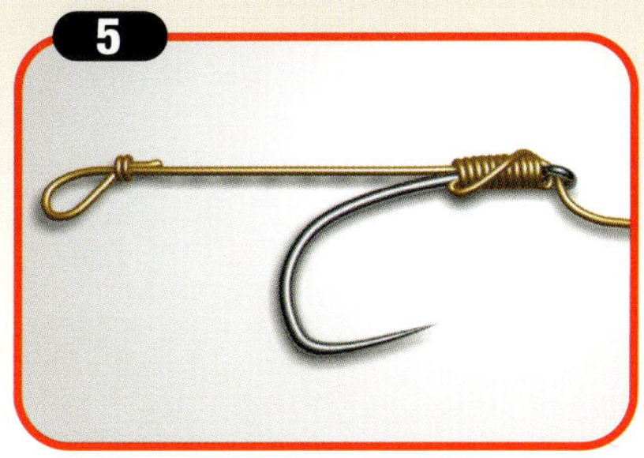

Maintaining pressure, draw the coils of the knotless knot tight. You'll be left with a strong knot which is ideal for most hook link materials.

There are three main types of meat used at Commercial Fisheries – standard luncheon meat, including flavoured and coloured versions; mini meatballs, either from bait companies or off the supermarket shelves; plus cat food.

We'll deal with the latter type, which has perhaps edged out standard luncheon meat in popularity terms in recent years but which also carries a degree of controversy, in the pet foods section which follows. So first to luncheon meat.

> **"Mini meatballs, also known as Meaty Fish Bites, are hook-sized balls of luncheon meat impregnated with a potent liquid such as squid juice"**

There are numerous popular types on supermarket shelves, many of which were household foods for the post-war generation including *Plumrose, Tulip, Princes, Ye Olde Oak* and perhaps the best known of all, *Spam*. Most cost in the 50p to £1.15 region and are based upon reconstituted pork, with various additives including salt, starch, milk protein and spices. They traditionally come in a rectangular tin with a special key which you turn to open, allowing you to extract the block of meat.

All the major bait companies also provide canned luncheon meats of various flavours including scopex, prawn and shrimp, strawberry plus pellet.

In addition to the many supermarket varieties of Luncheon Meat, the major bait companies also produce flavoured meat.

Supermarket meats tend to be very fatty and therefore far softer, which makes them great for feeding and for use on the hook. The bait company types are harder and better for using on the hook when fishing shallow, being less inclined to fall off when shipping out, dropping in or when striking without connecting.

Once out of the tin, there are several things you can do. Chopping the meat into various sized cubes or less regular shapes to provide baits for hooking or hair-rigging is one option. Punching out cylinders or cubes with a special bait punch – there are both square and round types in the Fox Match range - will provide a more aerodynamic hair rig bait. By using these, you can match your hook bait to your feed or plump for a larger piece which will stand out and attract the attention of a hungry fish. Fox also produce hair stops specifically for use with meat.

Alternatively, pressing the whole block of meat through a specially designed meat cutter – available in three sizes for around £50-60 for a metal type or £20 for plastic - can provide a finely minced luncheon meat feed. This is ideal for cupping, introducing through a feeder or adding to groundbait or paste base mix.

You can also use a maggot or pinkie riddle to achieve this but the process takes far longer. This was more popular prior to the development of meat cutters, and really is a time-consuming process. However, you'll be left with a finer feed which is ideal for adding to groundbaits or pastes.

Yet another alternative is to use a blender to create a meat flavoured groundbait. The softness and flavour create a virtual gravy of feed, over which the hook baits stands out like a juicy piece of steak.

Meat can be cut and cubed with a knife, or torn into rougher chunks, but one of the best ways to create a hook offering is with

POLLY'S COMMENT

Supermarket meats tend to be very fatty and therefore far softer, which makes them great for feeding and for use on the hook.

a special bait punch, available with various sided cutting heads. You can avoid handling the actual meat pellet too much in this way.

Luncheon Meat Stops are shaped to ensure hair rigged chunks of meat are secured on the cast.

Mini meatballs, also known as Meaty Fish Bites, are hook-sized balls of luncheon meat impregnated with a potent liquid attractor such as squid juice. Smaller than the *Campbells Meatballs* in various types of gravy which are also used on some Commercials, they sell for around £1.65 a tin as opposed to 85p for the table versions.

Other types of meat including the steak and mince combination plus sausage meat have been used for years with success on rivers for chub and barbel, but their use is very limited on Commercials. There's perhaps scope for experimentation here, as carp are sure to take them and a change bait can often produce excellent results before others cotton on to its effectiveness.

Fox Match Series 2 Barbless Eyed Hooks, in either Standard or Extra Strong Wire, are a good choice for meat but use a Carbon Carp if targeting bigger fish. Size 14s and 16s are the norm but a size 12 can be used with bigger chuncks of meat. Even when fishing up in the water, it is advisable to hair rig meat because it is such an effective presentation.

It is important to carry a selection of meat punches. Bites will often be forthcoming on a bigger chunk one day, while a smaller piece will work the next. A round piece on the hook can work wonders for wary fish.

USING A MEAT CUTTER

Place a slice of meat in the cutter. Varying the thickness of the meat at this stage will produce different sized cubes.

Push the meat smoothly through the cutter one way to create long columns of meat.

Then push the meat through the opposite way to create cubes of meat.

Turn the meat over a few times to ensure the meat is broken up into lots of little cubes.

One of the oldest 'man-made' baits, bread is also one of the cheapest with prices starting from as little as 20p for a loaf of 'economy' white sliced bread at some supermarkets. More typically, at around 40 to 70p per loaf, it's still a bargain basement bait of the highest order.

White bread seems far better than brown for all types of fishing. This is probably due to its extra visibility and also its texture, which stays on the hook better. On Commercials, its use falls mainly into two areas – firstly, as a floating or sub-surface bait to intercept cruising carp in the hot summer months, and secondly as a visible 'target' hook bait, perhaps in conjunction with a little liquidised bread feed, during very cold winter conditions.

Bread is naturally buoyant, especially the denser crusts, and lends itself to the pole tactic known as 'dapping'. This simply involves tying a hook to the end of a piece of line and lowering it onto the surface. If carp can be seen, you can attempt to anticipate their path and intercept them by dropping it onto their noses. Either a roughly torn chunk of flake or, in cases, an entire slice rolled up and wrapped around the line with the hook point left to dangle free, can be used.

The latter presentation is often known as 'the cigar'. However, bear in mind that many fisheries prohibit surface baits and/or the use of line without a float attached, so check first.

Winter bread fishing can be done either on the pole or the tip. Most anglers use large bait punches to produce one or two circular pellets of bread which can then be nicked onto a wide gape hook or, sometimes, threaded onto a hair rig. Once submerged, these will expand and fluff up.

When it comes to choosing the type of bread to use, the long life supermarket varieties – commonly packaged in foil-style bags – are a good choice. They have a high oil content which helps keep them on the hook. Another favourite is Warburton's.

A Standard Fox Match Series 2 in size 14 is the ideal choice for a decent sized piece of punched bread. A size 12 Series 7 is preferable for larger pieces such as used for surface fishing.

POLLY'S COMMENT

A standard Fox Match Series 2 Hook is my choice for a decent sized piece of punched bread, or a size 12 Series 7 Hook for larger pieces when surface fishing.

Even in winter, bread can dry out fast. Remove slices for punching from the airtight bag one at a time.

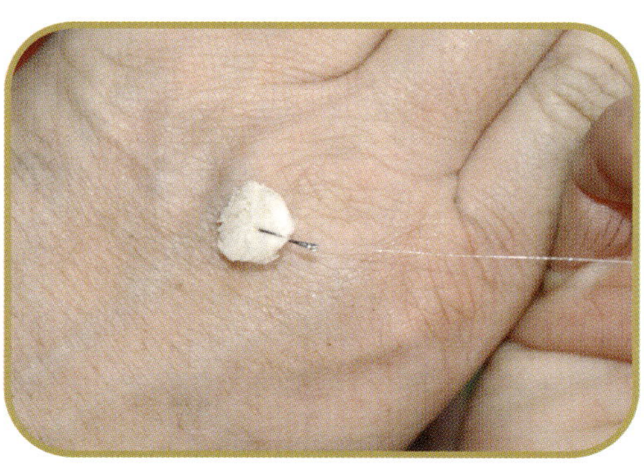

Once submerged, a piece of punched bread will swell up to around twice its size, hiding much of the hook shank.

The potent pulling power of hempseed for river roach and barbel has long been known, but carp love the stuff too. The natural oil exuded by cooked hemp is a superb attractor, even on those rare occasions when fish aren't interested in eating the actual seeds. This makes it an excellent winter feed on Commercials.

Hemp is actually the seed of a plant in the cannabis family. But don't worry, the stuff sold for angling won't germinate and won't get you high. And it does no harm whatsoever to the fish. Several types are available, but the cheapest is the basic uncooked seeds which you can get from tackle and pet shops or animal feed wholesalers. The latter can be your most economical place to bulk buy the stuff, typically at around £7.50 per five kilos.

You should soak hemp for around 24 hours, then bring to the boil in a saucepan before reducing the heat to simmer the seeds until they start to split. The shell will turn dark brown or black, with the inside kernel remaining a brilliant white which provides a contrast that makes for a highly visible bed of bait.

Some bait firms offer giant hemp, which are the larger grade seeds. These are best for hook baits if you opt to target roach, which reach excellent sizes in many Commercials. But you may also be surprised to catch a wide variety of other species.

Many bait companies now offer tins and jars of cooked hemp, vacuum sealed in the oil-rich water it was cooked in. A small can generally costs around £1.50. An aniseed flavoured version is available too in this format, with crushed and grilled hemp available in bags for use as groundbait additives.

Hemp is not allowed on all Commercials; nor does it work to maximum effectiveness all year round. However, towards the end of April or early May, following a consistent period of warmer weather, the 'demon seed' comes into its own when fed with meat, using meat on the hook. Hemp produces a loud noise when fed, and Commercial Fishery fish are notorious for associating noise with food. It is sometimes good to feed by hand for this very reason.

"Towards the end of April or early May, the demon seed comes into it's own when fed with meat"

In the colder months, hemp is an excellent feed in association with a few grains of sweetcorn, using a grain of corn on the hook as a stand-out hook bait.

One useful dodge used by roach anglers is to liquidise cooked hemp into a mush, perfect for cupping in. This has yet to be widely tried on Commercials but seems likely to pull other species too.

Aside from hemp, there are several other particle baits available in either dry form or in large jars from *Dynamite Baits*. Tares, mini maize and maples are all proven carp-catchers and so long as fishery rules do not state they are banned, all are worth a try if you're seeking a different bait to the norm for a pleasure session.

Left: If time is limited or you can't cook hemp in the kitchen at home, some excellent pre-cooked versions are available in jars and tins, with the added bonus of oil-rich water being sealed in.

"A huge choice of tinned or sachet cat food is available, usually in jelly or gravy. Carp absolutely love them"

A bit like bread, the use of pet foods as bait on commercial fisheries can be split neatly into surface and bottom fishing categories.

The surface part comes with the use of dog biscuits, widely known as 'Mixers' after a very popular brand from *Pedigree Chum*. However, many supermarkets offer 'own brand' biscuits, and there's also a wide variety of dry cat foods which float and therefore perform similarly. Prices are typically around £2.60 for four kilos of 'own brand' mixers.

Their main advantages over floating bread is that you can catapult out freebies with minimal effort, and they they'll last a lot longer once dunked onto the water and don't come off as easily. On the downside, they're harder to hook so they tend to be either banded (see the section on pellets for more information on this), superglued or drilled out with a Mini Nut Drill then hair-rigged. As with bread, Mixers take on colours and flavours well.

Like many baits 'borrowed' from the specimen carp world, the use of Mixers is somewhat limited at Commercial Fisheries. Although carp love them and they can be highly effective, on many fisheries they're banned. Surface baits by their very nature are effected by surface conditions. If there's a strong wind blowing, any free offerings tend to end up in one position of the lake, normally the bank into which the wind is blowing.

However, the same can't be said for the other type of pet food, widely known as 'cat meat' but more accurately as cat food. After all, it's not actually the meat of a cat…at least we hope not! There's a huge choice of tinned or sachet-packed meaty chunks - usually in jelly or gravy – intended to feed the family moggy. But carp in particular absolutely love them too, and costing as little as 25p a can, they are yet another popular and affordable convenience bait. Favourite brands include *Coshida*, *Whiskas* and *Katkins*. Some anglers swear by fishy flavours, others meaty varieties.

However, be aware once again that many fisheries ban or limit its use meat due to fears over its reputedly low nutritional value, and also its effects on water quality when introduced in large quantities.

Love it or hate it, cat food certainly seems to attract the larger stamp carp where it's allowed. Reason enough to give it a try at some stage, surely?

PERFECT CAT FOOD PRESENTATION WITH HELP FROM A BAITING NEEDLE

Cat food is messy stuff, and it's wise to have a bait box containing water to wash one's hands after handling it. Being very soft, it can pay to use a Paste Coil to keep it on the hook – certainly if attempting to cast it on float or leger gear rather than ship or swing it out carefully on the pole. It's important to use a good size hook - a size 12 Series 2 is perfect, either Standard or Extra Strong wire. Here's a couple of useful tips which allow you to present the bait without using a spring or coil. Here's how…

1

Thread a chunk of cat meat up the shaft of a baiting needle.

2

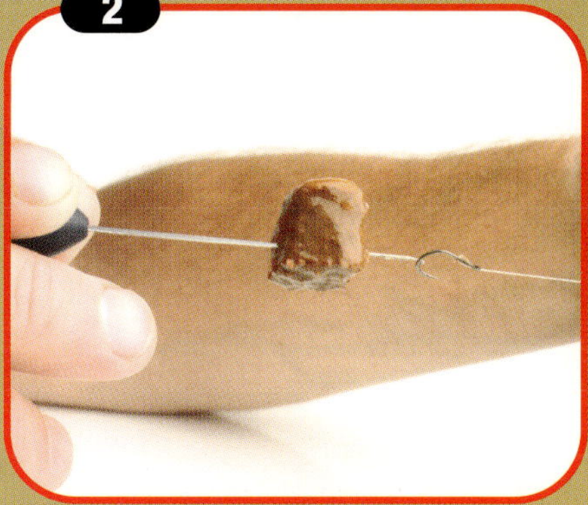

Place your hook in the needle's hook.

3

Pull the chunk of meat over the hook and onto your line.

4

Remove hook from needle, then turn the hook point through 90 degrees.

5

Pull the hook back into the bait. You're left with a totally concealed hook, which will strike easily through the soft cat meat when you get a bite.

The soft nature of Cat Food means the concealed hook method is highly effective. However, if you're missing a lot of bites then try the following which gives you a kind of reverse hair rig:

1. Repeat steps 1 to 3 in the above procedure.
2. Instead of pulling the meat into the hook, leave it resting on the hook's eye with the hook exposed below, as shown in step 4 above.

If this doesn't work, use the hair rig and coil method shown in the Paste section.

Despite all the many and various groundbaits and additives on the market, Mark Pollard relies on just a small selection for his Commercial Fishery angling when carp are the prime targets. "Experience leads me to believe that using groundbait on commercials attracts too many silver fish. To get round this you must use a bigger bait such as corn or meat on the hook if you do decide to feed it," says Mark. Here's his favourite mixes.

Groundbait Feeder

Mix 1

1 bag Green Marine
1 bag Ringers Carp Mix

Mix 2

1 bag Ringer Carp Mixl
1/2 a bag of brown crumb

These two mixes cover all my commercial fishing. At relatively new fisheries or where F1's and smaller carp are the quarry, I always opt for mix 1. Marine Green and Ringers Carp Mix are both fishmeal based groundbaits and as most stocked fish are raised on a diet of pellets, I feel this mix serves as an excellent attractant whilst still offering some feed value. On more established fisheries, or if the carp are predominently of a slightly larger stamp (5lb or above) mix 2 comes into play.

The fishmeal in the Ringers Carp Mix serves as the attractant while the brown crumb provides more feed value to the mix, which is essential for bigger fish. Although I've stated half a bag of Brown crumb, this is purely a starting point and I'll add a full bag of crumb if a big weight is expected. Bream are also lovers of brown crumb so on fisheries where big bream weights are expected, I will also use the second mix.

I tend to mix these two options fairly damp but not oversaturated, otherwise it sticks in the feeder. When feeder fishing for carp you must be certain that when you have a fish on, the bait has emptied from the feeder so while you play the fish you don't spread bait all over the peg.

After mixing either option I put it through a maggot riddle, although in winter I use a pinkie riddle to create a finer mix. A riddle produces an even, consistent mix and helps break up any big lumps. Unlike some anglers, I don't push any big particles left on top of the riddle back into the riddled mix. I prefer to add any free offerings such as corn,pellet or meat aftewards.

I also use these mixes with a Fox Toss Pot. For this task, the groundbait needs to be mixed slightly drier but once again must be run through a maggot riddle prior to fishing. This creates a softer, slower falling bait which creates a bigger cloud as it passes through the water.

What I do is to sprinkle the groundbait into the Toss Pot loose, along with any other freebies such as a few pellets or the odd grain of sweet-corn, then very lightly compress it down with my thumb. This helps to keep everything in place while shipping out. You mustn't press down too hard though, as this will make it hard to release the bait once you've reached the spot and inverted your pole. A gentle tap of the butt should send the contents tumbling into the water."

Apart from a few large pieces of flaked maize, a Method mix should be riddled to a nice fine consistency just like any normal groundbait.

Method Mix

For most of my method fishing I use a fairly simple mix, comprising Van den Eynde Method mix with a little crushed hemp. The ratio is about 95% Method Mix to 5% Crushed Hemp.

Although only a small proportion of the hemp is used, it plays a vital part in the mix. Firstly, it produces a cloud of oil which 'fizzes up' through the water and serves as an attractant to fish. Secondly, the crushed hemp helps to break down the mix when on the bottom as the oils are released.

By their very nature, Method mixes need to be fairly sticky and quite damp. However, it is important to achieve the correct consistency; one where the groundbait will adhere to the feeder yet still break down over a relatively short period of time – say 10-15 minutes. To achieve this you need to add water to the mix gradually, leaving it to stand for five minutes before returning and adding more water. Remember, you can always add a bit more water but you can never take it out once it's in.

As with all groundbaits, I always pass the final mix through a riddle.

At venues where there is a high proportion of bigger carp, in the 7lb-plus stamp, I find Van den Eynde Hi-Pro Carp Method Mix good on its own. But that's about it as far as my Commercial groundbaits go," concludes Mark.

MIXING GROUNDBAIT

Mixing your groundbait correctly is as important as choosing the right mix in the first place. When mixed incorrectly the action of the groundbait can become 'dead' and will not attract the fish. Here's how to create the perfect mix:

1

Combine the dry baits in a round mixing bowl with ample capacity.

2

Using a bait box add water to the dry mix but do not over wet it. Then leave it to stand for 10 minutes. After this time you may need to add more water as the groundbait absorbs this.

3

Even carp mixes should be pushed through a riddle prior to use, to stop big lumps forming.

4

Return larger particles that won't go through the riddle, such as flaked maize, to the mix.

5

The final mix looks like this.

RINGERS FISHMEAL LIQUIDISED WITH LUNCHEON MEAT AND A LITTLE PREDATOR PLUS

1

Place half the Ringers groundbait in the liquidiser.

2

Depending on the power of your blender, cut the meat into four or more equal size pieces.

3

Set the liquidiser running and drop a piece of meat into the mix. Leave the liquidiser running for at least a minute. A good tip here is to occasionally stop and start the liquidiser to produce a really fine cloud.

4

With the blender running, add a good egg cup full of the Predator Plus liquid. This, along with the juices, of the luncheon meat, will help to bind the mix.

5

Repeat step three with each of the remaining chunks of meat.

6

Once all the meat is added, it is good idea to give the mix a quick pulse to ensure it is completely blitzed.

7

The final mix should be fairly fine. You should be able to take a handful and squeeze it gently to create a ball but when you rub it between your hands it should crumble back to fine particles.

8

This mix is best prepared at home either the night or morning before a match or a session. Seal the mix in a plastic bag to ensure none of the flavours escape whilst en route to your venue.

Moondust – or space dust as it's sometimes known - is still a fairly hush-hush Commercial Fishery groundbait being used by those in the know with increasingly effective results over recent seasons.

A valid option in the warmer months whether you are pole or feeder fishing, to make up your own batch you need the following items:.

- 1 bag of Ringers Bag-Up Carp Mix groundbait
- 1 standard sized tin of luncheon meat
- 1 bottle of Van den Eynde Predator Plus
- A liquidiser, blender or food mixer.

Basically a blend of fishmeal groundbait and finely ground luncheon meat, Moondust is a sure-fire winner with carp, tench, bream and many other species from mid-spring right through to late autumn.

Before you learn how to create your own, you will need to check fishery rules as the groundbait content may result in this being banned at certain venues. Also, if there's a limit on the amount of meat then you must enquire whether the tin used in a Moon mix forms part of this, and regulate your remaining amounts accordingly. Happily, Moondust seems to have very few bans to date, so it's something you should be able to try out at most of your local Commercial fisheries over the coming months.

So, just why is this stuff so effective? Top anglers liken the mix to a rich gravy, in which your hook bait stands out like a prime chunk of steak. In a nutshell, it's giving carp a combination of the meaty taste they find so irresistible but without filling them up, combined with the fishmeal/pellety flavours they've known since birth.

The Predator Plus liquid adds a tinge of attractive red colour, plus extra scent, whilst also helping the mix to bind together better. That said, you mustn't overdo it with the squirty bottle as you can create something far too sloppy. A couple of generous squirts is ample. Combined with the meat's inherent moisture, this will ensure the entire kilo of Ringer's groundbait gets dampened down sufficiently once you've given it a good whizz in a blender.

POLLY'S COMMENT

Moondust creates a rich gravy, in which your hook bait stands out like a prime chunk of steak!

Either pack a pinch of Moondust into an open-end feeder, or cup some in on a pole line. Lower a bait in over it, sit back and await action. Be warned – it can be quick and seriously explosive!

POLLY'S COMMENT

For a typical five or six hour session or match, I prefer to use mini boilies on a hair rig with size 14 to 18 Fox Match Barbless Extra Strong Series 2 Hooks.

No chapter on baits would be complete without mention of Boilies. The success story of the past three decades in the big fish world, these little round balls are basically a mix of powdered ingredients bound together with eggs and dunked briefly into boiling water for a minute or two to create a tough skin which is resistant to the attentions of small fish.

Mainly based upon a fishmeal or seed 'base mix', boilies come in a myriad of flavours and colours and in several sizes from 'mini' – typically 8mm diameter – through to 20mm-plus 'gobstoppers'.

A 14mm diameter is the typical specimen carp angler's choice, though the size of fish encountered in Commercials generally finds this a bit too much of a mouthful. Furthermore, boilies are on the 'banned' list at many venues.

Where permitted though, boilies can work well although regular match and pleasure anglers tend to find they take longer to

A hair-rigged boilie can be left to hang beneath a Method feeder (top), or be placed in the mix for fish to dig out (bottom).

Ready-tied hair rigs are available for several specific baits, including mini boilies.

"A 14mm diameter is the typical specimen carp angler's choice"

draw an initial response compared to the likes of pellets, meat and corn. For the average length session you are therefore advised to avoid using boilies as a feed, but they're certainly worth a try as a hook bait at waters which see a fair amount of their use by specimen anglers.

Mark Pollard prefers mini boilies for the five or six hour session which form a typical match. He'll hair rig one on a size 14 to 18 Fox Match Barbless Extra Strong Series 2, below either a groundbait or Method feeder, or a bomb.

Other Alternative Baits

As well as all of the many and various baits already mentioned in this chapter, there are several others which you may come across or feel inspired to try. After all, fish – especially carp and chub - are catholic eaters which will sample most things.

And you may encounter 'local favourites' – baits which seem to work especially well at certain fisheries – in your travels. The likes of potato pellets, prawns and cockles and even macaroni cheese are a few of the better known examples. Keep an open mind and don't be afraid to experiment from time to time.

But generally speaking, sticking to the baits we've already mentioned will see you succeed wherever you set up. Just be sure to always check the fishery rules to ensure your chosen bait isn't on the 'banned' list.

Chapter 2

float tactics

"Any Commercial Fishery visitor will benefit from packing at least one float rod in their holdall"

When it comes to float fishing with a rod and reel as opposed to a pole, for 95 per cent of Commercial Fishery tasks you should reach for the waggler. This is the commonly used name for a float attached bottom end only, as opposed to top and bottom which almost all pole floats are.

Good as the pole is, there are occasions when most or even all of the fish – or perhaps just the bigger ones – are swimming around beyond pole range. This usually happens when the sun is at its highest during the middle of the day. Despite the generally well coloured water on Commercials, they can see you and the shadow of your pole, and know this spells danger. Any Commercial Fishery visitor will certainly benefit from packing at least one float rod in their holdall, and learning the various techniques to help them get the best from it.

Most wagglers have an eye at the bottom which you can pass the line through. Once accomplished, you can set the float at the desired depth by either locking it either side either with shot, or doing likewise with rubber float stops. Remember to thread the first stop onto your line before your float.

Wagglers can be made from many different materials including peacock quill, cane, plastic and balsa.

ATTACHING THE WAGGLER

As well as simply using locking shot or rubber stops, you can fit a float adaptor which allows you to change styles and sizes of waggler quickly and efficiently without having to tackle down. This is helpful if the wind strength suddenly increases or decreases and you find you now need a larger or smaller float carrying greater or lesser amounts of loading to cast to the desired spot.

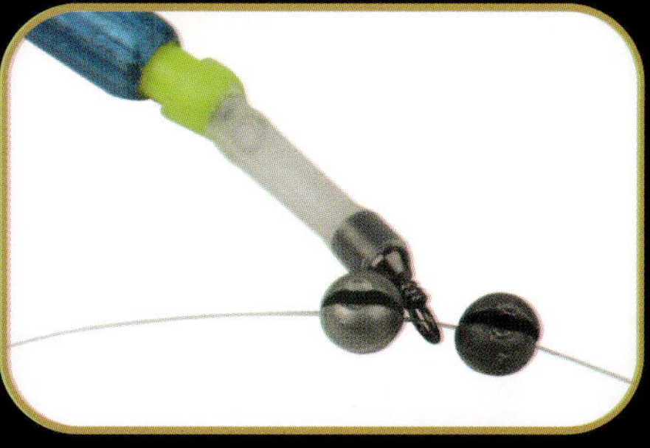

Locking shot with a swivel adaptor, a type good for reducing line twist.

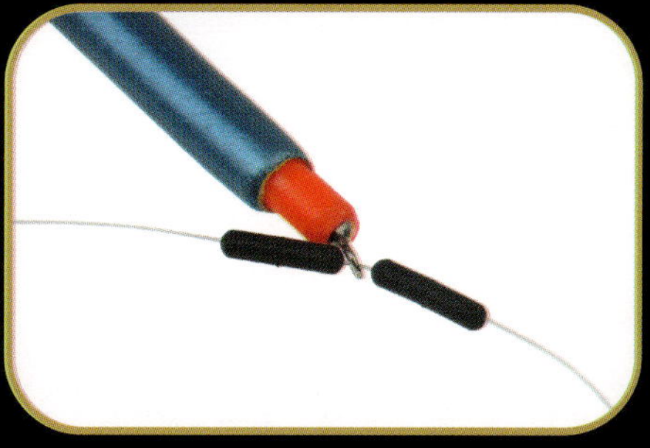

Locking your float between sliding rubber float stops is very kind to the line.

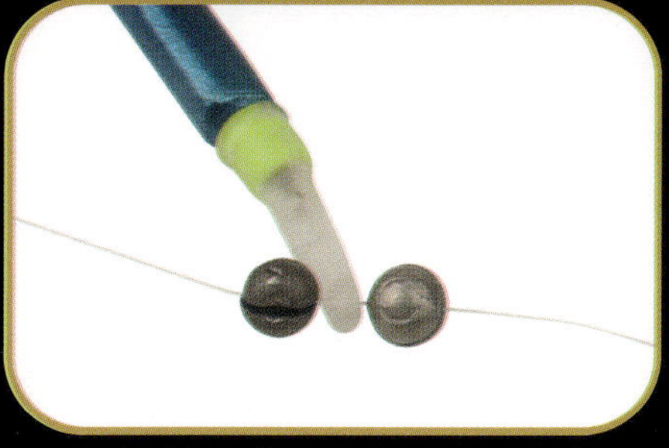

A basic silicone float adaptor allows fast float changes, but the line can sometimes cut through.

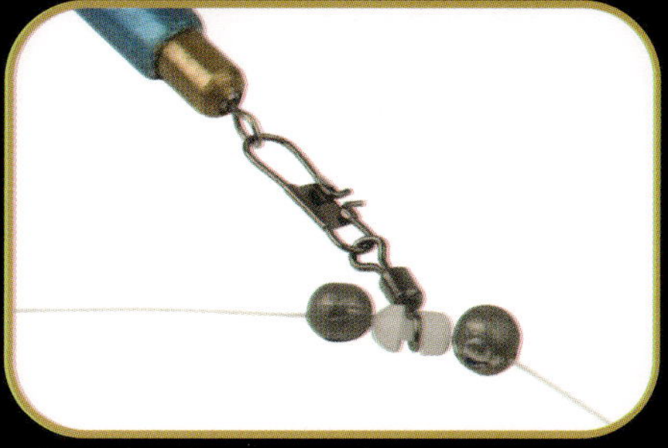

Mark Pollard likes these quick-release link swivel adaptors for waggler fishing.

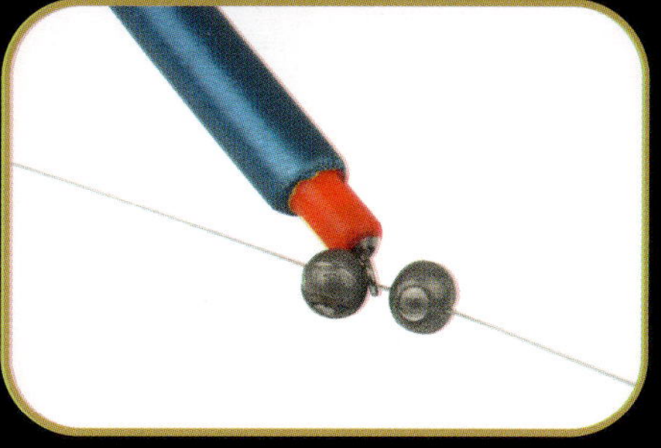

Straight through the base eye with locking shots is the most basic attachment method.

Having established that 'Wagglers' is a broad term covering all bottom-end floats, it's time now to examine what amounts to massive range of shapes, colours and sizes in greater detail.

All these many and various floats can be sub-divided into a handful of categories, as detailed on this page. Some are better suited to Commercial Fishery applications than others. Indeed, quite a few were invented specifically for use on carp-packed stillwaters.

Mark Pollard is an exponent of keeping things simple and only carries a small selection of wagglers.

In the subsequent pages, we'll go into greater depth about how to fish different types of wagglers – whether overdepth, tripping bottom, mid-depth or shallow. Once again, as with all fishing, you'll see that it pays to keep things as simple as possible by using just a small selection of the various types of wagglers that are on the market.

Peacock quill (left) and plastic wagglers.

That said, when you enter your local tackle shop and peruse the vast range of floats on offer, you'll be able to select something broadly suitable for your own favourite fisheries by using this guide as a 'rule of thumb' checklist.

All the major float-making materials - peacock quill, clear plastic (widely known as 'crystals'), balsa and occasionally sarkandas reed – can be used to make straights.

Different tip colours suit different backgrounds.

Quick Colour Tip

You'll notice that wagglers, like all floats, come with different colours of tip. The most common are orange, red, yellow and black. This is because some colours show up better than others against different backgrounds.

Red and orange are good all-rounders, but when faced with open water reflecting a grey sky – perhaps with a ripple making visibility even harder – most anglers find a black-tipped float best. In dark water beneath trees, yellow is reckoned by many to be the most visible colour.

POLLY'S COMMENT

It's a good idea to carry a black waterproof marker pen plus some white correction fluid and, if you can locate some, other fluorescent coloured marker pens. If you don't have a float of the right size with the right colour tip for the conditions, a quick bit of DIY on the bank will solve the dilemma.

SHOTTING WAGGLERS

It's important that when you strike a bite on the waggler, the float itself doesn't hinder the process in any way. For this reason, Mark Pollard likes to attach his to the line via a small link swivel, which allows the waggler to 'collapse' and offer minimal resistance through the water.

1

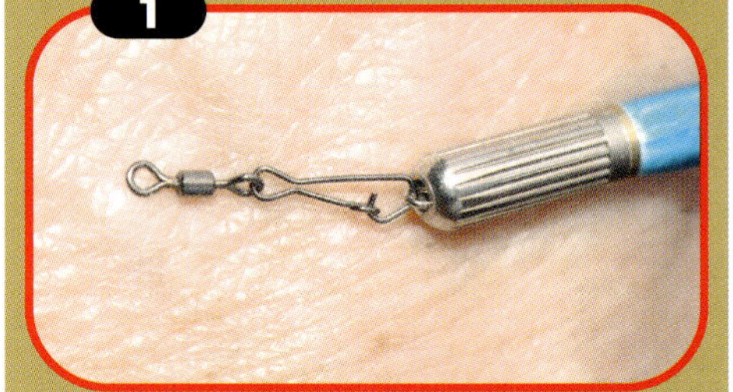

A clip swivel also allows instant changing of floats if conditions demand

2

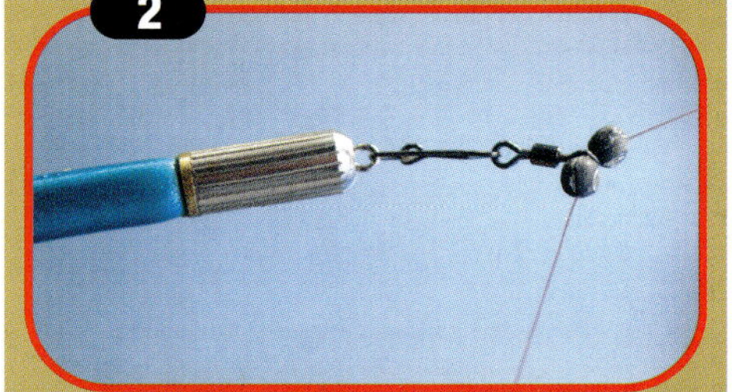

Attach a shot each side of the clip swivel's eye to lock the float at the chosen depth. As an approximate rule of thumb, at least two-thirds of a waggler's capacity should be used as locking shot (commonly known as 'lockers'). The float in this picture has a base weight, so two BBs are all that's needed

3

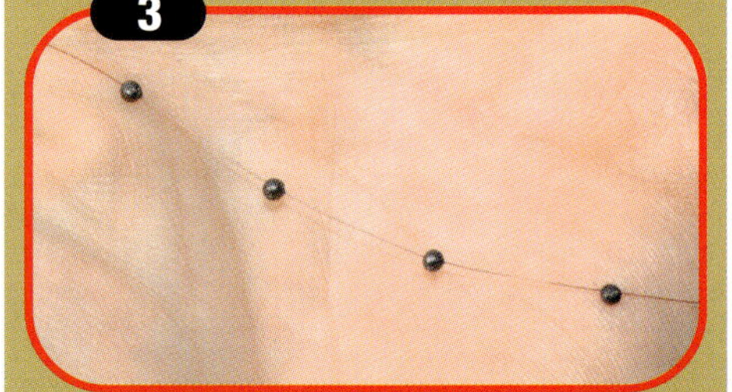

Dropper shot is the term given to shots placed down the line between float and hook. These are usually small shot such as No.8s and No.10s, though occasionally you may need to use larger ones.

4

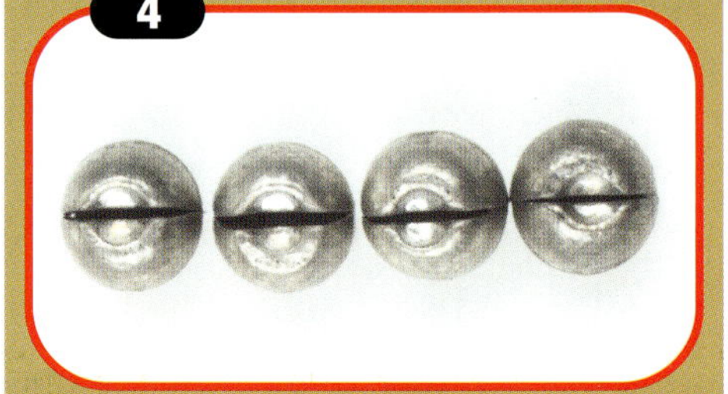

On occasions when you want more weight down the line, such as to bomb the bait down past smaller nuisance fish or when fishing a Slider, a bulk shotting pattern is required. This is basically a group of three to five shots, anything from No.4s to AAAs, with one, two or three smaller droppers set below. Ensure the slots all line up when you squeeze on your bulk shot, as this helps to prevent line twist and makes the cast more streamlined.

Straight wagglers can be long and loaded (left) for deeper swims and longer casts, or shorter and thicker (below) for shallower water and bigger baits presented off bottom.

Straights

The standard waggler, is hugely versatile and justifiably popular. As their name suggests, they are of uniform thickness and can range from around six inches to more than a foot long.

A good choice when fish are biting freely or when you need to fish overdepth, they cast straight and true and their tip's inherent buoyancy allows overdepth presentation of fairly big baits without the risk of repeatedly dragging under, signalling false bites.

Straight wagglers allow the option of placing more shot down the line than finer and more specialised models. This makes them useful for getting smaller baits down quickly when nuisance small fish are marauding in the upper layers.

Straights are also your first choice in choppy conditions, where you would struggle to see a finer tipped float, let alone detect bites.

FULL DEPTH WAGGLER RIG

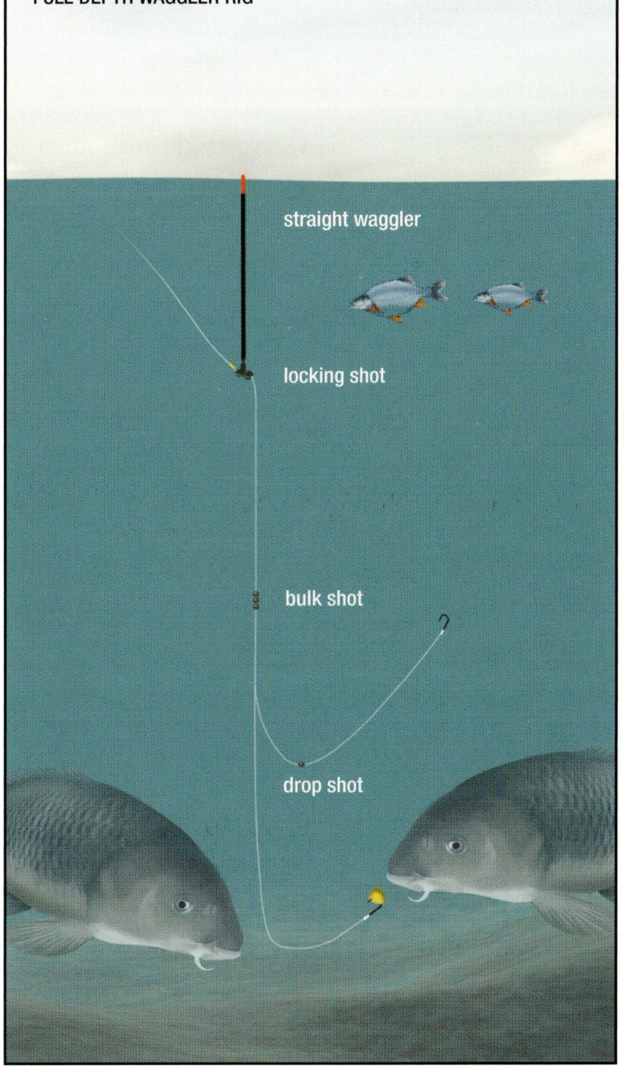

Loaded versions of the classic straight waggler are also available. They have part of their shotting capacity built in via a metal rod in the base, or add-on weights which slot over the base peg. These tend to dive deeper into the water upon entry, and are therefore best avoided if you expect to catch shallow later in a session.

SHALLOW WAGGLER RIG

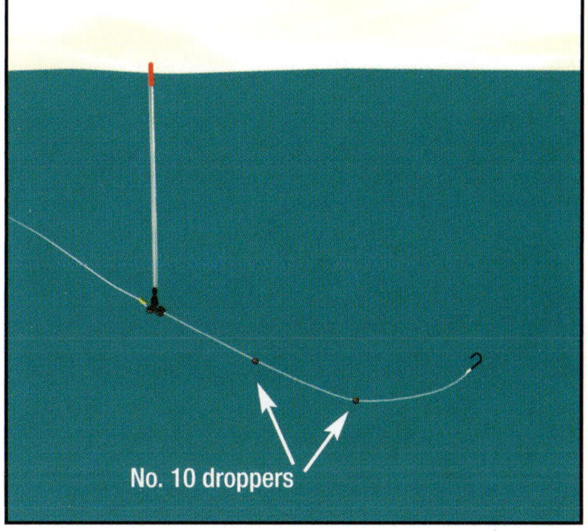

Shallow

Short wagglers designed for fishing up in the water can be either straight, insert or bodied, and equipped with or without a loaded base. Often made of an unobtrusive clear plastic, their purpose is to catch fish in the top layers of water. Instead of an eye at their base, some models have unique methods of attachment that eliminate the need for shot to be placed either side of the float to lock it in place.

They can either be cast into shallow water or set to fish shallow over greater depths. Choose a fat-topped version to present big baits and a more slender insert when the fish are more finicky or a smaller species such as rudd are the quarry.

Shallow wagglers can also be constructed from more traditional float materials such as balsa and peacock quill. Of the two, balsa is the more versatile as it can be shaped to feature a wider base which offers greater resistance to the water upon entry, limiting the depth to which it dives. Balsa is also better able to accept built-in loadings.

Often known as 'Stumpys', shallow wagglers made of balsa tend to have a greater shotting capacity and are therefore good for casting greater distances than plastic models. They are capable of withstanding a lot rougher treatment than their more fragile peacock quill equivalents, which is what you need when chunky carp roll on them and bash them about before being unhooked in the landing net.

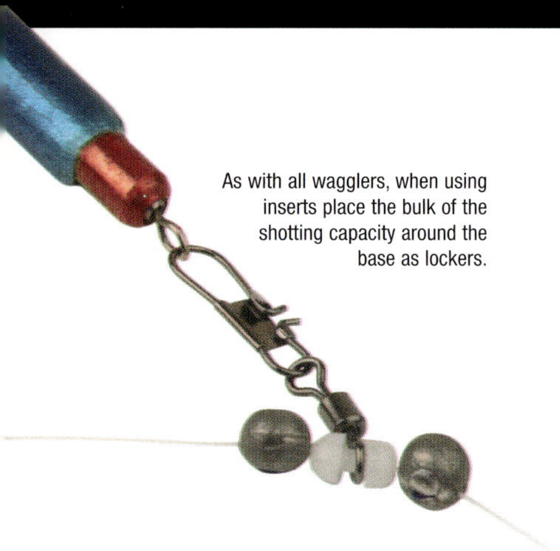

As with all wagglers, when using inserts place the bulk of the shotting capacity around the base as lockers.

Inserts

Similar to a straight waggler, with the same range of materials used but with a finer diameter tip section inserted into the top of the float.

Inserts offer less resistance than straights to a biting fish.

This finer section offers less resistance to a biting fish, thus making inserts ideal for hard winter days and/or smaller venues where you're fishing at closer ranges. Their only disadvantage is the fact that their finer tips do not cope well with choppy surfaces, registering false bites too often due to their lack of buoyancy.

In recent years, a less pronounced type of insert waggler has been produced. Rather than using cane to produce the insert, it involves blending in a finer section of peacock quill. This type will ride a choppy surface better than the usual ones, but still gets defeated by bigger waves. When this happens, try a straight waggler or go on the tip.

When shotted correctly, less than a centimetre of an insert's tip is left protruding from the surface. Shy bites are easily detected to allow a fast strike, likewise those from fish that intercept the bait as it falls through the water - a type of bite widely referred to as being 'on the drop' or a 'hold up'. In this latter case, you'll notice more of the insert standing proud of the water when the bottom dropper shot should have settled it down. A fish has taken the bait, so strike!

If the insert fails to settle properly, a fish is holding the bait up - so strike!

Before baiting up, cast out an insert waggler and observe the effect each dropper shot has on the tip. If the float fails to settle properly when you cast out with bait then it has been intercepted by a fish on the drop.

The size and thickness of a bodied distance waggler's body can vary.

A slider is best used in depths of 10ft and above, or if there's considerable tow. The bulk of shot is positioned about 4ft from the hook.

Bodied

Bodied wagglers feature a thicker section – usually curved and elongated to give a streamlined oval profile – towards their base.

The body has the effect of stabilising the float in windy conditions. It also boosts shot carrying capacity, allowing longer casts.

Whilst straights may get dragged unnaturally through a swim by wave action, the body acts as a kind of anchor and can help pick up the undertow.

Although seldom required on Commercial stillwaters, bodied wagglers can also be fished in a style known as The Slider. As the name suggests, the float is set to slide on the line which is useful in depths greater than the length of the rod, as you often find on deep quarries or farm irrigation reservoirs.

A bulk of shots is set well down the line and the float rests against these on the cast, sliding freely up the line until coming to rest against a stop knot which is tied at the actual depth of the swim.

Distance

Basically a bodied waggler with added loading at the base. Used to cast well out, typically on large lakes, the distance waggler is sometimes known as a Missile or Scud. Most feature a series of circular brass or nickel screw-on plates set over a special threaded base peg.

With a full set of plates, the float will cock by itself meaning little or no extra shotting is required around the base or down the line. Alternatively, you can remove one or more to allow extra shot to be added down the line.

The largest versions are commonly known as Splashers, due to the noise they make on impact with the water. With a built-in weighting of up to 20 grams, they can be cast to extreme distances. Another variation is the 'Bagging Waggler', a very thick and relatively short balsa float featuring a swimfeeder frame at the base for moulding groundbait around. We will look at this further, later in the chapter.

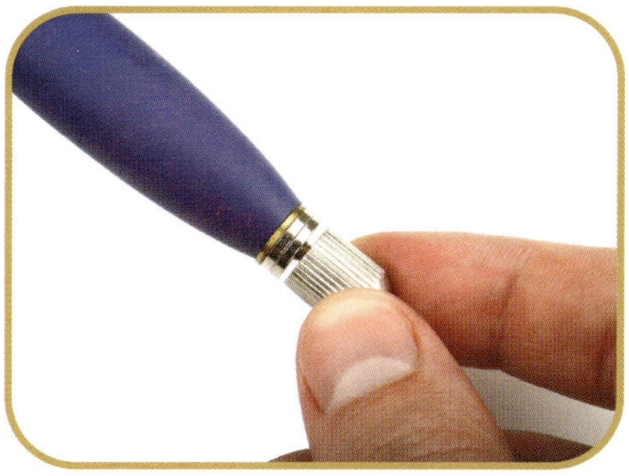

Some bodied floats have screw-threaded base weights which hold a series of removable plates in place.

If you want extra shots down the line, remove the required number of plates before screwing the base back on.

Surely there must be even bigger advantages to fishing a bottom-end only float on stillwaters than those briefly outlined on the previous page? After all, pole floats are attached top and bottom, and they work pretty well don't they?

Absolutely correct. The biggest difference between pole fishing and waggler fishing lies in the amount of line between the tip of the float and the top of your rod or pole. On the pole, the distance is seldom more than two or three feet – and often a great deal less when it comes to presentations for Commercials, as you'll see in the next chapter. This allows a very fast, almost instant response to a bite, and, most crucially there is not a lot of line for the wind or drift to catch hold of so the rig stays in position. In windy conditions, a back shot can be used with a pole rig, something not possible with a running line set-up.

However, if you attempted to fish a top and bottom float any further out than just beyond the rod end with a rod and line set-up, you would soon notice how the line between them formed into a large semi-circular shape, commonly known as a 'bow'. Even on days with minimal wind, there's often a significant drift in one direction at the water's surface. The upshot of all this is that the float would begin to 'skate' along, being pulled by the bow in the line.

"You may be surprised to find that the undertow often moves in a different direction to the wind"

Try next to imagine what is happening below the surface. Your hook bait would be motoring through a swim where all your freebies are far less active. No self-respecting fish is going to take a bait moving unnaturally like yours now is, except for maybe a few immature rudd or perhaps a greedy perch or two. The larger residents of Commercial fisheries such as carp and tench certainly aren't stupid! To catch them consistently, you need to present your hook bait in a natural manner as possible.

Beating The Bow

So to overcome the problem of a bow in the line, reach for the Waggler. Because the line is only attached at the float's bottom end, the first foot or so above the float will sink anyway. In many cases, it's also desirable to sink the entire remainder between float and tip as well. To do this follow the instructions in the panel on the opposite page.

By sinking the line between rod tip and float, you eliminate the negative effects of wind and drift as well as putting you in more direct contact with the float. Although there is still some movement beneath the surface – known as undertow - this is far less; indeed, picking up the undertow often helps natural bait presentation.

If you've not waggler fished on stillwaters before, you may be surprised to find that the undertow often moves in a different direction to the wind. This tends to be most noticeable on larger, more open venues where the prevailing wind blows the upper layers towards the leeward bank which in turn causes the lower layers to flow in the opposite direction to the wind, as shown in the diagram below.

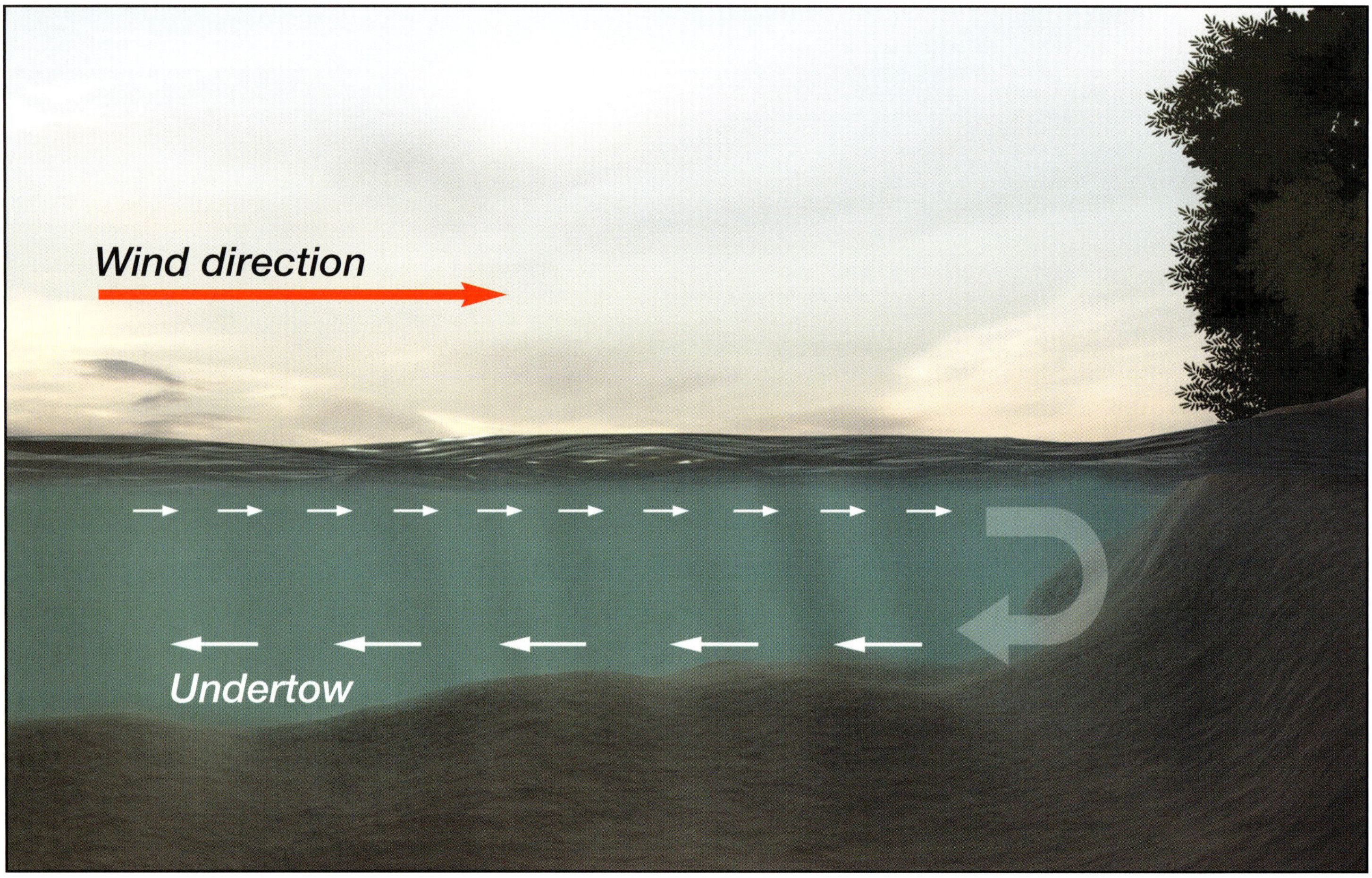

Bear in mind, that in most instances, the undertow will be moving in the opposite direction to the wind and surface current on still waters.

POLLY'S COMMENT

I prefer an upward strike rather than a sideways sweep. By striking upwards you can see which direction a fish is heading at the earliest opportunity.

The second benefit of a sunken line waggler approach is that you create a much more direct line to the float, improving control and allowing you to easily twitch the bait to induce bites, and, of course, to strike into bites. Because there's far more line between rod tip and float than on the pole, you will need to exert some force to drive the hook home. That's not to say you should try and pull them out of the water though.

Specialist Soft Steel Mono comes on handy sized spools in Commercial-friendly breaking strains

Mark Pollard's preference is for an upward strike, which he feels allows you to gain control of a fish quicker than with the sideways sweep style of strike preferred by some anglers. By striking upwards you can see which direction a fish is heading at the earliest opportunity.

Finally, there are instances when you have to fish a floating line on the waggler. We mentioned casting tight to islands or other features. Sometimes, you need to stay so tight to the feature get bites that even the 'striking under' line sink technique will result in your float coming too far away.

Doing nothing with your line, other than an initial 'mend' – meaning a sweep of the rod against the wind – to lay the line on the surface as straight as possible, is the only option. In instances like these, bites usually come fairly fast anyway as the fish are feeling confident tucked beside cover.

Using The Drift

As with most rules, there are occasional exceptions. One is when you are seeking to fish a floating bait such as bread crust or dog biscuits, to fish which are taking off the surface. Here, you should use the wind to your advantage and deliberately seek to avoid sinking your line. Floats for this task are Controllers or Bubble Floats. Although some controllers are attached bottom-end only, this is more for ease of casting. One attached top and bottom to lay flat on the surface would work perfectly well provided you can avoid too much of a bow forming.

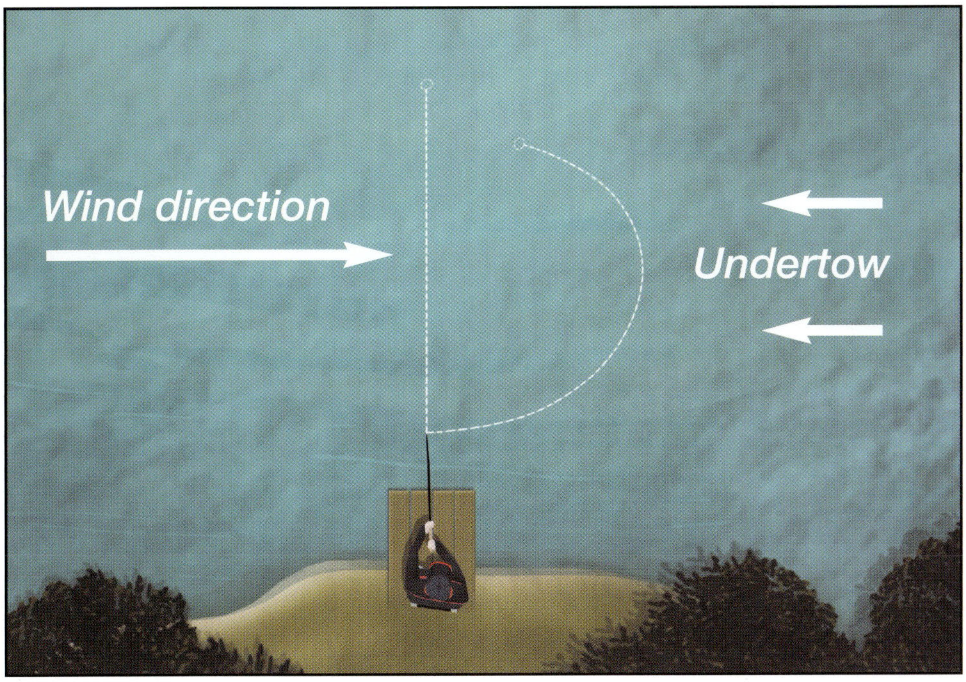

By not opting for a sunken line, the wind can form a bow in the line and your float can be pulled out of position in an unnatural manner.

SINKING THE LINE

There are several ways you can help ensure that your reel line sinks when fishing the waggler. Here's how.

1

Choose a brand of line known to be a good sinker.

2

Douse your reel's spool with a generous blast of line sink spray or a solution of water and washing-up liquid before tackling up.

3

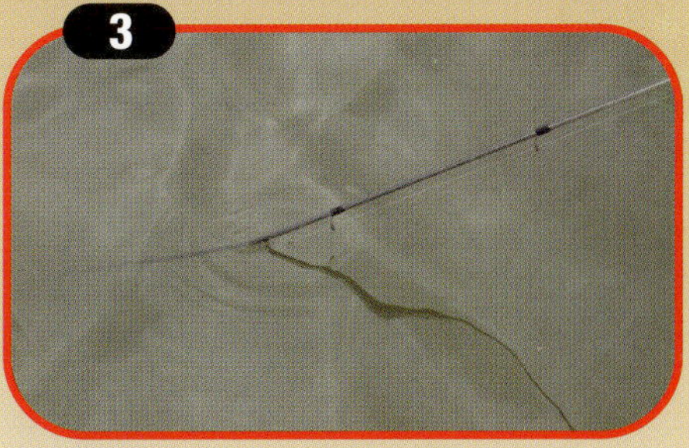
Once you've cast, sink your rod tip beneath the surface in the margins.

4

Strike sharply upwards but stop your rod on a horizontal plane. The line between float and rod tip will now be sunk, and the float should not have moved too far back from the spot you cast it to.

5

If you prefer, overcast then dunk the rod tip and give your reel handle three or four quick turns to sink the line. However, this is obviously impractical when fishing tight to features such as island margins or overhanging vegetation, and is only really viable in open water.

The way you cast will to some extent boil down to personal preference. However, on some occasions the swim you are in will dictate. For instance, overhanging vegetation may rule out a full-blooded overhead cast. In this case you will need to master the side cast technique.

More of that on the next pages. But first, some essential advice which is often overlooked but, if heeded, will ensure you can cast exactly where you want time after time after time.

POLLY'S COMMENT

Always select a slightly heavier float than you think is needed to cast the distance. It is better to reach your distance with ease than it is to struggle with a lighter float.

Choose Far Bank Marker

Whether you're casting tight to far bank cover or simply into open water, accuracy is important. Selecting a marker to aim at is an excellent habit to develop.

Be certain that the object is immovable. A shadow, for instance, is not. One well-known angler is said to have chosen a cow in a field opposite, with disastrous consequences! Popular legend apart, many others have come unstuck by choosing a patch of shade of a reflection on the water onto for this to later vanish as the sun moves round in the sky. A tree or a telegraph pole are obvious examples, but not every peg has these so you may need to select a smaller target such as a reed bed or a certain piece of vegetation.

In the picture on the left, the clump of tall grasses on the island corner plus the distant tree form a double target for the angler.

Accuracy sorted, you next task is to gain uniformity of distance. We'll look at the role of line clips in greater detail in the Legering chapter later in the book, but provided you're casting to an island where hooked fish can only run left or right then clipping is also a viable option on the waggler.

Match Float To Required Distance

A useful rule of thumb when waggler fishing is to always start by selecting a slightly heavier float than you think is needed to cast the distance.

Casting should be a smooth, almost effortless operation, but if you pick a float which is too light then this won't be the case. The familiar 'swish' of anglers struggling to punch out a too-light waggler in a vain bid to make the distance is still commonly heard on the banks of Commercial Fisheries.

Provided you use a quick change adaptor of some description, you can change floats in seconds if your initial choice is either too

heavy or too light. You may also need to do this if the wind picks up or changes direction and you are suddenly struggling to reach a spot which you'd hitherto been reaching with ease.

With most waggler fishing being done at beyond maximum pole range, a cast of more than 15 metres generally requires a float which takes a minimum of 3BB shot, and more typically 2AAA+. Some of this weight capacity may already be built into the float in the form of a permanent loading at the base, as seen in the larger straight waggler in the picture above. The smaller insert waggler is unloaded, so the bulk of its shot are placed either side of the adaptor's base eye.

FIll Spool To Rim

Loading the line onto your reel in the correct manner is another vital element of successful casting. Get it wrong and you'll struggle to make the distance, or line twist will make your life a misery when you should be enjoying yourself!

The reel pictured here is filled to perfection, with the line about three millimetres short of being level with the spool's front lip. If you don't put this much on, a more acute angle will be created between the line and the spool lip and the added friction will reduce potential casting distance.

Most good fixed spool reels come with two or more spools, one of which is usually a fair bit deeper than the other. We'd suggest placing a heavier mono such 6lb breaking strain - a typical summer choice for when carp fight their hardest - on this one. The shallower spool can take a finer 4 or 5lb mono for winter fishing.

To load your reel, attach it to the the butt section of a rod then pass the line through the butt ring then round your reel's spool with a simple double overhand knot. Ensure your bale arm is open so that it engages the line in the roller once you click it back over.

Draw the line tight and bed it down towards the lower end of the spool, trimming back the tag end as tight as possible to the knot.

Ask someone to hold the spool of monofilament with the label facing towards the front of the spool with one hand, and apply some tension to the line by having it pass through the thumb and forefinger of the other hand. The intention is to wind the line off the spool in the opposite direction to which it was loaded in the factory to remove any inherent line twist.

The line should come off the spool smoothly, without any coils which can create nightmare tangles once fishing.

OVERHEAD CASTING

With heavier tackle I always use an overhead cast, unless I'm in a 'parrot cage' swim with awkward branches above and behind me. Assuming there's none, the basic overhead cast is the best way to deliver your waggler to the chosen spot.

With your index finger trapping the line on the reel's open bale arm, hold the rod directly upwards and slightly behind you with the float dangling three to five feet beneath the tip (depth permitting).

Keeping your eyes fixed on a marker such as a reflection or immobile object on the far bank, sweep the rod overhead and release the line as it comes past the vertical, with the rod tip still pointing towards the spot. Feather your tackle down by batting your index finger lightly on the open spool as the float nears splashdown.

Once you have mastered the basics detailed on the previous pages, it is time to fine tune your casting technique. Specifically, this involves learning different methods of casting and the art of feathering.

Right! The ideal length of line from rod tip to float.

Feathering describes the use of your forefinger to slow down the line's exit from the reel's spool in the final stages of a cast. It's best likened to dabbing the brakes on your car in a controlled manner as you approach traffic lights where you may be able to proceed without reaching a complete stop.

Wrong! With so little line from rod to float you'll never cast far.

Feather your line too hard and the float's flight through the air will be prematurely halted, causing the rig to crash down into the water in an untidy heap still some way short of the desired distance.

Get it just right, with a light and fast series of fingertip touches as the cast nears the end of its arc, and the float will hang in the air for a crucial split second whilst the baited end tackle continues on to land in a perfect straight line ahead or to the side of it. Like so many of angling's finer arts, this is harder to describe and imagine than it is to see somebody do it and explain it on the bank. Don't be afraid to ask a good float angler for a lesson. Provided he's not in a match at the time, he will usually be happy to do so.

A failure to feather at all will result in the float and tackle landing noisily in a heap, with an increased likelihood of tangles. Or, worse of all, overshooting the mark to snag far bank vegetation with the possible loss of a float plus the near-certainty of a time consuming re-tackling task ahead of you. As previously mentioned, you can rely on your line clip to brake the float's flight short of far bank snags. However, this can produce the kind of sudden jolt which pulls the float those crucial few inches short of the target.

SIDE CASTING

This cast can lay your float and end tackle down on the water with barely a ripple. Best of all, its low trajectory allows you to cast beneath obstacles such as overhanging branches on the far bank as well as dodging tangles in any behind you.

The key is to use the rod's inherent flexibility to fire the float to the desired spot. Holding the hook length in your spare hand, a couple of inches above the baited hook, create a bend in the rod tip by tensioning the rod then quickly sweep it around on a parallel plane, simultaneously releasing the hook length.

The rod should end up pointing towards the desired landing place. It's not uncommon to catch round the rod's tip or second ring down when you first start, but practice makes perfect.

It is far better to practice hard at learning to feather a split second before the float hits the water to straighten the rig out. When doing so, it's wise to make a couple of dozen casts without any hook length attached. This way, if you get it wrong and catch the far bank then you've got far more chance of being able to retrieve the rig without snapping off and loosing the float. Choose a waggler that will only just reach the required distance, not one that will overshoot by ten yards or more. Always use a waggler adaptor so you can change the float later in the session if the wind picks up. Once you are happy with accuracy, tie a hook and start fishing!

Feathering line with your fingertips is an essential skill to learn towards float fishing success.

You can make a float land with minimal disturbance by feathering it down in the final stages of a cast.

Instead of landing in an untidy, tangle-prone heap, feathering will cause the line beneath the float to straighten out, making for a smooth descent of the bait with instant bite detection.

Carp on Commercial Fisheries will feed at all layers of the water, though not always at the same time. As with pole fishing, the decision on what depth to target them is one which can make the difference between success and failure; enjoyment and disappointment.

Experience plays a big part, but carp are not shy at showing themselves when they are feeding in the upper layers of the water and this is a big help. Generally speaking, the warmer the weather the more likely they are to be up in the water. It therefore follows that on cooler days and through the winter months, they are more likely to be found close to or on the bottom.

> **"In most instances you should aim to present the bait just touching the bottom"**

Other species, especially bream and tench, are even more reliable in their bottom feeding habits. That said, Commercial Fisheries are a unique environment with no hard and fast rules on where even these two species will intercept a bait.

It's therefore fair to say that you are most likely to benefit from waggler fishing at full depth a) during the colder months from late autumn onwards or b) during rough conditions with extreme undertow in shallow open water lakes. In this latter case, it can pay to set your float around 12 to 18 inches overdepth in a bid to slow the bait's progress through a swim.

But in most instances you should aim to present the bait just touching bottom. During winter, when the fish can be very tightly shoaled in a small area and unwilling to move, a wise ploy is to reduce your loose feed to an absolute minimum and cast around your swim with just the bait on your rig.

This will require knowledge of all the depths in the different areas you cast to. Plumbing the depth accurately is therefore essential. You can follow the sequence on the opposite page to learn the correct approach. But first, let's look at the type of tackle required for full depth waggler fishing.

Tackle For The Job

For full depth waggler fishing on Commercials, Mark Pollard recommends a standard float rod such as the Envoy 13ft or Signature Series 13ft 2in models. His current reel of choice is a rear drag Fox Match prototype fixed spool, loaded with reliable 4lb monofilament.

In summer he'll generally use 0.12mm Micro Plus hook lengths carrying a Series 2 barbless spade-end hook of size 18 or 20, which can cope with all the likely baits such as maggots, pellets, casters and sweetcorn. In winter he may scale down to an 0.10mm bottom as the fish don't fight as hard.

Mark favours loaded straight peacock wagglers for full depth fishing. He shots these with the bulk of the weight either side of the bottom eye, with a maximum of

The versatile 13ft 2in Signature Series waggler is a good choice for waggler fishing at full depth.

Bump Bars are handy to drop your rod onto when firing out bait via catapult.

three No.8s and No.10s spread down the line below.

In most instances he's aiming to present the bait at dead depth. However, the are times – especially when using pellets on the hook – that he will go overdepth by a foot to 18 inches.

Mark likes to attach his main line to his hook length via a loop-to-loop knot, but stresses that you must tie the loop in the correct way – a figure of eight – and avoid a weaker double overhand knot.

Finally, Mark does not use any type of rod rest when waggler fishing other than his beloved Fox Match Bump Bar, positioned in front of his seat box as when pole fishing.

The wind never blows his rod along or out of this rest due to the bar's ridged rubber surface, its height setting is fully adjustable and it locks up nice and securely unlike a rod rest on a bank stick or a long, unstable arm fixed to a seat box leg.

Which plummet to choose?

Plumbing the depth is an essential part of float fishing. Even if you opt to fish off bottom or overdepth, it's important to know by how much. So it's wise to get into the habit of plumbing your swim before every session.

The sequence of pictures on the right, plus the diagram below, will help you understand the basic principles. However, before you even get to the bank you'll be faced with a variety of different styles of plummet to choose from in the tackle shop.

Cork base plummets are most popular. There's also clip-on sprung versions. But both can be prone to damaging the line if not used with great care. Mark Pollard prefers a Stonfo plummet, seen below.

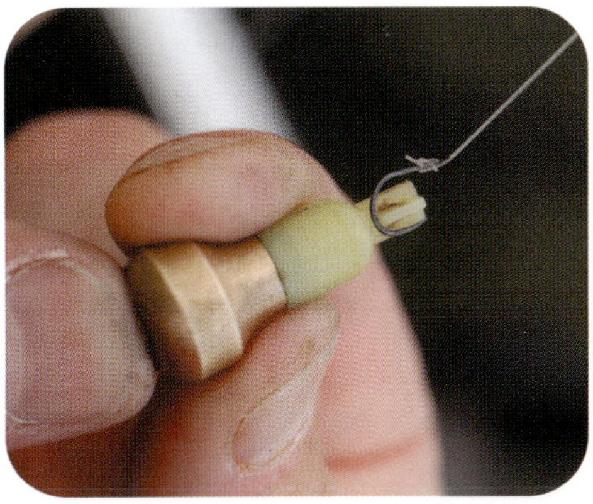

Depress button with thumb and slot your hook beneath the protruding tab's central catch.

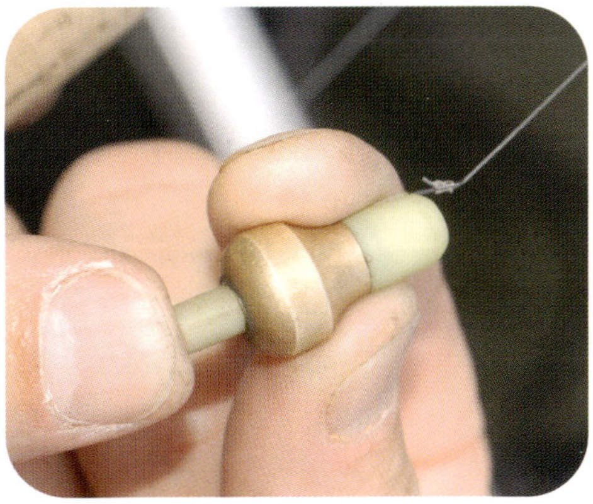

Release thumb pressure on the button and the hook is drawn safely and securely into the plummet's upper section. There's zero risk of line damage here.

This diagram shows the importance of ensuring your float sits directly above the plummet. By allowing the plummet to travel ahead unchecked, and keeping a tight line to the float, the angled line will make your float appear to be set correctly, although it will be set over-depth.

PLUMBING UP

Place a plummet on your hook then grip the hook length line around six inches above this. Point your rod tip at the place you want to cast to and flex the tip by applying steady backward tension on the line above the plummet.

Raise your rod and simultaneously release the plummet, ensuring the tip is pointing at the target spot. Feather the line so your float sits directly above the plummet upon entry for a true depth reading.

To plumb up at longer distances you need to cast overhead. This requires you to leave the plummet dangling free behind you. A slow, smooth overhead sweep is the favoured casting motion. Again, ensure the float sits directly above the plummet on entry by feathering the line on the descent.

For Mark, full depth waggler fishing is mainly a task for the colder months. A popular and sensible tactic is minimal feeding, or on occasions no feed whatsoever.

Using a single grain of sweetcorn on the hook, it's wise to cast widely around your swim and locate the fish which are likely to be very tightly shoaled and unwilling to move far in search of bait. Therefore, firing out any more than just the occasional grain of corn runs the risk of overfeeding these sluggish fish, and is a waste of time as they won't move to it like they would in warmer weather.

> **"Ensure you shot your float down well, only a couple of millimetres of tip showing"**

By casting around the whole confines of your swim, occasionally twitching the bait and moving it back towards you by a foot or so at a time, you should eventually locate some fish which find the golden grain in front of their noses irresistible. Of course, that grain has your hook in it!

Ensure you shot your float down well, with only a couple of millimetres of tip showing if the conditions permit. Winter bites can be very shy and you should strike at anything suspicious.

If for any reason you want to fish at full depth in summer, it's important to introduce enough feed but in a manner which doesn't encourage the fish to rise up from the bottom. Three or four generous pouchfuls of your chosen bait – hemp, pellet and corn are good – then fish out your bites before repeating the process is the way to go.

However, warmer conditions on Commercial stillwaters usually only mean one thing in terms of successful waggler fishing – shallow fishing to intercept carp which are cruising around and feeding in the sub-surface area.

Winter Searching Tactics

The number of matches won every winter on waggler and sweetcorn demands a closer look at the intricacies of what, on the face of it, is a very straightforward tactic.

Even if you're pleasure fishing and therefore competing only against the fish, you'll gain extra pleasure from a session if you get the approach right and end up catching more than others on the lake.

The golden rule is to get the depth absolutely spot-on, so that the sweetcorn hook bait is just tripping bottom. Although you may consider there to be advantages in fishing overdepth in winter, when the fish are hugging the bottom and totally unwilling to chase about for food, there is one vital reason why this approach is inferior to a 'dead depth' presentation.

So sluggish are these fish on most occasions that the bites they give when half-heartedly sucking at a grain of corn - probably more as a reflex reaction to its arrival in front of their noses than an actual desire to feed – are best described as feeble.

On a float set at dead depth, these shy bites will at least register as a dip under the surface, giving an alert angler time to strike. But if there's line dragging along the bottom, you may not even see the float tip move before the bait is blown out once they realise it's not a free meal. That's a chance missed, and you don't get too many chances in winter!

Time spent plumbing the depth ahead of a winter waggler session is never wasted. It can pay to separate your swim into several zones; straight out, to the left and to the right, maximum distance and halfway back.

Why? Because drift and undertow cause a float to move through a swim. This may mean your bait gets dragged away from a spot where you've set the float to precise depth, into deeper or shallower water. There's no easy answer, but bear in mind that most bites come within a minute of casting. Despite it being winter, this remains an active method with frequent casts needed to ensure accuracy.

The technique described earlier of moving the float back a foot at a time works best in swims of uniform depth, as the grain of corn will still be just touching bottom, not suspended off it or lying on it by an inch or two. If your swim is uneven then regular adjustments of the depth to suit different parts of each zone is necessary. Keep on working at it and you'll reap the rewards on more occasions than not.

Shotting Specifics

The fact that winter carp are often extremely shy biting is the main reason why a float tip dotted down to a mere pimple on the water's surface film is best.

Feature finding in cold conditions is critical. Search out all the contours by carefully plumbing the whole swim.

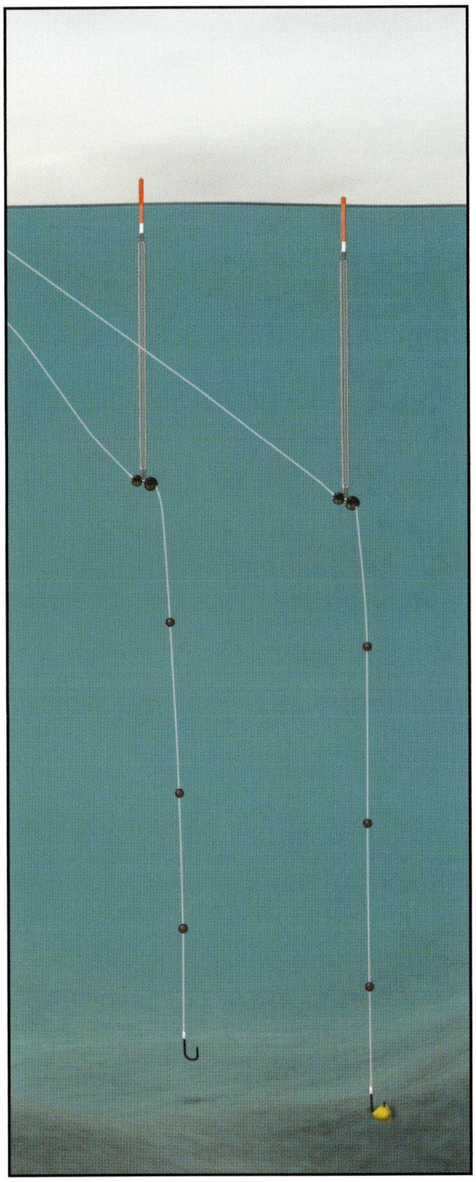

The addition of a grain of sweetcorn just touching bottom provides the perfect fine tuning for a winter waggler set-up.

However, it's important to remember that a grain of sweetcorn weighs around the same as a No.10 shot. If you shot your float to perfection without factoring this in then it will sink once you bait up and cast.

With bites on-the-drop unlikely, it can pay to place a small group of four No.8 shots around two-thirds down the line, with one or two No.8 or 10 droppers evenly spaced below. This bulk steadies the rig in strong winds, acting as a mini anchor beneath the faster moving surface layers of water.

The 'spread bulk' system, where the No.8s are spread out evenly across five or six inches of line rather than in a tight group, is a good approach in better conditions. This is easier to cast than a tighter bulk arrangement.

Tackle And Alternative Baits

Although corn is the No.1 winter bait on many waters, you should never discount maggots – either single or double – and even 4mm pellets.

Despite 'full depth' waggler working well in winter, it is also a successful technique in the summer, particularly early in a session before the fish move up in the water. When targeting big fish in summer which are out of pole range, a waggler fished at full depth coupled with hair rigged meat, pellet or another big bait can be devastating. If you're casting a shallow waggler into a channel between islands or the island slope, it's often worth deepening up in these circumstances if bites cease.

For full depth waggler work, Mark Pollard's favoured rod is the 13ft Envoy Carp Float, with the 12ft Envoy Carp Waggler during summer when fish fight harder. Both rods have the right action to control hard fighting fish on relatively fine hook lengths.

Reel line is generally 6lb Soft Steel, which should be sunk in a bad skim. Hook lengths are a foot of 0.10 to 0.12mm Micro Plus in winter, stepped up to 0.14 to 0.16mm in summer. A loop-to-loop attachment is fine with single maggot, corn or pellet, but with double maggot use a mini swivel to avoid line twist caused by the bait's propeller-like action when winding in.

Winter hook choice is a Series 2 Fine Wire in size 18 and 20, with either the standard or extra strong Series 2 equivalent preferred in summer. Barbless hooks will be required by the rules at 99 per cent of Commercial stillwaters.

To Feed Or Not?

This is a tough call in the depths of winter, but Mark believes the introduction of the occasional grain of corn or pellet can help in the early stages of a match or pleasure session. By occasional, we mean just one or two. If fish are willing to feed straight away, even such tiny amounts of bait can act as a stimulus. But if there's no response, put your catapult away and simply rely on your hook bait alone.

Whatever the case, you must confidently expect a response at some point in the day. At this point, you can feed a tiny amount once more, and gauge the response. Confidence is everything in winter fishing, and this sparse or no-feed tactic really does work.

Tackling Up

Mark favours loaded straight peacock wagglers for full depth fishing. He shots these with the bulk of the weight either side of the bottom eye, with a maximum of three No.8s and No.10s spread down the line below.

In most instances he's aiming to present the bait at dead depth.

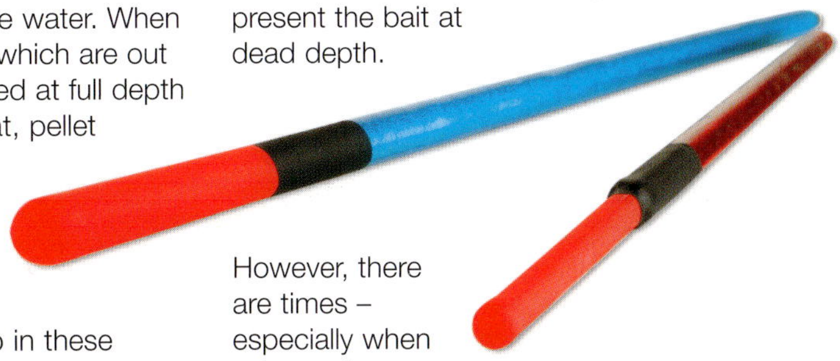

However, there are times – especially when using pellets on the hook – that he will go overdepth by a foot to 18 inches.

Mark likes to attach his main line to his hook length via a loop-to-loop knot, but stresses that you must tie the loop in the correct way – a figure of eight – and avoid a weaker double overhand knot.

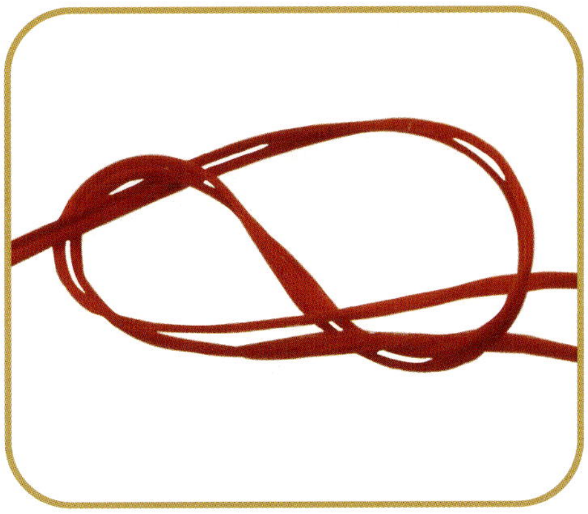

The most essential knot to learn!
This is the correct way to tie a loop

Widely used for attaching pole rigs to connectors plus hook lengths to main line. To tie, double the end of the line back then pinch it tight against the line in your hand, forming a loose loop of approximately 2cm. Next, pass the end of this doubled section back round and over the line trapped in your fingers, then back through the loop in the original direction.

At this point, twist the larger remaining portion of the doubled line round to form a second loop, trapping the bottom between fingers, then pass the original loop's end through this. The formation it now resembles the figure eight, hence the knot's name. Lubricate with saliva then draw tight.

Shallow waggler – or 'up in the water' as it's often known - is a tactic which accounts for scores of massive weights on Commercial Fisheries during the summer months.

As with the full depth waggler, it comes into its own when fish are beyond pole range – often patrolling island margins on bright sunny days. Even in murky water, their dark shapes can be clearly seen. But even if conditions are overcast and windy, there are still tell-tale signs to look for which betray the presence of carp feeding in the upper layers of the water. These may take the form of a glimpse of a dorsal fin breaking the surface, a distinct swirl, the occasional splash or even a fish jumping clear out of the water.

All the aforementioned signs indicate the presence of carp sub-surface, and issue an invitation for you to try and catch them there rather than on the deck.

This visual aspect makes for a very busy and exciting method, but as with everything there are right and wrong ways to go about catching carp shallow. Get it wrong and you can be left feeling severely frustrated. But follow Mark Pollard's advice, borne out of years of experience on a wide variety of Commercial stillwaters, and you'll be well on the path to success. As with so many aspects of angling, a large part of the key rests with how you feed. But it's no use getting this part, which we'll deal with overleaf, right unless your kit is up to the task. So we'll start on that right here.

The shallow margins of distant islands are often excellent places to intercept carp on shallow waggler tactics - but they could also be patrolling in open water.

The biggest fish are often margin huggers, but also trip up to shallow baits beneath a float at long range on occasions.

Tackle For The Job

Due to the more frequent casting, shallow waggler fishing places greater demands on your tackle than full depth style. Also, the larger fish in many waters are often more inclined to dominate a shallow swim. All the more reason to step up a level throughout your set-up.

For most of his shallow waggler fishing, whether to islands, weed beds or open water, Mark favours an Envoy or Challenger Carp Waggler rod. He sticks with the same reel as for full depth fishing, but opts for a 6lb main line rather than 4lb.

Typical hook length will be 0.16mm Micro Plus with a Series 2 Extra Strong hook, still in size 18 and 20. Pellets, corn and maggots remain top shallow wag baits.

Prototype dumpy wags, loaded and unloaded, are perfect for short to medium ranges.

Set your rod to the side on a rest or bump bar while your feeding and watch the tip out the corner of your eye. That's a bite!

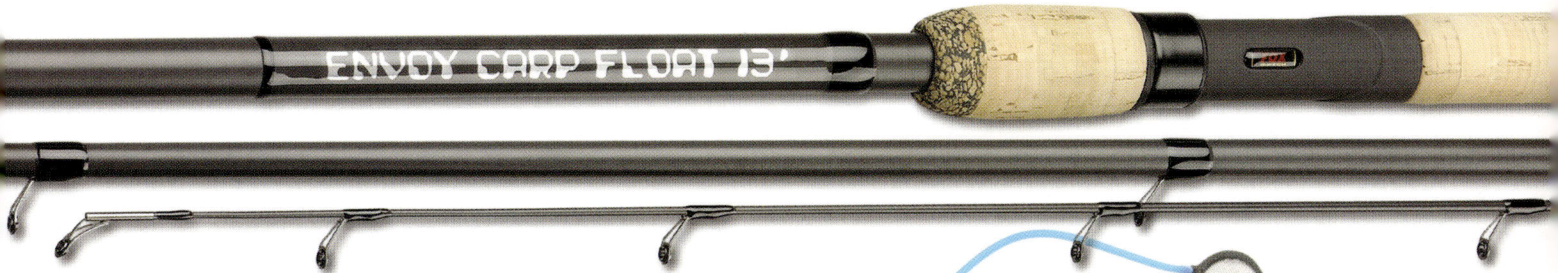

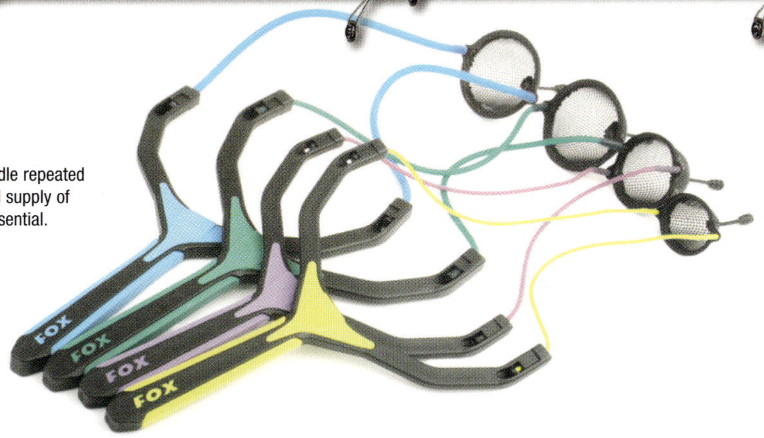

A powerful rod to handle repeated casting, plus a good supply of catapults, are essential.

Floats-wise, small dumpy carrot-shaped balsa wagglers of 2-4 inches long – sometimes loaded and sometimes unloaded – are Mark's favourites at modest ranges. They don't dive deep on the cast like larger and longer versions, and therefore spook fewer fish.

On waters where longer casts are required, thicker straight balsas of still no more than 4-5 inches long but taking up to 2SSG are used by some anglers to catch shallow.

Again, Mark usually favours his Bump Bar by way of a rod rest, although at times it's better to angle the rod sideways by about 45 degrees so biting fish hook themselves against the tip while you're steadily loose feeding with catapult in hand. On these occasions he reaches for a round sculpted butt rest fitted onto a feeder arm. With an angled rod, the tip's curve provides better shock absorption on the line than a rod pointing straight out, which in fact offers zero. You'll certainly notice when one hooks itself!

A reliable catapult is a must for shallow wag work. Mark favours the new Fox Easy Feed type, in the Match and River strengths. We recommend taking spare elastics to fit on the bank in case of breakage.

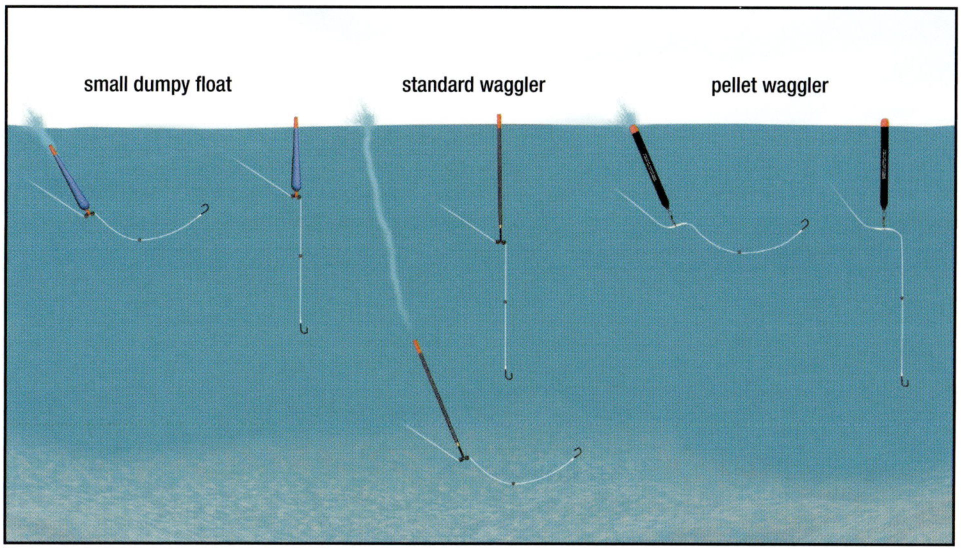

Short dumpy buoyant wagglers are perfect for fishing shallow because they don't dive deep on entry and settle quickly, compared to standard straight wagglers. The new highly bouyant 'Pellet' style wagglers are also good for this style of fishing as they settle almost immediately and attach to the line without shot.

Rig-wise, shallow waggler is simplicity itself. It's feeding, rhythm and playing your fish which tend to make the difference between a poor or just-about-OK day's sport and a truly memorable one, which it can often be when you get it right.

One frequently asked question concerning shallow waggler fishing is how deep to set the float. This leads on to how much, if any, shot to place down the line.

Really shallow island margins and plateaux speak for themselves. After all, you can only fish as deep as the water is. But in open water, Mark Pollard's general rule is to start at 3ft then change by 9 inches to a foot at a time, according to response. This will usually be heading in the shallower direction. Any deeper than five foot no longer counts as shallow, unless you're over exceptionally deep water of 12ft-plus and that is seldom encountered in Commercial-style stillwaters, other than the occasional farm irrigation reservoir which has been stocked and given over to angling.

If he's fishing a foot deep, Mark places no shot at all down the line. The baited hook alone is enough to sink the line. Two feet deep may require a single No.10, with another No.10 added when he's at 3ft and another for 4ft.

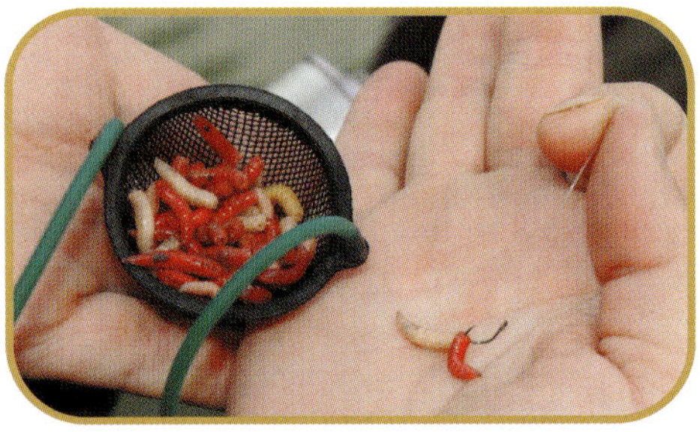

Although you can feed and fish many different baits on the shallow waggler, the fact that good old maggots are fast to hook and stay on well means they're still a popular choice. Their only downside is a tendency to attract small nuisance fish.

POLLY'S COMMENT

As a general rule, when setting the depth I start at 3ft then change by 9"-12"; shallowing up if I miss bites and deepen if none are forthcoming.

More important is your feeding tempo. But don't make the mistake of thinking that you need to blast big pouchfuls of bait in simply because you're fishing shallow. Half a standard sized catapult pouchful of feed every cast is ideal for maggots, casters and pellets. The idea is to keep them shallow, not to risk them following the feed down to the bottom as can happen if you get 'trigger happy' and overdo it.

As with all fishing, feed to your bites. As long as you are catching you are getting it right. If they're coming really thick and fast you will naturally find yourself feeding more regularly – but ensure it's always the same steady amount whether that be 10, 15, 20 or 40 pellets (or maggots, casters, cubes of meat, grains of corn etc).

To become really good at catching up in the water – and the same applies to pole fishing as you'll see later – you must strive to extend that regularity and consistency of amounts to feeding when you're playing or unhooking fish.

Finally, no matter the duration of your session, be it match or pleasure fishing, if the fishery in question has a bait limit then you will need to work out an hourly amount and pace yourself accordingly. Believe us, you'll do far better than with a more haphazard approach.

When you get the feeding pattern right, shallow 'wag' sport can be fast and furious.

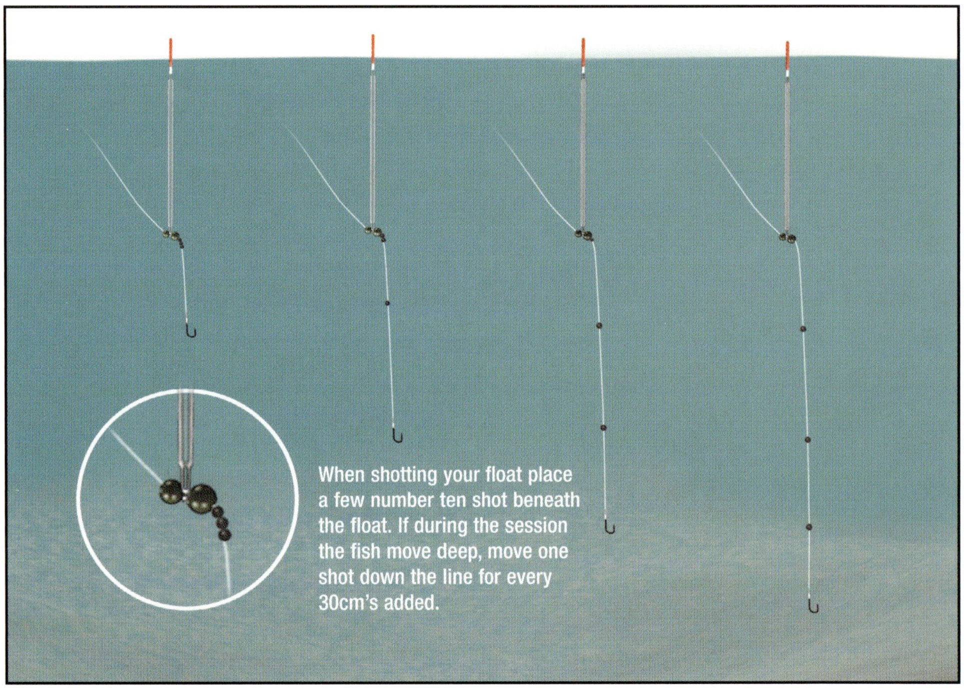

Depending on the depth you fish at, shotting patterns can vary from none at all to up to 3 No.10s down the line.

CAST, FEED & CATCH

Try not to strike. Shallow-feeding carp usually hook themselves anyway. A gentle pull and it's game on. If you're fishing really shallow, say at 1ft or less, the tiniest of movements to the side is all you need.Anything heavier-handed risks bigger carp snapping your hook length on impact.

1 In open water, start by casting your float beyond your chosen catch zone.

2 Drop your rod onto the Bump Bar, pick up your pult and fire out some feed.

3 Pick up the rod again and wind a few turns of line back on, drawing your float and baited rig into the feed zone.
Being slightly heavier due to the hook's weight, you hook bait will catch up the sinking freebies and appear totally natural to the fish.

The Splasher and the Bagging Waggler (or Feeder Float as some call it) are certainly not for the faint-hearted.

Both involve the use of big heavy floats which are specifically designed to announce their presence – or rather that of the hook bait dangling just below – to the fish upon their entry to the water. It's that old 'banging the dinner gong' theme again. Unlike their wild counterparts, commercial fishery carp often associate noise with food.

Both methods work best during high summer, but don't rule them out at any time of year. Be sure to check they are permitted at your chosen fishery, as they are often banned – in part due to their devastating success rate, and in part due to their unsuitability on smaller venues.

Splashers are bodied wagglers, normally with thick bulbous tip sections which aid visibility at long range and boost the method's self-hooking properties on the take. Balls of groundbait or Stickymag – maggots stuck together to form easily catapulted balls which break up on entry to the water - are fired steadily at the tip to further announce the presence of a feast.

Bagging Wagglers incorporate a frame-type swimfeeder in their base, removing the need to catapult bait out. The method first rose to prominence in the late 1990s at Drayton Reservoir near Daventry, Northamptonshire, where anglers like Steve Gregory and Geoff Ringer and his sons Steve and Phil pioneered the technique. Long range fishing for fish of a high average size, 6lb-plus, saw them employ light carp rods instead of the usual stepped-up waggler tackle.

Tackling Up

For the Splasher, Mark Pollard suggests the 12ft Envoy Carp Missile is a good choice of rod. He'll team this with a fixed spool reel carrying 6lb monofilament.

The heavier Feeder Float requires a beefier rod, and Mark's current choice is the new Challenger XT 13ft Baggin' Stick. With a 1lb test curve and larger guides than the average match rod, this is part of a new crossover breed of rods developed specially to cope with the larger carp found on today's Commercials. Mark steps up to 8lb reel line and a 10lb shock leader at long distances.

With the heavier floats used in these techniques, Mark opts to include a micro swivel between main line and hook length rather than connecting them loop-to-loop like he does for less demanding float techniques.

Proof of the pudding - Polly with a splasher-tempted carp.

POLLY'S COMMENT

When bagging, you need a beefy rod. My current choice is the new Fox Match Challenger XT 13ft Bagging Stick, which has a 1lb test curve and larger guides than most average match rods.

At the business end, hook lengths range from 0.18 to 0.22mm Micro Plus, with hooks invariably being a Series 2 Extra Strong. Sizes vary according to baits.

Although big wagglers are often fixed within a six to eight inch loop on the main line, you need to be aware of the potential danger of your line breaking above the float. Mark uses a Safety Lead clip, popular with big fish anglers, with the baggin' wag as it will release the float in such an instance rather than leaving a fish tethered. However, experience leads him to believe that a loop is safe on the lighter Splasher floats providing all the tackle is properly balanced.

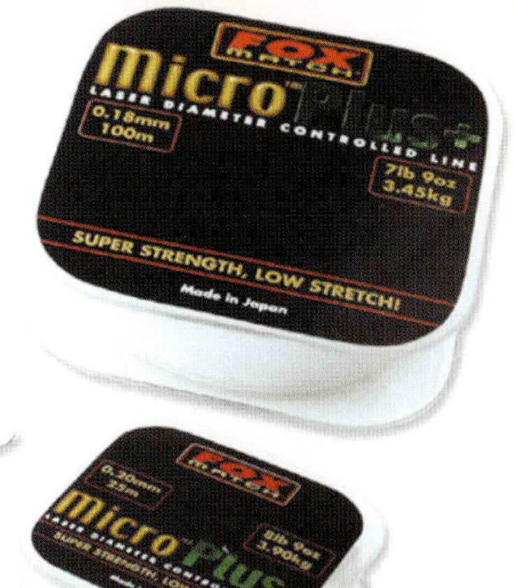

Strong rods, reel lines and hooks are essential for the two most demanding float techniques.

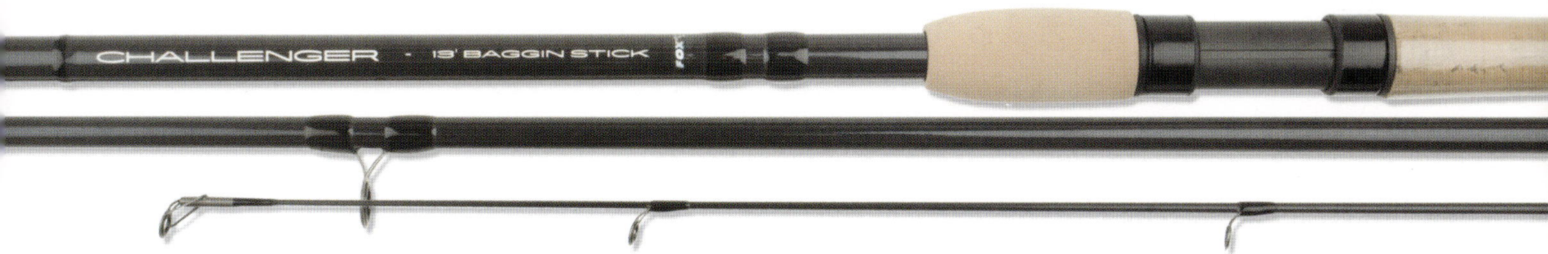

SAFETY FIRST WITH BAGGIN' WAGS

Rather than running the risk of fish trailing heavy floats around in the event of a snap-off on your main line, the use of a Fox carp safety clip is recommended to attach your Baggin' Waggler. Here's how to set them up.

1

Safety clips come in two pieces; tail rubber and the clip itself. Slide both onto your main line, tail first.

2

Next, tie a ring swivel to the end of your main line using a reliable knot such as the Palomar.

3

Draw the swivel back into the clip's housing.

4

Click the small peg, seen in picture 3, into place to hold the swivel's top eye securely inside the clip.

5

Next, attach another ring swivel to the base of your Feeder Float, using a speed link.

6

Pass the swivel's ring onto the clip's safety arm then push the tail rubber down. Safe and sound!

If you're facing islands or other prominent features you'll have an obvious target to fish towards. But one of the beauties of the Splasher is that over a period of time you can make the fish come to you in an open water swim.

Just because you're using big heavy floats doesn't mean you have to cast to the horizon. In any case, even at large open venues like Drayton and the many other British Waterways-managed Midlands reservoirs where the Splasher rules supreme at certain times of year, casting distance may be limited by anglers on the opposite bank. Halfway is a gentleman's agreement. Please don't be tempted to cast further just because the angler opposite happens to be fishing the pole at the time!

There are two main ways of feeding a swim to entice the carp which will undoubtedly be interested by the noise of your Splasher hitting the water. The first involves soft groundbait, the second Stickymag.

Soft Groundbait

In Commercial Fishery terms, groundbait is normally associated with fishing on the bottom, having been introduced either with a swimfeeder or via a pole cup. Surely the use of softer groundbaits, which break up before hitting the bottom, begins and ends with catching bleak on rivers, right? Not so!

"Anglers realised a softer groundbait mix and more regular feeding were needed"

In the early days, fishing shallow meant loose feeding maggots. But once the British Waterways reservoirs were stocked up with carp, longer range fishing became essential and groundbaiting techniques previously only used for long range bream fishing on natural lakes and wide rivers, came into play.

Anglers in the know realised a softer groundbait mix and more regular feeding were needed to concentrate feeding carp in the upper layers of water, and before long many anglers' long-redundant groundbait catapults were enjoying a new lease of life along the famous boards and dam wall at Drayton.

SOFT GROUNDBAIT IN SEQUENCE

Based around Mark Pollard's favourite feed for the Splasher waggler, here's a step-by-step guide to the mechanics of feeding soft groundbait when you're fishing a Splasher waggler. Just remember that the more you practice using a groundbait catapult, the more your accuracy and results will improve. What's more, it really is great fun once you're in the swing. Don't worry too much about the occasional stray ball - it happens to the very best at times!

1 Mix up at least four kilos of groundbait in a large bucket, aiming for a mix which errs on the wet side but still holds together in a ball on the palm of your hand. A 50-50 mix of Van den Eynde Marine Green and brown crumb is Mark's choice.

2 Form a ball of groundbait - or several if possible in advance of a session. A sausage shape suits the wide shape of a groundbait 'pult's pouch better than a ball, and is faster to form with one hand too.

3 Cast your Splasher rig into the swim and place your rod down on the bump bar or rod rest.

4 Using a Fox Midi Groundbait Plus catapult, aim and fire the feed out as close to the float as possible.

5 It should break into an attractive cloud on impact. A gentle lob with a high trajectory is best.

The Splasher actually originated in the days before fishmeal groundbaits, which we take for granted these days, were available in the tackle shops. Anglers did indeed use the finer mixes developed for bleak. For a couple of seasons in the early '90s, matches at Drayton were won by anglers who mixed up and fired out 12 kilos of Sensas Surface!

A fine groundbait is required because large particles would risk dragging some of the fish lower down in the water. Fortunately, most of today's fishmeal-based mixes are very fine textured and fit the bill perfectly.

Stickymag

With feeder fishing banned in matches across the majority of Europe, with the exception of Holland, the preferred long range feeding method of continental anglers has long been Stickymag.

> **"In essence, the method involves binding maggots into suitable sized balls"**

In essence, the method involves binding maggots into suitable sized balls for catapulting, through the use of fine powders which, when wet with the spray from an atomiser, go sticky. The powders are sometimes flavoured, hence you can get strawberry or vanilla stickymag. This is undoubtedly an area where the continentals are still some way ahead of the UK anglers in knowledge and application.

We've got a couple of good tips to pass on when it comes to Stickymag fishing, over and above the picture sequence on the right which takes you through the basic preparation steps.

Firstly, always keep a tub of fresh maize meal on your bait tray. Wear waterproof over-trousers, and dust generous amounts of the maize regularly onto the thigh parts. This allows you to wipe your palms across them regularly, preventing a build up of annoying sticky residue.

Secondly, whenever possible, chill your maggots right down in a fridge at its coldest setting, or even overnight in the freezer section, in an airtight plastic bag. Keep them cool on the way to your swim. The reason for this is that the less the wriggle, the faster the binding process will be.

HOW TO MAKE PERFECT STICKYMAG

Surprisingly few anglers in the UK have used Stickymag, a method of feeding maggots far beyond the normal loose feed catapult range. As the name suggests, it involves sticking maggots together into balls which can be catapulted out to the require distance, but which then break up in the water. It can be a bit of a messy process, but there are occasions when it can outfish everything else so ignore it at your peril!

1

You must have your maggots in sawdust rather than maize. Run a minimum of a couple of pints over a riddle, discarding the dust. Do this more than once with the same batch. The cleaner the better!

2

Slightly wet your hands and give the maggots a good stir. More dust particles will adhere to your hands. Wash it off and repeat until you are happy that the maggots really are as clean as possible.

3

Sprinkle some Stickymag powder, available in special shaker tubs including various flavours, over the cleaned maggots. Err on the side of caution. Leave for a while to disperse.

4

Next, grab a handful of maggots and check if you can squeeze together a ball which stays stuck once formed.

5

If they won't stick, add a bit of water via an atomiser spray. Only if this still doesn't work should you add another light dusting of Stickymag powder.

6

You'll be left with a thin sheet of sticky maggots.

7

These can be broken off and rolled into balls of various sizes for catapulting out to your float. Cover the tray up at the first hint of rain.

POLLY'S COMMENT

Be prepared for an instant and aggressive bite from a carp which responded to the splash by racing to the spot and devouring the first bit of food it finds.

The Bagging Waggler does away with the Splasher's need for a catapult and relies instead upon delivering groundbait to your chosen spot via the plastic frame feeder set at its base.

Again, different sizes are available although in this case they are usually limited to just two – big and very big!

Unlike the soft groundbait which you can catapult at a Splasher, a stickier mix is required to ensure it stays put during the cast of a Bagging Wag. Mark Pollard's chosen groundbait is the same one he uses for the Method feeder. After all, a Bagging Wag is a basically Method Feeder fished at the surface rather than on the bottom. It's mixed exactly the same, with a small proportion of grilled hemp added to the main element - Van den Eynde Method Mix.

When casting a Bagging Wag, a high trajectory is desirable. A groundbait-loaded float creates a seriously heavy weight on your line and this is no time for snatchy or jerky casts. A smooth, steady lob with the rod left pointing high but in line with your target is the way to go.

The float will land with an almighty splash, but quickly bob back up due to the thick balsa's inherent buoyancy. Be prepared for an instant and aggressive bite from a carp which responded to the splash by racing to the spot and devouring the first bit of food it sees before any of its shoal-mates can.

This is why no other loose feed is added to the Method mix. Other than fragments of groundbait breaking away, your baited hook is all a carp will encounter when it swims up to inspect what caused the commotion. Obviously this maximises your chance of a fish taking it!

If you get a fast bite, remember not to strike but instead to merely bend into the fish, anticipating the direction of its run and applying the necessary side-strain. On other occasions there may be no carp in the immediate vicinity after casting, and your float may sit motionless. Don't leave it longer than three or four minutes before retrieving and recasting, as it's the noise which will ultimately tempt them in. Sometimes you may get nudges and tweaks on the float, usually a sign that small rudd are attempting to take the hook bait. Don't be tempted to strike.

Robust baits such as corn or mini boilies will stay on better than a softer pellet after the impact of a Bagging Waggler cast.

BAGGING WAGGLER TACTICS

It's tempting to say that the groundbait needed for wrapping around the frame feeder base of a Bagging Waggler requires less attention to detail than a comparable mix for legering. But, as always, the top anglers like Mark Pollard are very particular about achieving an even consistency through riddling the mix. So don't be tempted to cut corners.

1

Mix Van den Eynde Method groundbait with Grilled Hemp, adding water, riddling and stirring vigorously as per the instructions in the baits chapter.

2

Attach a Feeder Float via a quick release Fox carp safety clip. Ensure the float's bottom eye moves freely on the clip, and that the tail rubber can slide off easily in the event of breakage.

3

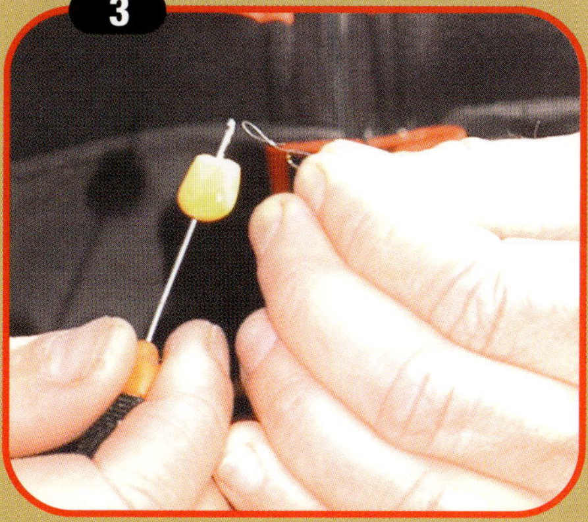

Attach your hook length and bait up. You can either hair rig baits or nick them directly onto the hook.

4

Mould groundbait around the base of the float, squeezing firmly and rounding off nicely.

5

The grilled hemp adds the necessary 'stickability', enabling the baited float to withstand the cast without the ball breaking up.

6

Cast to the chosen spot. Be prepared for bites within seconds of touchdown. Bend into fish steadily rather than striking. They'll hook themselves more often than not, but you must avoid snapping off.

The final section of the running line float chapter of this Commercial Fisheries book is reserved for the one tactic which incorporates a non-waggler. In other words, a float attached at top and bottom rather than bottom-end only.

Fat-tipped, dumpy bodied pole floats are best suited to the long rod margin approach.

Exclusively a tactic for the near margins, it's aimed at landing larger than average sized carp which have a habit of tearing off at great speed and bottoming out even the strongest pole elastics, leading to inevitable line breakage.

Although you can fish for carp in the margins with a standard 13 foot rod, a longer rod – up to 20 feet in some cases – is preferred because it allows you to search further along the margins in each direction from your swim. It also allows excellent control of your tackle, plus a fast strike from directly above a fish. This can sometimes allow carp well into double-figures to be bundled into the net in under 30 seconds, as if they don't seem to know they've been hooked. But on most occasions they get their bearings and set off on a run which sets the spool spinning at a rate of knots!

The tactic first emerged at Gold Valley Lakes in Hampshire, before special beefed-up long rods were commercially available. Anglers teamed Bolognese-style telescopic rods with centrepin reels. Up in Yorkshire, much-capped England International Denis White even adapted the top six metres of a strong pole to carry a centrepin and rod rings, enjoying success at venues such as Fleets Dam.

Although Mark Pollard may only use the long rod margin tactics two or three times a season, he rates it as an important part of his armoury – notably during evening matches in summer. The bigger size of the fish this method is aimed at, means you can go from last to first with just a couple of fish.

Tackle For A Margin Ambush

Mark favours an Envoy Multi-Stick 17/19ft rod, which can be fished at either length with the addition or removal of a two foot section. He favours a normal fixed spool reel instead of a centrepin, generally fishing with 6lb line in open water. Where bigger fish are expected or potential snags such as weed beds exist, step up to heavier lines. Mark uses normal poles rigs with 0.20 or 0.22mm Micro Plus and attaches these to the mainline with a simply loop-to-loop knot; meaning he can be ready in a matter of minutes.

Float for the job is a standard thick tipped pole float such as those in the MP1 or MXP7/8/9 series. Size depends on depth and conditions. Go heavier in deep water or on windy days. Shotting is simple, a small bulk of No.8s or 10s then couple of evenly spaced droppers. Hook is a Fox X-Strong Series 2 in size 16 or 14.

The largest carp in a lake are often found 'kerb-crawling' in the margins, often late in the day when most anglers have packed up and gone home.

Below: Store your rigs for the long rod on a winder to save time tackling up.

> "Exclusively a tactic for the near margins, which is aimed at landing larger than average sized carp"

Floats And Knots

We've already stated that the size of float depends on two factors - the depth of water alongside the rushes, bankside or beneath the platform you're targeting - plus the size and therefore weight of the bait you're using. But let's look closer at what that really means in terms of the weight carrying capacity of your chosen float.

It's fair to say there are more Commercial fisheries with less than three foot of water in their near margins than there are with more than three foot. Also, the proximity to the rushes plus the short line from rod to float tip means your rig is not subjected to strong gusts of wind. All this suggests a light rig will be best, as indeed it is on many occasions.

Mark favours the MXP9 pattern of float for most of his long rod margin fishing, in sizes from 4x110 to 4x14. But in deeper margins or with bigger baits than the usual pellet or piece of paste, he'll step up to as heavy as a gram. Mark stores his margin rigs on winders, tying a figure of eight loop at the top of each, just as for pole fishing. He attaches this to his main line via a grinner knot. Mark feels this is stronger and also neater than a loop-to-loop attachment.

Although we've emphasised throughout the book that Commercial fishery carp associate noise with food, it still pays to be quiet and avoid any sudden movements when margin fishing on the long rod. They seem to spook easier at close quarters.

As always, plumb the depth accurately and set the bait to touch bottom. You'll either need to feed by hand, which is no problem because accuracy is assured at such close range, or via a pole pot if you want to lay a big bed of bait at the start of a session. If you're fishing a match, remember that feeding with a pole pot is not permitted unless you wind the float rod in first.

Mark stresses that this tactic works best in snag-free water. Whenever possible, let the carp run – provided they don't charge through another angler's peg. Once beaten, netting carp is much harder on long a rod than with a standard length or a pole so you must be patient and never be tempted to lunge at them.

With a fixed spool reel, you should set the clutch to yield line easily. Alternatively, you can backwind – but can you backwind fast enough? Mark has been known to flick the bale arm off when a big carp charges off. On one occasion at Gold Valley, he landed an 18lb 12oz mirror carp which had torn across to the far bank on its first run in this manner. It was a crucial fish which boosted him to a 61lb section-winning weight that day.

Remember to continue feeding your margin line whilst playing fish. There may be more to come, and you won't need too many of them to post a winning total.

LINE BITES - DO NOT STRIKE!

A large carp feeding in a margin swim can create vortexes of water which in turn drag a light float rig to move around or even drag under. The fish's fins and flanks brushing against the line will do likewise. You must learn to distinguish these line bites for what they are and never strike at them, as the upshot will be a spooked or foul-hooked fish which you've got little chance of landing.

PLUMBING THE DEPTH

Although a bait just touching bottom is ideal in perfect conditions, we all know these occur all too seldom. For instance, if the wind is blowing into your bank, the float can easily get pushed right into the reeds. In such instances you're better off going a little overdepth, with your lowest dropper shot just touching bottom and acting as a mini anchor. Either way, you'll need to know the exact depth. A clip-on plummet can be useful here, as you can open it up then slip it over the lowest shot before gently closing it to avoid any damage to the line. Lower the rig in as you would when plumbing up on the pole and adjust your float until the precise depth is discovered.

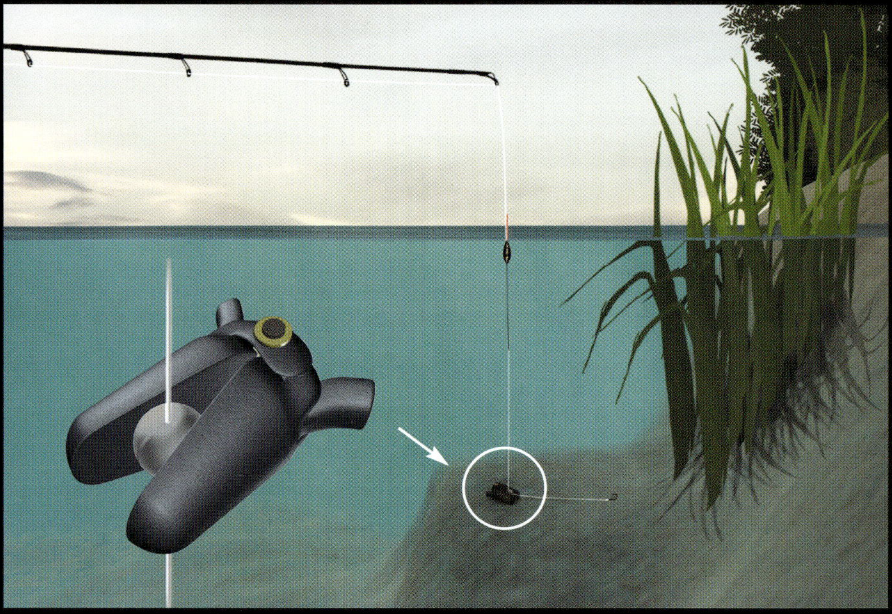

PRIME LONG ROD SPOTS

Two of the best spots to search around with a long rod and pole rig combo are overhanging near bank vegetation, plus platforms on adjacent swims. In the case of the latter, it's obviously vital that another angler isn't sitting there at the time! But if you stay on after the majority of anglers pack up, your opportunity will come. One of the main reasons why these areas are so good is the fact that the fish are used to mopping up free bait there from around 5pm onwards. Most anglers dump leftover bait straight into the water as they pack up, and it's this regular feast which draws the carp in. What's more, they never seem to get caught there so their natural caution falls.

Stagings get a constant drip feed of bait either by accidental spillages or end-of-session discards. Bailiffs sometimes sweep them clean, and fish associate them with food.

SLOW AND STEADY WINS THE RACE

One thing you'll soon appreciate when you first try long rod margin fishing is that you can't hurry things. The fish is in charge during the early stages of a fight, but gradually you can begin to exert increasing pressure and take control of the situation.

1

Hooking a big fish in the margins can be like hooking into the National Grid, assuming you stay connected for long enough. Hook pulls or line breakages avoided, you'll often find the fish heads out into open water. After the first run it may now go into 'sulk' mode, moving only grudgingly. It's wise to get your rod up now, but don't try to pull too hard just yet. Cushion the rod with your spare hand ahead of the handle in case it lunges.

2

Judging the right moment at which to push out your landing net is another tricky stage of a long rod battle with a big fish. The very sight of the net may create a panic reaction in the fish, which if it has any fight left could suddenly surge off and snap the line. The floatation device which Mark Pollard always fits to the business end of his net handle can prove invaluable in such situations, when you suddenly need both hands back on the rod and reel again.

3

As soon as you manage to draw the fish into the net, flick the reel's anti-reverse off and drop the rod down onto your rest or Bump Bar, simultaneously raising the net's frame back above the water to minimise the chance of the fish flopping back out. Do not attempt to lift it until you have shipped back the net pole and taken a firm grip on the frame.

LANDING YOUR FISH

When the long rod technique first emerged, most of its exponents insisted that a centre-pin reel was superior to a fixed spool. They argued that you could control a fish's run plus the rate at which you yield line under thumb pressure, and also lock right up if a fish is inches away from perilous snags.

Whilst its fair to say that a centrepin represents a wise investment if you do a lot of this type of fishing, the vast majority of anglers will find a quality modern fixed spool reel perfectly adequate, using either the clutch/drag system or backwinding to yield and gain line at the right moments.

The key to winning the often-prolonged battles with fish hooked on long rods down the margins is understanding when to take it easy and when to put on the pressure.

A considerable amount of pressure can be exerted via 17 feet of progressively powered carbon. One of the best times to step it up is when a fish starts moving back towards you. Now you can simultaneously gain back some line and draw the fish up in the water.

It's likely to surface two or three times before diving back down, expending energy each time. When it comes up and just wallows around feebly then it's time to reach for the net and make it count. Despite the fact that the longer you play a fish the greater the chance of the hook hold loosening, never try to rush things. Just take it steady.

Chapter 3

pole fishing

POLLY'S COMMENT

For beginners, investing in a pole elastic kit is a wise idea. Priced around £5.99, you can choose from various grades of elastic with a bush, connector, bung plus diamond eye threader – an essential length of wire used to pull elastics through pole sections.

The pole fishing revolution was already in full swing when commercial fisheries began to spring up across the UK.

Most match fisherman plus quite a few pleasure anglers already owned carbon poles of 11 or 12.5 metres, while those on the elite team circuit were forking out around £2,000 for the all-new 14 metre versions. And understandably, many were loathe to use them on venues stocked mainly with carp. Indeed, many of these anglers had never caught a carp at this point, the late 1980s. Surely it would be foolhardy to risk using expensive carbon on a species with a reputation for fighting so hard they'd probably smash it?

Even those brave enough to take the plunge were severely handicapped by the tackle at their disposal. Most either cut back a spare top section of pole or removed it altogether, running a length of No.8 elastic – the heaviest available - through this plus the next section down. They knew they'd rather have three sections of elastic, but there were no suitable sized bungs available. Finding bushes large enough for No.2 sections was no easy feat either.

Hilarious 'action shots' in the match pages of the angling press from the likes of Moorlands Farm showed anglers netting carp in the 2-3lb range holding a full 11 metres aloft, just to counter the stretch of the woefully undergunned elastics.

Over the next few years, the gradual exodus of anglers from natural waters to managed stillwaters gathered pace. Thankfully, so too did the development of pole tackle. Before long, robust floats with secure side eyes, unbreakable stems plus bristles thick enough to support big baits were on the market.

Elastics also beefed up, with grades 10, 12, 14, 16, 18 and 20 soon available. No more netting fish with 11 metres of carbon sticking skyward. Bigger bungs also came into play, allowing three sections of pole to be elasticated - a necessity as tip sections had to be cut back to next to nothing, or even removed completely in some cases, to house these bigger grades of elastic. Quality co-polymer lines emerged in a greater range of diameters and strengths.

Shortly after, the actual poles themselves began to change. Most anglers had already gone down the route of having a dedicated 'carp pole'. In most cases this was an oldie or cheapie, but not necessarily all that strong! But manufacturers responded to demand and the carp pole was born; ultra strong models designed to handle fish into double figures with special wide-bore top twos -close to the length of an old top three - for strong elastics. These days all you need to worry about is elasticating the pole. Turn the page and you'll find our fuss-free elastication guide.

MODERN DAY POLE CHOICES

In the modern era, the quality of poles plus the sheer scale of the 'extras' package they come with or are available for ordering seem light years ahead of the earliest poles. Nowadays poles are made for specific applications and mainly fall into three catergories: competition/light liners, all rounders and carp poles. Manufacturers indicate the application by the grade of elastic the pole will accomodate.

At the top end of the scale are 'go-anywhere' all round match poles like the 16 metre Envoy Competition, which Mark Pollard and Derek Willen use for every conceivable task including Commercial carping on beefy elastics. The Envoy comes with two top three kits, two top four kits, and a rigid holdall to carry and protect it.

Short 4th's are included on most Fox poles. A more recent introduction, short fourths help stiffen poles at the shorter lengths and help with leverage when netting big fish on the usual section that anglers break down at.

Power Top Twos are all the rage and most poles used on Commercials, including Fox's acclaimed Matrix, have the option of these thicker, stronger top sections. However, always try poles with both kits before you buy them to see how the pole feels; the Envoy has none as they were found to unbalance it.

Finally, when choosing a pole think carefully about the venue or venues you are likely to visit. On canal type venues many fish are caught close to the far bank and not being able to reach this cover can be a significant disadvantage. If the water you fish has heavy snags close in which the large fish tend to patrol, a dedicated margin pole could save a lot of broken sections.

There's a huge choice of poles and accessories to suit every pocket these days.

Get your elastic right and it's possible to tame 20lb-plus carp on the pole.

Just like lines, pole elastics come in a wide variety of thicknesses – not to mention colours. Whilst colours vary from brand to brand, thickness (and thus strength) is measured in a common number scale, normally known as grade or size.

Grade 1 is the finest, running right through to grade 20 or even 22 at the thicker end. In recent years a new breed of hollow elastic has come to prominence and most anglers now rely on these at the upper end.

In Commercial Fishery terms, lower grades can be disregarded except for winter silver fish when finesse is essential in all aspects of your end tackle. We'll look at this niche area later in this chapter. But for 90 per cent of situations on managed stillwaters, you'll be targeting powerful carp and tench with elastics of grade 6 minimum.

Standard fluorescent Fox Match elastic comes in grades 1 to 16, in six metre lengths on winders. The new Fluro Carp Elastic, with a hollow inner core of a uniform bore, comes in five grades from 6+ to 20+, with diameters from 1.8mm to 2.8mm.

Hollow elastics are reckoned to provide an extra cushioning effect, allowing you to use lower diameter lines than with equivalent solid elastic grades. This is a boon when it comes to gaining extra bites on tricky days. It's sold in three metre lengths.

Choosing the right elastic for the task in hand is often a tricky balancing act. Stronger elastics inevitably cause more small fish to fall off barbless hooks, but go too fine and you risk being 'bottomed out' – a term meaning the elastic reaches the limit of its stretch – when you hook larger fish. At this point your line - or if your luck is really out, your pole - will break.

Most successful anglers on Commercial Fisheries err on the side of caution. Their whole feeding pattern is aimed at attracting the larger fish, normally carp, so they will assess the average size and decide on an elastic to suit. This generally means grades in the 10 to 20 range.

Elastics To Lines Guide

Having explained the general concept of teaming your elastic to suit the size of fish you're targeting, Mark Pollard has provided the following guide which lists the line diameters he's happy to use with different elastics grades for different target species and situations on Commercial Fisheries.

HOLLOW ELASTICS

Grade	Line Diameter	Targets
Blue 6+	0.09 - 0.12mm	Mixed bags of mainly sub-2lb fish
Orange 10+	0.12 - 0.16mm	Open water, carp mainly in 2-4lb class
Red 14+	0.16 - 0.20mm	Open water and shallow, carp in 2-8lb class
Yellow 16+	0.20 - 0.25mm	Bagging work and bigger fish
Purple 20+	0.20 - 0.25mm	Venues with high average size of carp including doubles

STANDARD (SOLID) ELASTICS

Grade	Line Diameter	Targets
4	0.09mm	Silver fish
6	0.09 - 0.12mm	F1s, skimmers, sub-2lb carp in winter
8	0.10 - 0.14mm	Open water carping, fish to 4lb, bigger bream, harder venues
10	0.12 - 0.16mm	Open water or shallow carping, 2-6lb fish. Also big tench
12	0.12 - 0.18mm	Bagging work on carp to 8lb
14/16/18	0.14 - 0.25mm	Hit and hold work near snags for carp to 10lb-plus

Hollow (top) and solid pole elastics have different properties and diameters.

On lakes with a large head of skimmers in the 8oz to 2lb range it can pay to drop to grade 8. These are good weight builders, but do not fight too hard and are prone to falling off the hook on heavier elastics. Grade 8 can deal with occasional carp and is a good summer compromise.

Grade 6 is often selected in the depths on winter on venues stocked with F1s in the 12oz to 2lb range. It teams well with the finer lines required to tempt bites from these delicate feeding fish.

Lower than this and you're into the realms of silver fish. Again, you need to know the average size of the roach, rudd, perch and skimmers you are targeting. In many Commercials these are a healthy 6 to 10oz, meaning grade 4 or 5 is better suited than 2 or 3 unless you're on bloodworm.

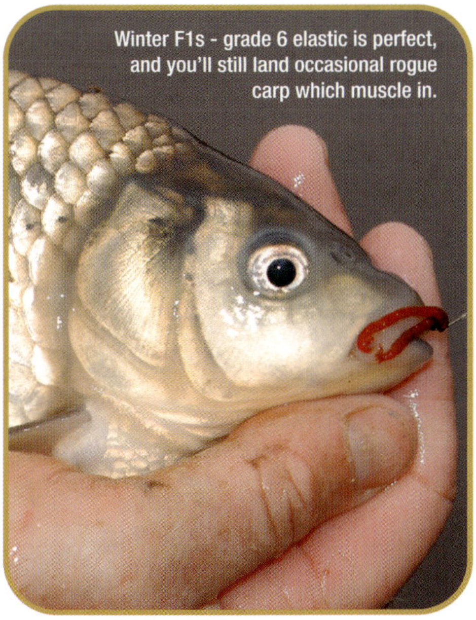
Winter F1s - grade 6 elastic is perfect, and you'll still land occasional rogue carp which muscle in.

Elastic Connectors

There are several ways of connecting rigs to pole elastics, but simplest and safest is via a purpose-made connector.

You may see some anglers advocating the use of a multi-tagged knot (known as a 'crow's foot' or 'spider') at the end of the elastic. Others favour a short length of dacron between elastic and line. But both are fraught with dangers for the inexperienced angler.

With connectors, provided you locate the overfit rear section properly over the plastic hook on the front section, you can't go wrong. There are five different sizes in the Fox Match range, coming in twin packs priced £1.49 with a variety of dayglow colours available.

The Mini model fits elastic grades 1-4, silver fish territory. More important on Commercials are the Midi (grades 5-8), Maxi (grades 10-14), XL (for hollow double core latex 6+ to 14+) and XXL (for the largest two hollow double core latex grades, 16+ and 20+).

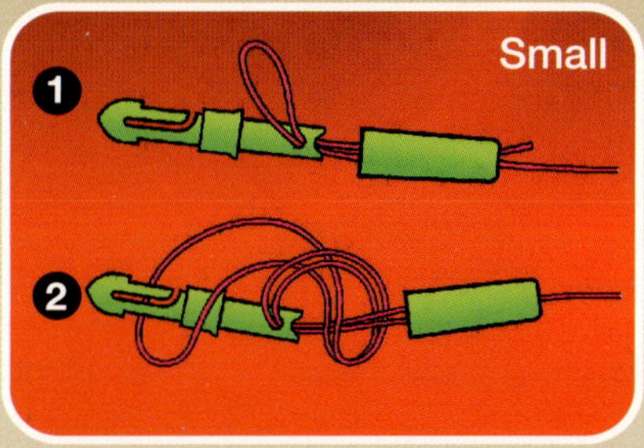

1. With the smaller three sizes, start by feeding a doubled loop through the connector's front section hole.
2. Tie a simple overhand knot, lubricate with saliva then snug it down in the rear recess before tightening.

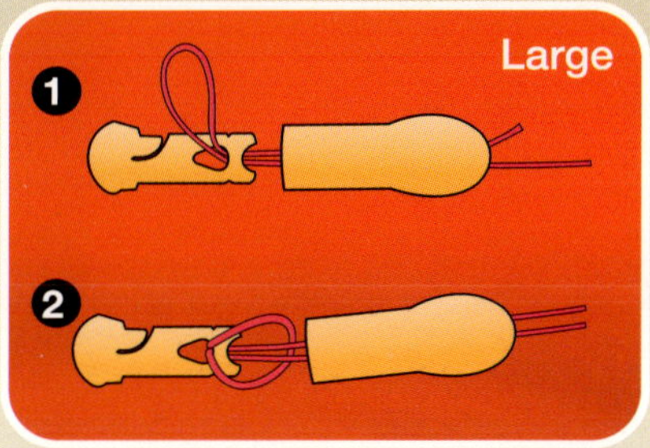

1. With XL and XXL connectors, pass a doubled length of elastic through the hole in the front section.
2. Loop the elastic round the front section, pull tight from behind the back piece then slide it over for a secure fit. Trim the tag end.

Match your connector size to elastic diameter. You can colour co-ordinate them too if you wish.

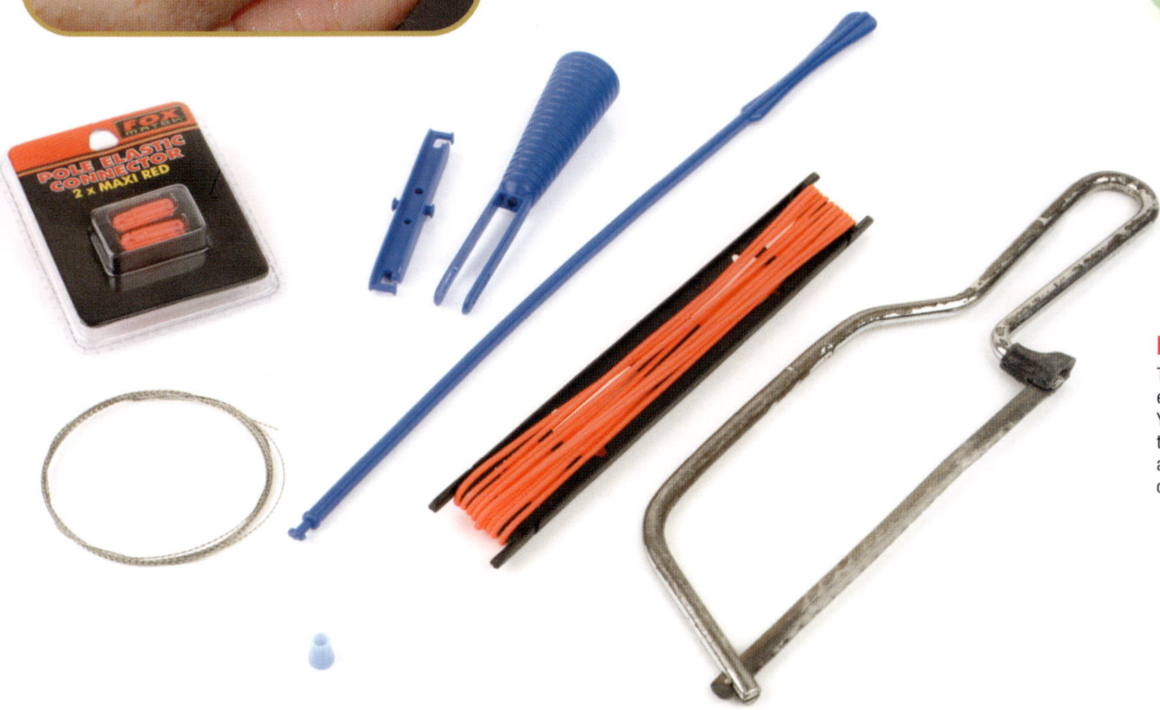

DIY ELASTICATION

Turn the page to learn how to elasticate your own pole. You'll need a junior hacksaw, threader, PTFE bush, bung and connector...plus of course some elastic!

HOW TO ELASTICATE A POLE

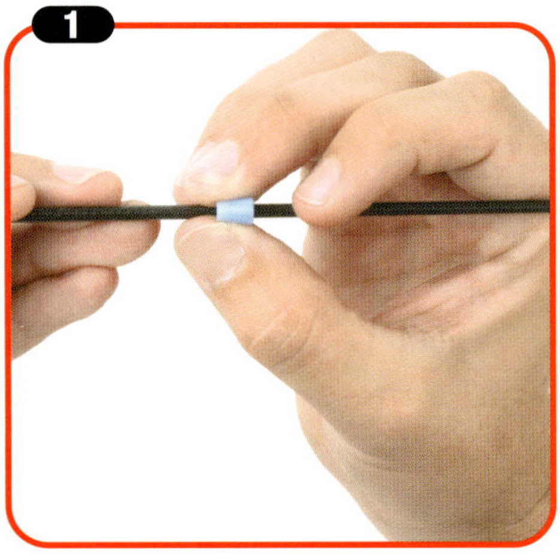

Hold the PTFE push so that your fingers are the same width as the tapered bush and slide along the pole to gauge where the pole tip needs to be cut. NOTE: It is better to go back to little than too far. You can always cut more off but you can't add it back on.

Use a sharp bladed junior hacksaw to carefully cut through the carbon of the tip section at the point identified in step 1.

Place a small craft blade inside the tip before slowly rotating the tip to clear up any loose pieces of carbon which the elastic could catch on.

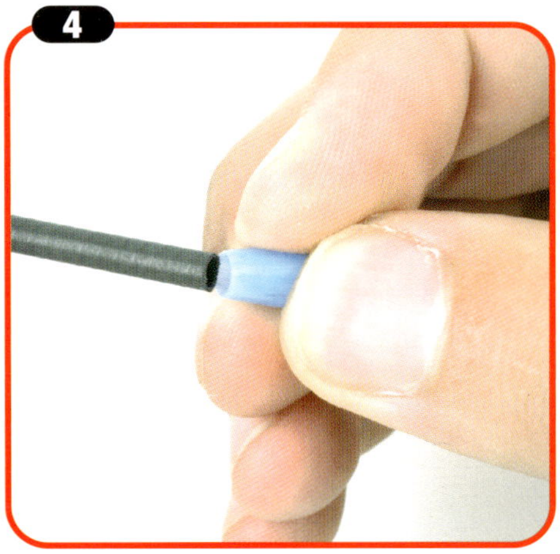

Push the bush over the tip. Gentle pressure should need to be applied which will ensure it is secured in place. If the bush proves to be to loose, repeat steps 1-3 taking back a little of the tip at a time until the bush fits.

Take the bung and place it inside the second section. Rotate the bung creating a scored line on the surface for reference.

The number 2 section of put over poles push over the number 3 section. To allow this, the pole bung needs to fit inside the number 2. Cut the bung one ridge closer than the marking.

Using the extractor rod, check the bung sits far enough inside the section. If not, use a stanley knife blade to trim more off the bung until it does.

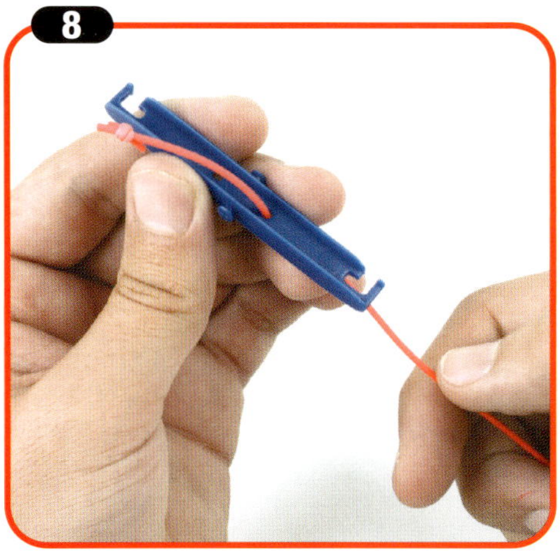

Thread the elastic through the hole in the winder and tie a double oven knot before trimming the ends.

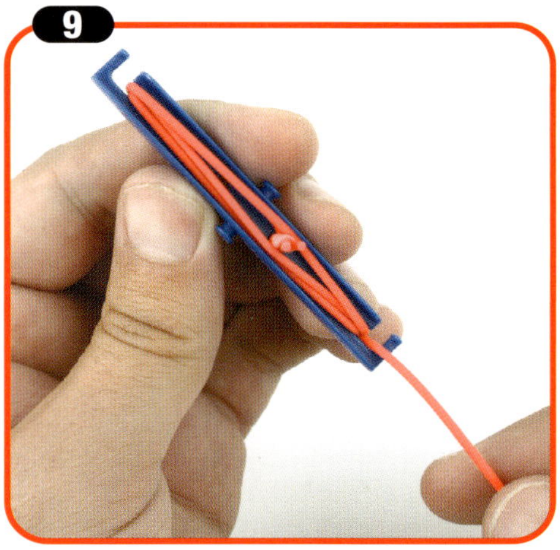

Wrap approximately three turns of elastic around the bung. When taking the pole elastic out of the winder ensure it exits over the opposite side of the bar.

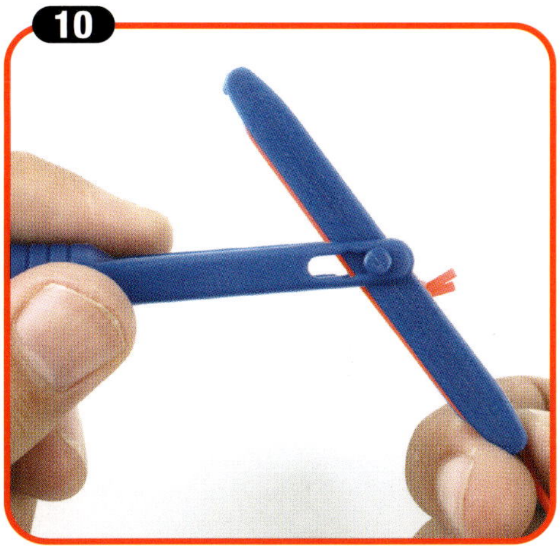

Place the winder inside the arms of the bung and slide it forwards, locking it in place.

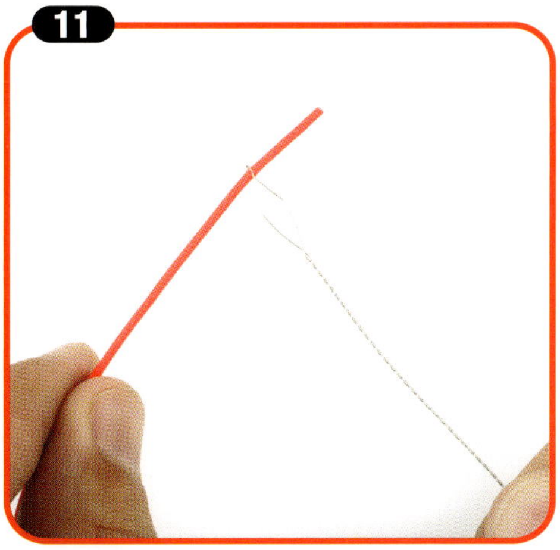

Push the pole elastic threader through the bush and down through the top section. It is usually possible to drop the elastic through number two and three sections using gravity. Once the end of the threader emerges through the top section, place the elastic through the larger hole in the Diamond Eye threader then pull upwards to secure it

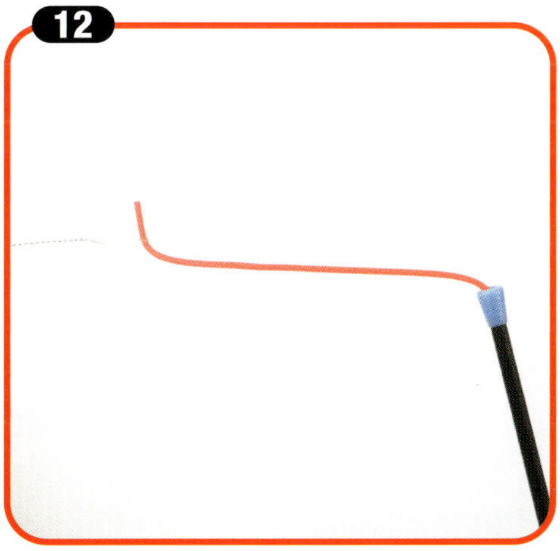

Pull the threader through the tip section which will in turn pull the end of the elastic out of the tip.

Thread the two parts of the connector on to the elastic. At this stage it is worth stretching the elastic somewhat as this tends to happen after some use.

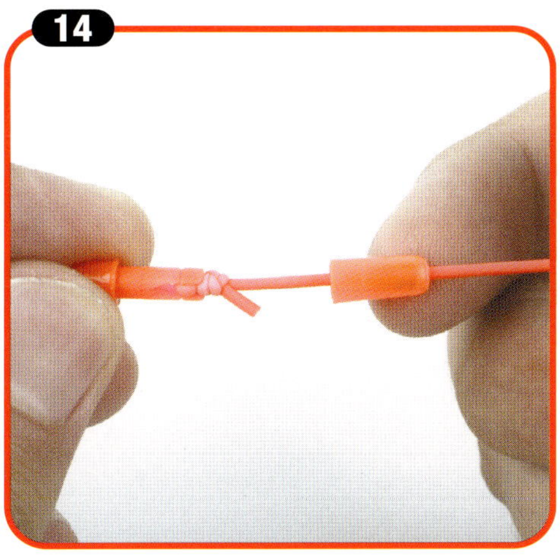

Knot the elastic to the connector. Various knots are available depending on the size of elastic and type of connector. These are detailed elsewhere in the chapter.

There should be enough tension so the elastic creeps back into the pole tip. If not, take more elastic off beneath the connector or see the panel on the right for quick changes.

TENSIONING ELASTIC

After prolonged use or after catching a large fish, the overall length of elastic running through the sections can increase. Slack elastic is unsightly and can cause tangles and lost fish. Conversely, when fishing venues in the winter or encountering smaller fish than expected elastic set too tightly can lead to bumped fish and hook pulls. A Fox Match Tensioner bung allows quick and easy changes without the need for knots or amends. In this sequence we will reduce the tension but to increase the tension simply add more turns of elastic to the winder.

Using the extractor rod, remove the bung from the pole.

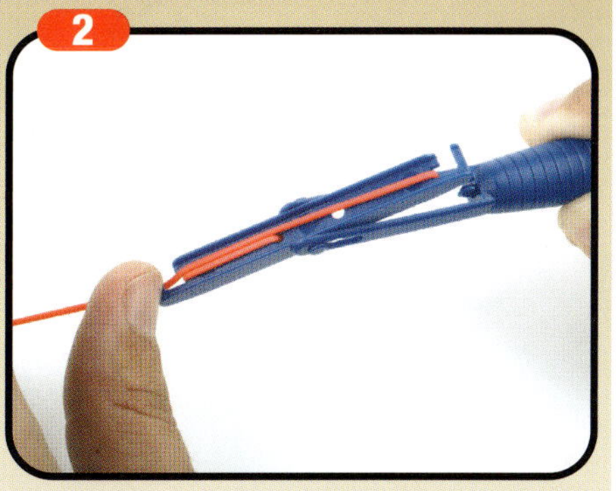

Remove a coil or number of coils of elastic by rotating the winder in an anti-clockwise direction.

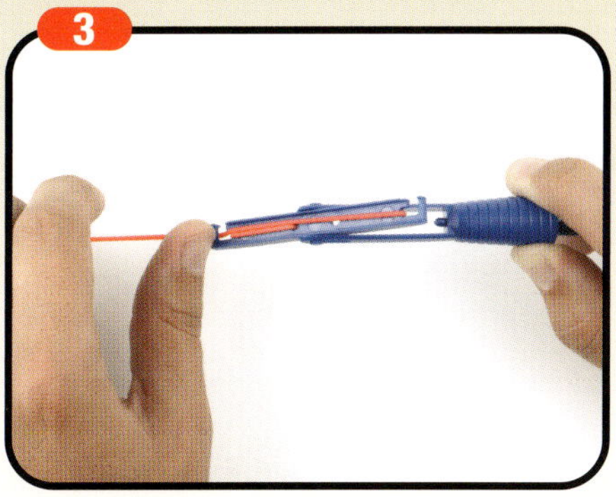

Ensure the elastic exits on the opposite side of the guide to the last length on the winder. This ensures the winder sits flush in the section.

Perhaps even more than with rod and reel, confusion often exists when it comes to selecting the right type of float for pole fishing. Once again, we hope to simplify and clarify matters over the forthcoming pages.

First and foremost, pole floats differ from the running line wagglers covered in the previous chapter in the fact that they are attached to the line at top and bottom rather than bottom-end only. With the pole being held almost directly above them, line control is far easier. Reacting to a bite is also faster. This means pole floats are also smaller and more delicate than wagglers.

Most pole floats feature a side eye fixed towards the top of their body to pass the line through. You then thread the line through two or three pieces of silicone rubber for attaching to the stem, trapping the float at the required depth. We'll show you exactly how to do this in the Rig Making section on pages 90 and 91. But first, we'll look at the different types of pole float and examine their uses.

The first thing to consider is depth of water, or more accurately the depth you're going to fish at. Few Commercial stillwaters are over five or six feet and many of the main catch areas – like marginal shelves and far bank reeds – are often around three feet or less. Also, on many occasions in warm weather you will be fishing 'up in the water' - between a foot and two feet deep – regardless of the actual depth.

Other considerations are the strength of wind and the type and size of bait you'll be using. A useful rule of thumb is: The stronger the wind, the heavier the float and the greater the length of line between float and pole tip. Why? Because extra weight helps to stabilise the set-up, and a longer line reduces the chance of gusts dragging the rig out of position when it inevitably causes your pole tip to bounce around.

"The first thing to consider is the depth that you are going to fish at"

Body Shape

Most stillwater pole floats have a body-down profile. However, there are different degrees of body down, from the outright pear-shaped to much more slender and subtle shapes (see image below).

They're all aimed at helping to further stabilise your rig in the surface drift. On stillwaters, once you've got the tackle basics right, drift and the wind's general influence is the main non-tackle related problem to combat in terms of ensuring you present the bait as naturally as possible.

Oval bodied floats are generally very sensitive and fast to strike with, leaving the water cleanly. Diamond shapes are good for holding on a tight line when fishing on-the-drop. Totally round bodied floats are another typeseldom used on lakes.

You will find some variations on the general body-down shape, namely the oval/rugby ball shaped body and the diamond shaped body.

Body-up floats are designed for holding back in running water and have little use on Commercials. The one exception is Dibbers, a short stumpy little balsa float used to present big baits in shallow water. They have no bristle, just a large domed top which tapers away to a small stem.

Tip Thickness

Another rule of thumb with pole floats is: The bigger the bait (or stronger the wind), the thicker the float tip.

Floats with thick bristles or domed tips have greater inherent buoyancy than fine bristles, meaning they ride the waves better and can support heavier baits.

It stands to reason that finer bristles are more sensitive, offering less resistance to a taking fish. As the weather gets colder, you should look to use finer bristles in increasing amounts – wind permitting.

Tip Materials

Dibbers and other shallow water balsa patterns with a more tapered neck and body-down profile have thick balsa tips and no bristles.

The very thickest bristles are generally plastic, a material widely used due to its high visibility in orange, red, yellow and sometimes black colours. Other tip materials include cane, which is far less visible and therefore not recommended on the long pole, plus fibre glass – a robust and flexible material though rather weighty and restricted to thin sections.

Stem Materials/Lengths

Longer stemmed floats are more stable, due to the surface layers of a lake being faster drifting then lower down where the reverse is often true with undertow taking an effect.

The stems of shallow water floats are necessarily shorter than those designed to fish on the bottom, as the bait may only be presented a few inches beneath the float. As natural as possible a descent is desired, and a long stem would inhibit this.

Stem materials vary, with wire being heaviest followed by fibre, carbon and cane. However, only fibre stems are flexible enough to withstand the rough and tumble of Commercial carping; being more rigid and brittle, other types are prone to bending and snapping.

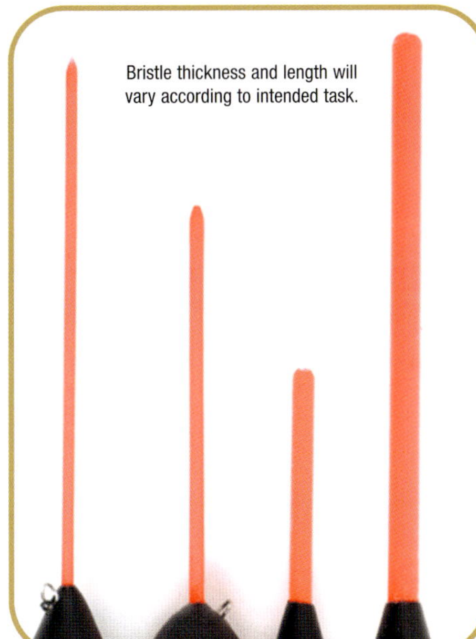
Bristle thickness and length will vary according to intended task.

Shotting Capacities

Further confusion can arise from the fact that three different systems which measure a pole float's shotting capacity are commonly used.

Modern pole fishing evolved in continental Europe where metric weights and measures were the norm long before the UK. Therefore grams, and parts of a gram, are the first of these three systems.

The second continental system involves capacity rating based upon Styl leads. Styls are small cylindrical weights seldom used in the UK, but their respective sizes and weights system remains widely used on pole floats of under a gram. For instance, a float marked 4 x 12 or 4 x 14 demotes a capacity of four No.12 and No.14 Styl leads respectively.

Finally, there's the well known and widely understood British system of round split shot sizes. Totally opposite to Styls, the larger the number the smaller the shot. A No.10 shot is smaller than a No.8. but in terms of Styls this would be the other way round.

Most Fox Match pole floats carry both metric and UK capacities. But to further simplify matters in the typical range of sizes of pole floats used on Commercial stillwaters, here's a rough guide to the three systems which should help you understand and memorise them.

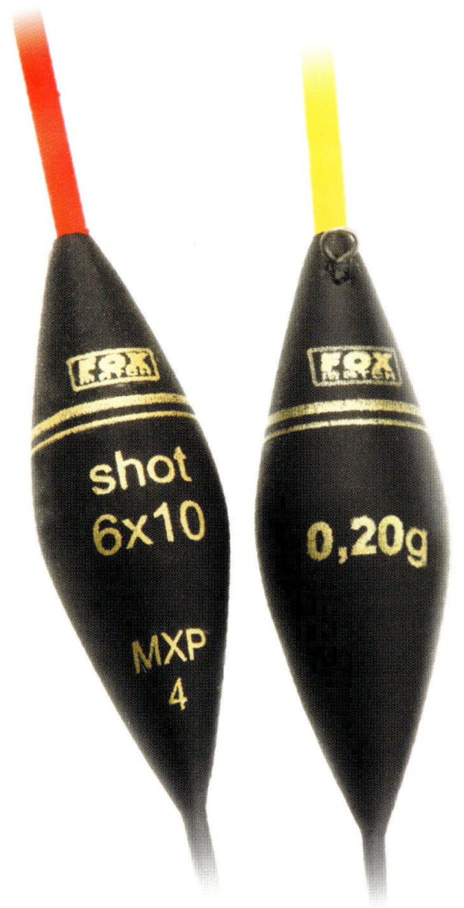

APPROXIMATE EQUIVALENTS

Metric (gm)	Styl leads	UK shots
0.1	4 x 9	3 No.10
0.2	3 x 10	4 No.9
0.3	5 x 12	6 No.9
0.4	4 x 14	6 No.8
0.5	4 x 16	4 No.6
0.75	4 x 18	3 No.4
1	6 x 18	4 No.4

STYL

STYL	WEIGHT (gm)	2x	3x	4x	5x	6x
7	0.010	0.020	0.030	0.040	0.050	0.060
8	0.017	0.034	0.051	0.068	0.085	0.102
9	0.025	0.050	0.075	0.100	0.125	0.150
10	0.035	0.070	0.105	0.140	0.175	0.210
11	0.046	0.092	0.138	0.184	0.230	0.276
12	0.064	0.128	0.192	0.256	0.320	0.384
14	0.100	0.200	0.300	0.400	0.500	0.600
16	0.125	0.250	0.375	0.500	0.625	0.750
18	0.170	0.340	0.510	0.680	0.850	1.020
20	0.302	0.604	0.906	1.208	1.510	1.812

Continental Styls are elongated weights with a central cut.

SHOT

SHOT	WEIGHT (GM)	2x	3x	4x	5x	6x	7x
#8	0.068	0.136	0.204	0.272	0.340	0.408	0.476
#9	0.049	0.098	0.147	0.196	0.245	0.294	0.343
#10	0.03	0.060	0.090	0.120	0.150	0.180	0.210
#11	0.02	0.040	0.060	0.080	0.100	0.120	0.140
#12	0.012	0.024	0.036	0.048	0.060	0.072	0.084
#13	0.009	0.018	0.027	0.036	0.045	0.054	0.063

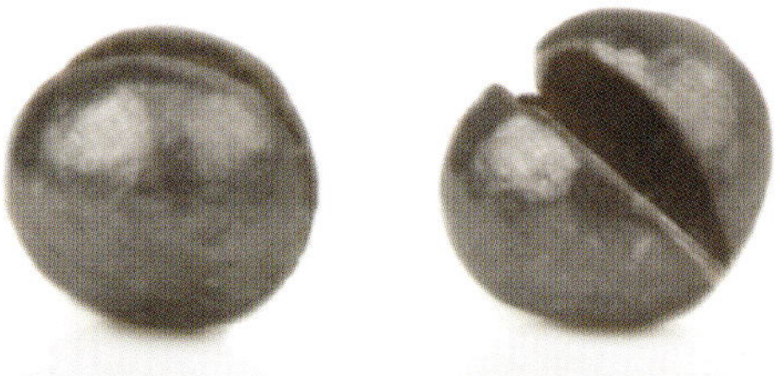

UK shot have a spherical profile.

Olivettes

Over and above 0.75 grams, olivettes are generally used to supply the bulk weight on a rig. On occasions, such as winter fishing, an olivette may be used with a lighter float to get the bait down quickly to the bottom; the fish's feeding zone .

Streamlined nose-down weights developed on the Continent, olivettes are rated on the metric grammage system. A wide range of sizes from 0.3gm to 5 gm, in both in-line (i.e. line through a central bore) and quick change (attached via twin silicone sleeves on pegs at top and rear), types are available in the Fox rannge.

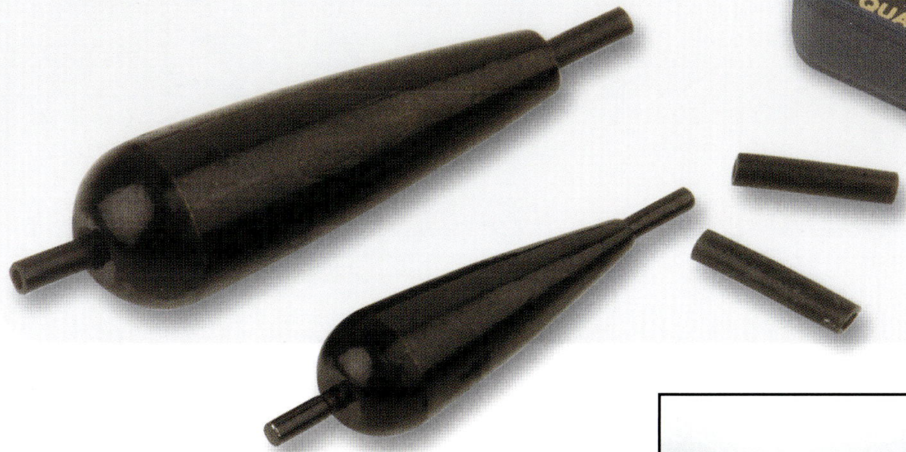

Both models of Fox Olivettes are supplied in handy lock close boxes with the weight clearly printed on the outside.

Fox Match pole shot has won a deserved reputation for perfect roundness, precision central cuts and an ability to move on the line without causing damage.

UK law bans lead shot of between No.8 and 1oz. In terms of Styl leads, this means sizes 7 to 12 are legal. They are often sold in multi-compartment dispensers. Above that, lead-free alternatives are required.

Using an olivette creates a more positive rig that takes the bait down to the catching area very quickly. A strung out rig, where shot or styles are placed at even intervals down the line, produces a slower more natural fall which is good when fish are feeding at different depths.

(Floats not to scale)

FLOATS	DEPTH: Shallow	DEPTH: Mid	DEPTH: Deep	DEPTH: Margin	SEASON: Summer	SEASON: Winter
	✓			✓	✓	✓
	✓			✓	✓	
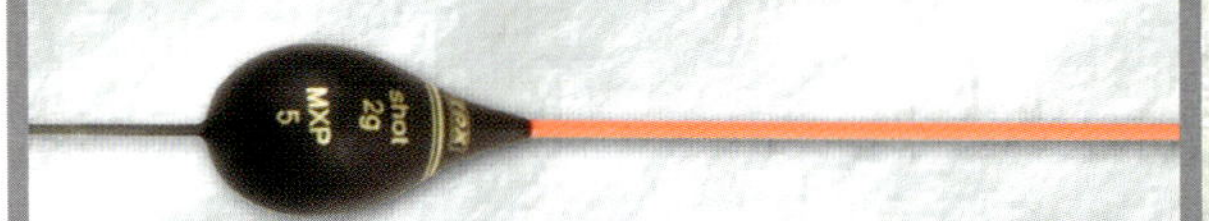		✓	✓	✓	✓	
			✓		✓	✓
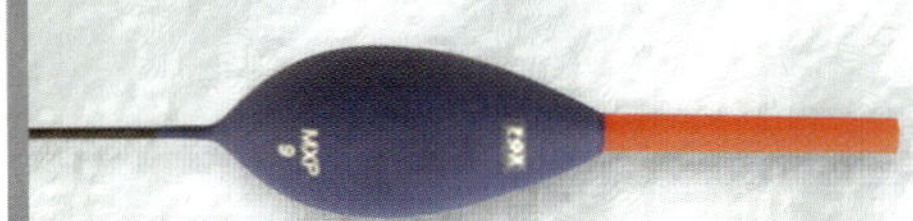	✓	✓	✓		✓	✓
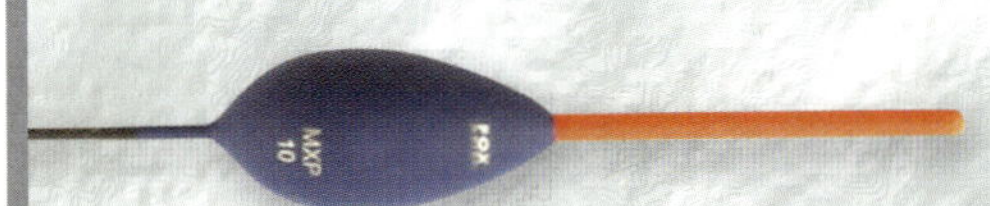		✓	✓		✓	✓
	✓	✓	✓	✓	✓	✓
		✓	✓		✓	✓
			✓			✓

BAITS

Bloodworm	Pellet	Paste	Worm	Meat	Maggot	Caster	Sweetcorn
	✓		✓	✓	✓	✓	✓
	✓	✓	✓	✓	✓	✓	✓
		✓		✓			
	✓		✓	✓	✓	✓	✓
	✓	✓	✓	✓	✓	✓	✓
✓	✓		✓		✓	✓	✓
✓	✓		✓		✓	✓	
✓	✓		✓	✓	✓	✓	✓
✓	✓		✓		✓	✓	

Although Mark Pollard tends to fine tune his rigs on the bank, there are other anglers who like everything down to the last No.13 shot to be spot on before they set off for the venue. One angler famed for his meticulous preparation is quadruple World Champion Bob Nudd, who demonstrates his rig making techniques and equipment in the series of photos on this page. But first, a few words from Bob.

"I guess there's some of you out there who know chapter and verse about rig construction. It's sometimes said - and only half in jest - that there are anglers who derive greater pleasure out of making up and arranging their rigs than the actual fishing.

At the other end of the scale are those who despise the entire process and do anything they can to avoid it. You all know one, I'm sure. Multiple loops where they've added or subtracted the line, immovable shots due to a little wind knot, float bristles blacked out then re-Tippexed.

Personally, I regard rig making as an absolutely vital part of the preparation process. It's not always especially enjoyable time, but it's always time well spent. If you follow my 12 Steps guidelines you may even come to enjoy it!"

1

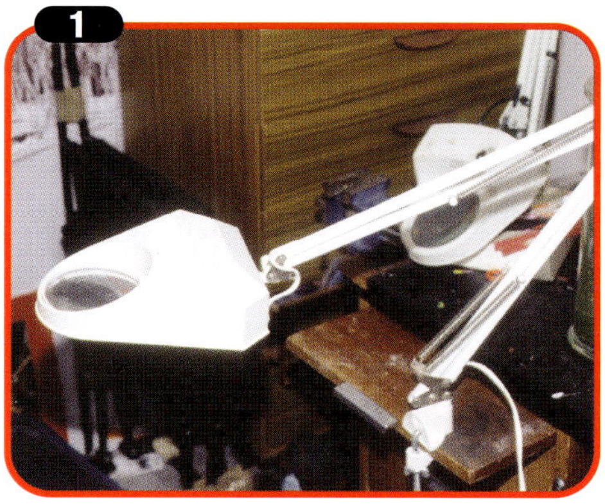

Magnifying Lamp
I would never be without one of these, but I bet plenty of you are! In fact I own two magnifying lamps. I take this portable one on World Championships or festivals. It screws to any surface via a wing nut clamp. The magnifying lens makes all those fiddly little jobs far easier, with a nice bright 100 watt bulb right where it's needed. I think it cost £17 from Argos. I've also got an older fixed base version.

5

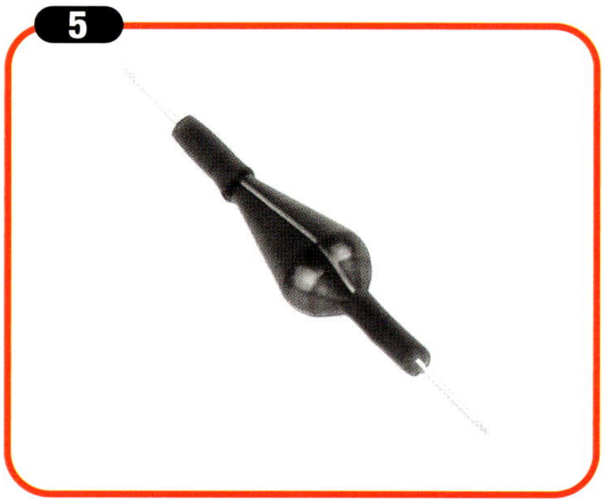

Add The Bulk
With floats over 4 x 14 I usually use an olivette. This one takes 0.6 grams, although you will sometimes find variations with what's printed on the side of a float. I add the next size olivette down, to allow for the addition of some dropper shot.§

9

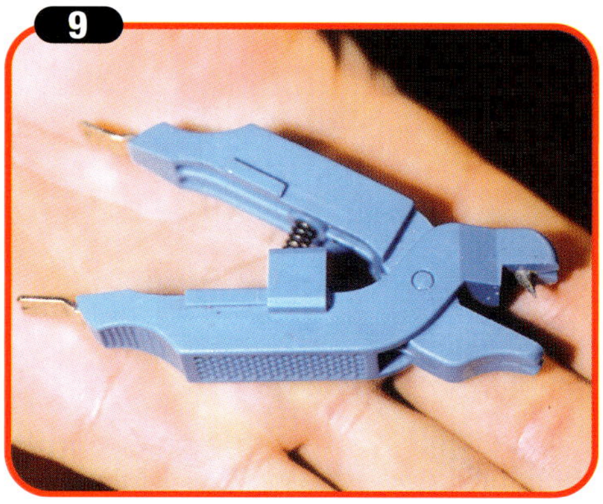

Rescue Remedy
I like to spread my droppers out evenly between bulk and hook length. Their distance depends on depth, bait and many other variables which are topics for another day. But let's say you've added too many. Here's a tool which gets you out of jail on the bank, a Stonfo shot remover. It has a little prong so you can careful open out a shot without damaging line. Absolutely essential!

2

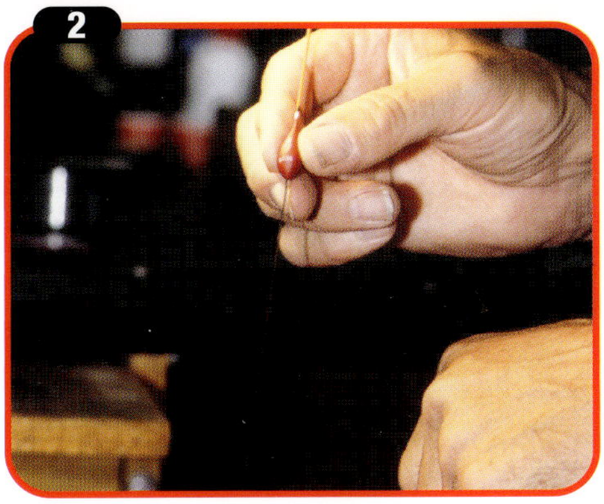

Fitting Silicone

The start point of all pole rigs is selecting a float. If it's one you've not used before, you'll need to cut some silicone from a length of the correct diameter tubing to fit onto the stem. You don't want the tubing to be too tight as this can damage the line, but too loose is worse than useless. Take your time and get it right and your rig will perform miles better.

3

Cut Three Bits.

Satisfied that the silicone is the right diameter? Next, take some sharp scissors and cut three pieces, ensuring the bottom one is a bit longer. I like to do this simply for a little extra security. If the line happens to cut through one piece, you can still use the rig with two.

4

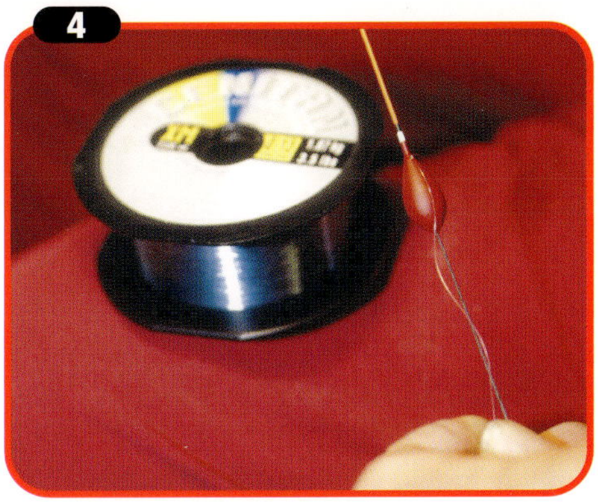

Thread Your Float

Pass the line from your spool down through the float's eye and the three pieces of cut silicone, then thread these up the stem and push the float up the line a bit further so you've got room to work with during the next stage, adding your bulk.

6

Test It Out

Once I've locked my olivette, I slide it up the line and cut off the section beneath which may have got damaged or weakened. Now it's time to test the float. You can see this old glass jar is well used by the algae on the sides! If there's a lot sticking out, I could plump for a 0.6 gram olivette instead and see whether there's enough left to play with to still add my desired number of droppers, three.

7

Fine Tuning.

On this occasion I opt to leave the 0.5 gram 'olly' on. I reckon I'll need five No.12 shots as droppers, but two can be left pushed up under the olly and brought into play if I need a more positive indication lower down later in a session. Note that I use Styl pincers – these are the Image type – to apply the perfect pressure to a dropper shot. You won't manage that on the bank.

8

Perfectly Dotted

The shots duly added, the rig is tested again. I actually needed six, but now it's perfect. If you look at this picture you'll see it's still some way off being shotted to a dot, but experience tells me that a float holding up this far in my jar will be just right on the canal, lake or river where the effect of surface tension will be significantly less.

10

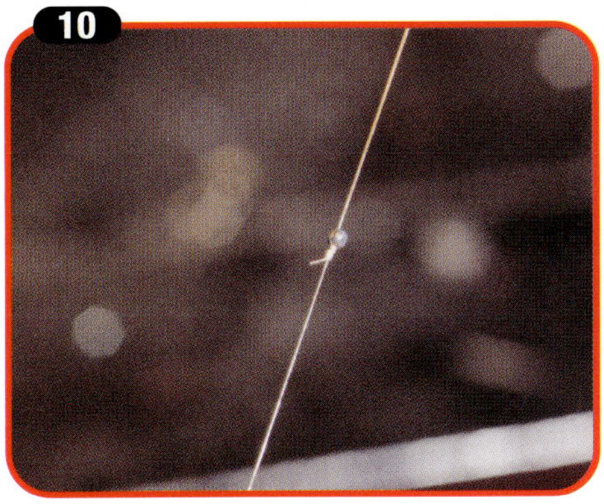

Add Hook Length

Loop-to-loop attachment of hook length to line can stiffen up a rig, resulting in a unnatural presentation right where you want everything to behave as naturally as possible. You don't get any doubled up bits of line with a three turn water knot. Learn to tie this one and your rigs will improve no end. I rest my bottom dropper snug against it.

11

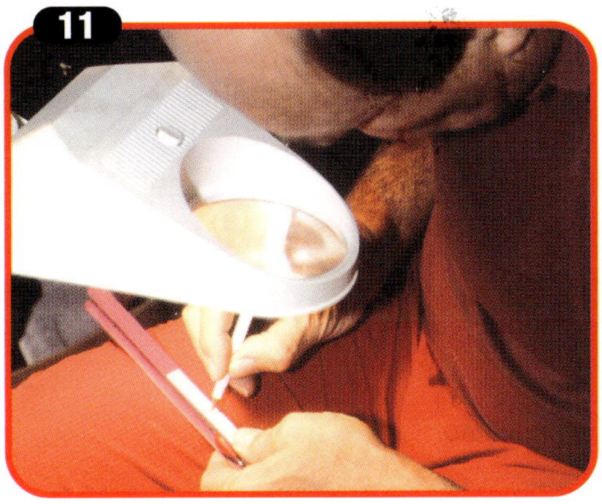

Note The Particulars

You'll waste a lot of time and make a lot of mistakes if you don't write down the line diameters or strength, hook length, hook size and pattern plus float capacity and rig length. I like to use some special paper stickers which have a space marked for each of these things. This is far better than writing onto each winder, as you can simply peel it off and add a new one of you change the winder's contents.

12

Gauging Depth

I'm surprised to be told that many anglers fit together their top kits when making up rigs and measure off their final rig depth using these. There's no need for this at all . Simply measure your winder and count the turns of line until you've got the right depth for the venue you'll be fishing. If in doubt, it's far better to have too much line then remove some on the bank. I almost always do this. Happy rigging!

Ensure all your bait and nets are close to hand, so you don't have to keep getting up from your seat box. Even on Commercials, too much unnecessary noise and movement risks spooking fish. And make sure you've also packed the following hardware...

Eight ESSENTIALS

1

A pole roller is an absolute must to enable smooth shipping– the process of passing the pole back behind you whilst playing a fish to the section at which you need to unship to net or swing it in. Ideally it should come on a solid stand or tripod which won't blow over in string winds, and which is adjustable both in the legs and height department to ensure you can cope with awkward banks. When fishing the very longest poles, some anglers favour two rollers to ensure the pole is supported properly.

2

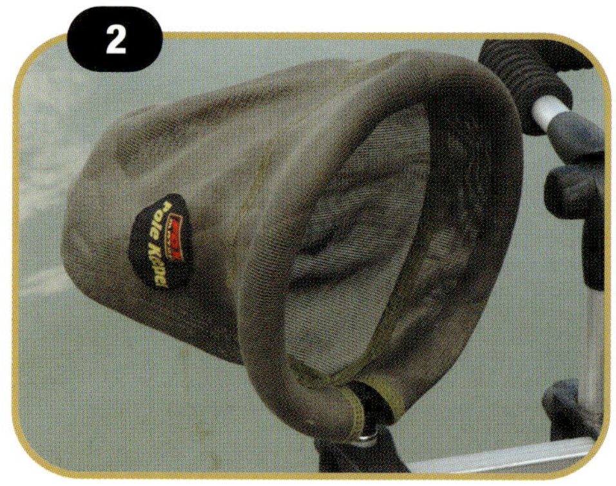

A Pole Keeper – a soft mesh is very useful to tuck the front end of your unshipped pole sections securely into while you deal with unhooking a netted fish. Without this the wind can cause your pole to skate out of reach on the roller, risking possible damage. Plastic grab-type devices serving the same purpose are available, but are less friendly on your expensive carbon sections.

3

Pole Shock Savers help protect your valuable pole from scratches and chips. These high density foam devices come in seven diameters to fit all your end sections, which are vulnerable when shipping back. As well as the damaging impact on hard gravel banks, you don't want small stones or pieces of earth rattling around inside your pole which can happen if you don't block the exposed end.

4

Holding a rig steady can be hard work, especially in awkward winds with long lengths of carbon in your hands. A standard rod rest on a bank stick doesn't provide enough stability, but Bump Bars which fix to the front legs of your seat box footplate are rock solid. These are height adjustable, with various widths available.

5

You can also fix on Bump Bar Rests to cradle the pole in. These devices ensure sudden gusts of wind won't drag the pole along the rest, risking potential collision damage.

6

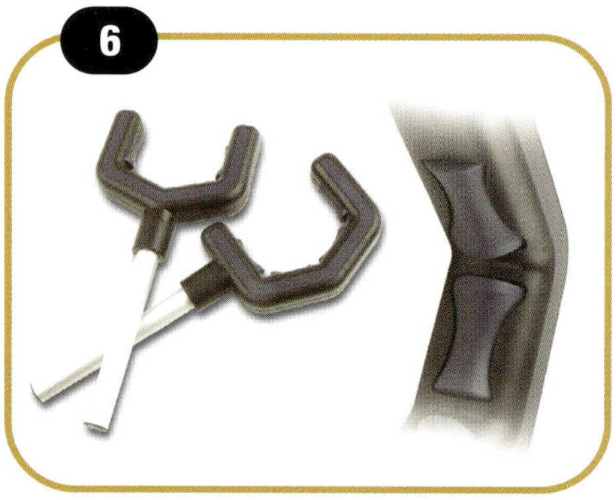

A standard U-shaped Pole Rest will do the job when secured to a standard keepnet bar. If you needs your hands free to ball in groundbait, Vertical and Horizontal System Roller Rests can be fixed at front and rear of your seat box. These feature mini rollers within to aid smooth and speedy removal and placement of the pole.

7

The right type of landing net – a rigid and strong frame with a wide diameter mesh which moves quickly and freely through the water – is a big help. Fitting a floatation device allows you to rest the handle on the Bump Bar or your knee without the net head sinking as you get ready to scoop up your catch.

8

Keepnets are banned other than in matches at 99 per cent of Commercial fisheries. Some venues provide their own for contests to avoid the possible spread of disease through damp mesh. However, if you're required to bring your own, you'll need at least two – one for silver fish and one for carp, or maybe more on venues with a 50lb per net rule. Features such as weighted end rings and pull-through inner handles make life much easier for the angler and also ensure the fish are returned in good condition in the minimum possible time.

So you've got your pole elasticated, your rigs made and your bait ready to hand. You're at your swim, ready to set it all up and start catching. Have you missed anything? Quite possibly...

There are several other essential pieces of hardware to aid success on the pole at Commercial Stillwaters, which we'll run through briefly on this page before moving onto the tactical area of feeding and dealing with different situations in the rest of the Pole chapter.

Above all, a level fishing station is vital when pole fishing. Most Commercial fishery pegs have nice flat slabs and wooden or metal platforms, but a seat box with adjustable levels is still a big bonus. After all, very few things stay totally flat forever. Stomachs and patios spring to mind!

Once you're sitting comfortably, a good posture becomes easier. By this, we mean sitting with as straight a back as possible rather than slumping forward. Support the pole across one thigh with your forearm beneath, or use a Bump Bar to take the strain.

Pole Fishing how to feed

By getting your elastication system, rigs and baits right, you're well on the way to Commercial stillwater pole fishing success.

Feeding is another key area. The use of pole cups and pots to deliver your loose feed with pinpoint accuracy is an absolutely vital skill to master.

Catapults also play an important part on occasions, and of course you can feed margin swims by hand. But first we'll look at cups, which come in many shapes and sizes each with their own specific uses.

The Fox Match range of cups and pots is reckoned by many top anglers to be the most comprehensive you'll find anywhere. There's a variety of larger capacity models designed either for attachment to a purpose-made cupping kit, plus a host of smaller Toss Pots for fixing to the top of your pole while you fish, then removing after the session.

Whatever bait you want to feed, from large balls of fishmeal groundbait right down to a sprinkling of hemp or micro pellets, there's something in the range to cover the task. Check out the pictures and useage guidance text below.

CUPS AND POTS

For kick-starting a swim with balls of groundbait, Conical Pole Pots are the ideal shape. Available in four sizes from 50ml to 250ml, there's a plastic set of four with special screw-in adaptors to fit onto the end of your pole's cupping kit. There's also ultra-strong and lightweight carbon conical pots in the same sizes, available singly. A spout in the side of the plastic models allows liquid attractants to be poured from the cup; a good method in colder months as it draws fish into the area without over feeding.

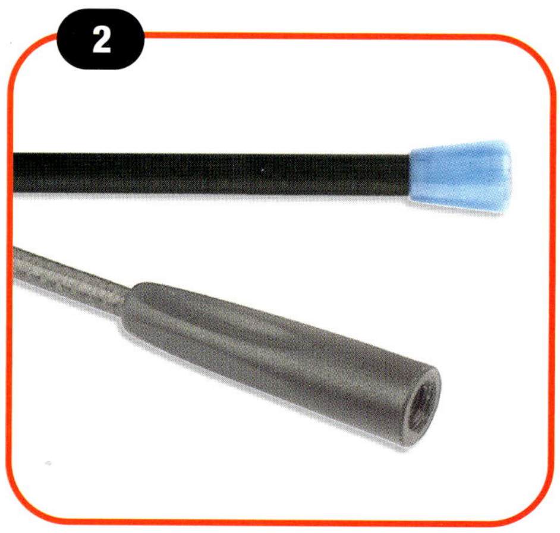

If your pole doesn't come ready supplied with a designated cupping kit, universal two-piece versions are available which fit over the third or fourth joint of most poles and trimmed to size. Fox Match's kit comes complete with an adaptor already fitted which conical pots screw into. See Over.

With a rounder profile, Pepper Pots come in 100, 150 and 200ml versions and fit the same screw adaptor as the conical pots. These allow the different models to be added or removed in an instant. Perferated holes in the detachable lids helps prevent spillage while shipping out and make the Pepper Pots perfect for introducing baits such as pellets, casters and hemp. Once at the spot, you can 'pepper' the freebies across one or more areas rather than dump the whole lot in one pile. Alternatively, the lids can be removed for rapid feed delivery.

One of the key elements of pole fishing success is a regular drip feed. Small, lightweight pot which stays attached to the tip section as you fish help acheive this. Toss Pots have swept the nation since their launch. They fix securely without damaging the pole via tapered grooves in their base. Three sizes of groove – Match, Mega and Power – ensure all pole tip diameters are covered. There's two sizes in a pack, each with removable rims.

In the same compact, lightweight and secure fitting format as Toss Pots, Sprinkle Pots come with removable caps with two different diameter holes. This makes them ideal for drip feeding baits such as micro pellets, casters and maggots – often allowing you to fish out several put-ins before a reload is necessary, especially in the colder months.

Cup Tips

As with all aspects of fishing, there are little tips and tricks which can help make the use of feed cups and pots even more effective. For instance, try scattering a few freebies into a conical cup before placing the ball of groundbait on top. These can help attract fish from the higher levels down to the bed of groundbait as they tumble through in the ball's wake.

With Toss Pots in rim-free mode, add a little dampened groundbait over the top of your freebies and firm it down under light thumb pressure to ensure it all stays in until you ship out to the desired spot. Once again, it's impossible to understate how important cups and pots are when it comes to maximising your catch. If you've not tried them yet, you really are missing out.

Catapults For The Pole

There are occasions when fish are feeding so freely, usually when fishing shallow in open water, that the time taken to load up a pole pot is better spent by rebaiting the hook, shipping straight back out and feeding by catapult instead.

If you grew up before the era of pole pots then using a catapult is probably second nature. You may even have mastered the art of feeding whilst still holding the pole.

But if you grew up using pots, this technique is well worth learning. After all, you may need to feed a secondary waggler line beyond pole range to visit later on in the session.

Accurate grouping of loose feed is still desirable when using catapults, but you are never going to create as tight a spot as with a pole cup. And when fish are cruising around shallow, they'd never stick in just one spot anyway.

So don't worry unduly if you spray bait around all over the place in the first instance. Keep the amounts small, keep on practicing and you'll soon improve. All the time, concentrate on trying to keep the pole as still as possible.

ONE-HANDED FEEDING

Here's a brief pictorial crash course in how to feed with the catapult whilst still fishing a pole. Of course you are not going to become an expert overnight, but it's worth the effort once it all starts to click. So practice as much as possible!

1

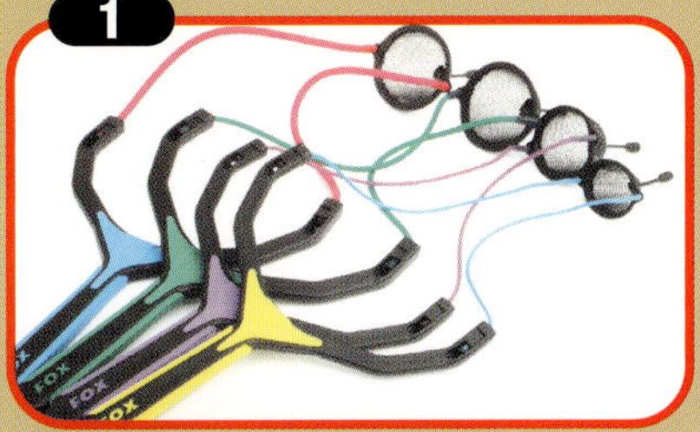

You will need a selection of catapults with different strengths of latex and sizes of pouch to cope with different feeds plus wind strengths.

2

Pick up the catapult and simultaneously scoop up the required amount of feed with the same hand.

3

Grip the tag on the pouch with your other hand and transfer the bait into the pouch.

4

Maintain your grip on the tag then extend the catapult frame forward to gain the required tension on the latex, keeping the pole steady across thighs or a bump bar.

5

Release the tag to scatter the feed around your float (or further out if baiting a waggler swim for later in the session), endeavouring to keep the pole as steady as possible in the process.

Having dealt with tackle and feeding, it's time to look at tactics. Pole fishing is synonymous with big catches at Commercial Fisheries, but in order to succeed you have to understand and master a number of techniques and approaches.

Over the concluding pages of this chapter, we'll break these down into the following sub-sections:

- FISHING AT FULL DEPTH
- FISHING SHALLOW
- MARGIN FISHING
- FISHING THE LONG POLE
- SILVER FISH TECHNIQUES

We'll show you some typical scenarios, and discuss how best to alter your approach as the seasons change.

Full Depth Fishing

Many commercial fisheries have been designed to give everyone a 'feature' - meaning an island, reed or lily bed or overhanging vegetation – to fish towards. Whenever this feature lies within pole range, it's an obvious place to concentrate a major part of your attack.

But not every peg or venue will have the luxury of a far bank feature within pole range. And even on those which do, you should also feed an area away from the feature in open water, or 'down the track' as the middle of the lake is often termed on canal and snake-type lakes.

On wider, more exposed venues, your pole options will be limited to open water or the near margins. More about that latter option later. But right now we'll kick off with a look at how to catch fish which are feeding on the bottom, at full depth, in what are often termed open water swims.

So where do you start? The first thing to do is to thoroughly plumb the depth across your swim. The best approach is a systematic one: start directly in front of you at the full length of your pole, then repeat the process to the left and right to see if there's any variations in depth. Work backwards a section at a time to find the depth at any place in the peg.

By swinging the pole slowly around to drag the plummet across the deck, you can also feel for any snags or changes to the make up of the bottom of the lake bed. Although most modern commercials have been created with fairly uniform bottoms, excavation is never an exact science.

RIG ENTRY OPTIONS

Another factor to consider is how you drop or lay your rig into the swim. A lot of anglers just ship out their pole to the required distance then raise the tip and swing the rig out beyond it. But if you do it this way, the way your bait falls through the water – on a tight arc back towards you – is very unlikely to appear natural to the fish. They are more likely to treat it with suspicion whilst mopping up the loose feed or freebies instead. Some more subtle and, usually, more effective options are outlined below. Experiment with all of the first three to discover what is best in any given venue or situation, and before long it will become second nature to pick the right one.

1

STRAIGHT DOWN

Lowering the rig directly down beneath the pole tip is a favoured option when fishing full depth. It ensures the tackle is in a nice straight line, with no risk of tangles plus the absolute certainty that you'll be right over your cupped-in feed or groundbait as the rig settles. Over the past decade, this has become the preferred technique of many top anglers including England internationals.

2

DOWNWIND

Just as river fish like to approach a bait facing into the flow, the same goes for undertow on stillwaters. As this is likely to be in the opposite direction to the wind, it can pay to swing your rig in at 45 degrees to the pole tip then hold it steady until it settles and begins to inch through the swim in the direction they'll be facing. If you expect bites on the drop as well as on bottom, it's well worth trying.

3

UPWIND

The direct opposite of the above, and not easy to accomplish in anything above a moderate breeze. But there are times, such as when the surface drift is moving faster than the lower layers, that you need to swing in upwind in the knowledge that your rig will be quickly moved away from the baited spot if you choose the downwind option. As with the previous approach, this can work very well if you're getting bites on the drop or just before the rig settles.

4

STRAIGHT OUT

Having declared this 'lazy swing' to be an undesirable option in the introduction, there are exceptions to the rule.
Most notably, if your pole is not quite long enough to reach a feature or an area where fish are showing, it's better to try swinging a heavier float on a longer line to reach the spot in the hope of catching a few than to sit biteless with perfect presentation at your previous maximum range. It's not pretty, but it can work occasionally!

Spend plenty of time plumbing the depth. Underwater features such as slopes, shelves, bars or any change in depth act as a magnet holding fish of all sizes.

You may find depth variations and undulations varying from a couple of inches to a foot or more. These are underwater features which can attract fish as much as something more obviously visible, and their exact location within the swim should be carefully noted and exploited.

In winter, the remains of dying lily beds are often excellent fish-holding spots and these can be located in this manner.

Where To Bait Up

Building up a mental picture of your swim's underwater topography helps you decide where to feed and fish. On busy weekends or under match conditions when every peg is occupied, it's often wise to fish as far out as you can comfortably get away with. Holding a pole of 13 metres or more is not the easiest of tasks in strong winds, but it can pay dividends as the bigger fish often retreat away from the disturbance.

Again, we'll cover long pole techniques in greater detail later. But suffice to say that in winter especially, when the fish are likely to be on or near the bottom, an approach based around targeting the deepest part of your swim is often wise.

Perhaps the main reason why the pole is such an effective tactic is the precision placement of bait which it affords, coupled with the subsequent placement and control of the baited rig over the very spot or spots.

Just as when float fishing or feeder fishing, it's important to visually line up your feed spot with an immovable marker on the far bank, ensuring your direction is spot-on as well as just distance.

POLLY'S COMMENT

Once you've plumbed a rig it's wise to mark the depth of the swim on your pole in case you need to re-rig or change the depth at any point. This is best achieved by hooking your hook into the bottom end of the section of pole to which you'll be unshipping at, then marking the position of your float's bristle or dome with a small blob of Tipp-ex. This can be wiped off easily without risking any damage to the pole.

Some of the biggest catches on Commercial stillwaters fall to shallow pole tactics. As with the shallow waggler technique covered in the floats section, it's a very busy method primarily used in the warm summer months when fish are actively seeking bait in the upper layers.

However, provided carp are catchable within range of your pole's length, the shallow pole is superior to the waggler for several key reasons.

- You can place a bait more accurately.
- You can strike a bite faster.
- The wind's adverse effects on the length of line between rod tip and float is greatly reduced.
- Provided your elastic and rigs are matched to the size of fish, you can land them faster and build bigger weights. (By referring back to the elastics/lines guide earlier in this section, you should be able to select a suitable combination).

Let's examine those advantages further, starting with the often all-important bait placement. Carp, and indeed many other species on commercial fisheries, love the security of features such as island margins, reeds, lily beds and overhanging branches. On some days you'll have to fish tight up to or even beneath them.

Even the world's best waggler angler will snag up sometimes when striving to get as close to these as possible, but with a short length of line between pole tip and float this will happen far less frequently.

A typical length from pole tip to float for shallow pole fishing is around 12 to 16 inches, though it can pay to go even shorter on occasions when fishing in really shallow water beside reeds and islands. Conditions and distance will dictate to some extent, as it's not really viable to hold 16 metres of pole in a stiff wind with less than a foot of line to the float tip. The inevitable movement of the pole will result in the rig being jerked and dragged around too much, with the hook bait never staying still long enough for a fish to take it.

Although backshotting – the placing of a shot on the line between pole tip and float – is an option which some anglers recommend to steady things up in gusty conditions, the advent of Bump Bars has largely removed the need for backshotting in Mark's opinion.

The less line from pole tip to float, the faster your reaction to a bite should be. On many occasions you won't even need to strike as the fish will hook itself against the pole tip, often at incredible speed so that before you know it the pole is bending round with elastic streaming out.

POLLY'S COMMENT

The less line from pole tip to float, the faster your reaction to bite should be. On many occasions you won't even need to strike as the fish will hook itself against the pole tip.

Feeding By Catapult

To really bag up you need to get the fish competing for bait. But don't overdo it. It's very easy to get excited and put too much in, which merely results in too many line bites as the fish charge around in a frenzy. You may also find that too much feed results in the fish following it down to the bottom. Not ideal when you're trying to catch shallow!

What you use on the hook for shallow fishing can be almost unlimited. There's two schools of thought – try to match your hook bait to the loose feed, or give them something a bit larger and/or brighter which will stand out and hopefully be taken quicker.

Experiment with hook baits to find what suits your waters. But remember, above all, the key to catching is how you feed. And invariably that means mastering the art of accurate catapulting whilst holding the pole.

Making A Splash

On venues where bait limits apply, you can fool the fish into thinking some more loose feed has just arrived by tapping the tip of your pole on the water as you fish.

Other variations on this trick include cupping in water or, in one memorable case a few years ago, using a toy 'super soaker' gun to spray a jet of water in the area around your float!

However, the ethics of these approaches are questioned by some and many fishery managers ban them, so always establish their legality before putting them into action at your venues.

Tapping your pole on the surface as you fish can fool curious carp into thinking there's some free food around!

"To really bag up you need to get the fish competing for bait. But don't overdo it."

"Kerb crawlers - a frequently heard Commercial Fishery term for big carp which frequent near the margins"

Before examining the finer points – or more accurately the stronger points – of this important area of pole fishing, we first need to define what is meant by the term 'Margin Fishing'.

After all, every venue has a near and a far margin - although the latter isn't always within reach of a pole.

But in Commercial Fishery pole angling parlance, references to Margin Fishing invariably mean the near margin. Far bank work comes under the Long Pole heading, even though presentations and rigs are often very similar.

On this page, we'll deal with ways to catch fish from the near margin – often in surprisingly close proximity to your platform or peg. It's one of the main features in your swim, and carp in particular love to feed in the often shallow and sheltered water close to the bank from which you fish.

The theory and substance of Margin pole fishing is very similar to the Long Rod float approach shown in the previous chapter. The obvious difference is that instead of a reel which can yield line when a hooked fish charges off, you're relying on pole elastic to take the strain and subdue your target.

Kit For The Job

You can either use your normal pole for margin work, or buy a separate margin pole created specially for the job such as the Fox Match Insider or Sideliners.

Margin poles typically run up to 8.5 metres and are specially reinforced to withstand the hit-and-hold shock tactics of close range carping. Rated for the strongest of elastics, they are ideal for situations which don't require too long a reach along the near bank to the left or right of your peg.

If you prefer to pit your normal pole against the might of 'kerb crawlers' –

Accurate feeding is never a problem when you're fishing the near margins.

Only small this time -
but the next one could be 15lb-plus!

a frequently-heard Commercial Fishery term for big carp which frequent the near margins – then you must have extra sections put together and ready to add on in an instant if a big fish surges off and threatens to bottom out your elastic. It's no good doing this but not having them at the correct angle for the direction you're fishing. More about that on the following pages.

Ultimately, your chosen rig, bait and feed approach depends on the size of fish a venue holds and the time of year. But as a rule of thumb, err on the heavy side when it comes to lines and hooks - especially when fishing close to serious snags such as bushes with trailing branches. And on the positive side when it comes to feeding, and size of hook baits!

Baits And Feeding

If you expect to fish the margins for the majority of a session, you'll need plenty of bait to throw in - preferably noisily! Whether you're expecting a regular run of carp in the 1-3lb class, or just a handful of double-figure lumps, you're targeting fish which have moved into the edge because they want to eat - and eat well.

Even if you feed a margin line purely as a back-up or with thoughts of only checking it out in the later stages of a match or a session, be prepared to introduce plenty of bait. You need to be sure that silver fish, or large carp, haven't moved in and cleaned you out. This may take the form of a couple of large cupfuls every hour rather than regular handfuls. Good feeds for the margin include pellets, corn, hemp and also fishmeal groundbait. The latter feed can either be dampened, riddled then poured in loose, or formed into balls. A lot depends on the depth of water. Casters have their day, often in cooler weather when silver fish are less active.

On the hook, you can present a large stand-out bait like a ball of soft paste, or cat food, over a bed of fishmeal or small particles. Alternatively, you could go down the route of matching your hook bait to the free offerings. The only downside to this latter choice is that it limits your hook size, and a hook as large as fishery rules allow is very helpful in what often amount to hit and hold situations.

Building A Big Weight

Overleaf, we'll look at some more ways to help you catch those kind of weights which will either put you in with a good chance of winning a match, or send you home from a pleasure session with aching arms but a big smile on your face.

Ten fish from the margins may give you 100lb on a well established venue on the right day. On a newer venue, you may need 150 fish for the same weight. Although carp are the likely mainstays on established fisheries, all species learn to associate the margins with food so do not be surprised to catch bream, tench, crucians, chub, orfe - everything with fins really!

Having looked at the basic principles of pole fishing the margins on the previous pages, we'll move on to cover some suggested tackle and tactics.

Tackle-wise, the elastic and lines you choose for margin fishing should pretty much mirror the at-a-glance guide seen earlier in this section on the elastics page. However, you also need to factor in the fact that you are fishing at much closer range than on the long pole.

The extra flexibility and 'give' in hollow elastics makes them a good choice in the majority of margin situations. They are less harsh than solid types, therefore there is less likelihood of a hooked fish splashing on the surface right where you are fishing, possibly spooking others nearby.

By contrast, if you are fishing close to snags such as lily beds or a bush with trailing branches then a solid elastic is best as you will want to strike into a fish and immediately try to steer it out into open water and away from danger.

As well as stepping up your elastics, it can be wise to use one stage stronger line than you otherwise would for an open water situation. Which brings us around to the question of hooks. Again, try to get away with as strong a pattern as possible whether you go the big baits or small baits route. You can always scale down if bites are finicky.

Spare Sections At The Ready

One of the commonest errors when margin fishing is the failure to give yourself adequate back-up in case you hook an unstoppable fish which threatens to bottom out your elastic and smash the line.

Many anglers either forget to assemble a number of pole sections into one long length for fast shipping to follow a runaway carp, or do this but fail to position them in alignment with the direction they are fishing in. The two pictures on the right demonstrate the right and wrong ways.

Multiple Margin Spots

You needn't feed only one margin spot. It can pay to alternate between areas to the left and right of your fishing position, and even right in front of it beside your keepnets!

Just remember to switch the position of those back-up sections accordingly. If there's no handy vegetation to rest them on, reposition your pole roller and use that.

BACK-UP SECTIONS: GET IT RIGHT!

When margin fishing for big fish, if your back-up sections aren't positioned at a similar angle to which you are fishing at, the upshot will be lost carp and trashed rigs!

With back-up sections within easy reach and pointing the right way. Providing you move quickly, the fish should be safely landed.

Dedicated Margin Poles

If you don't fancy subjecting your main pole to a possible beasting from big 'kerb-crawlers', consider buying either a secondary carp pole or best of all a dedicated Margin Pole.

Margin poles are typically between six and nine metres long, and have a thinner overall diameter but much stronger carbon walls than normal poles.

With reinforced joints and in some cases a cross weave for extra strength, they are rated for elastics in the grade 16 to 20+ range. Although there's no such thing as an unbreakable piece of pole kit, these are they closest thing to it. In any case, it's anglers, not fish, that break poles - but that's another story!

Margin poles require little if any cutting back of the tip section, which has a wide bore suiting thick elastics and external PTFE bushes.

Despite the tough-wearing image of Margin Poles, they are also excellent tools with which to introduce young anglers to the joys of Commercial stillwater fishing. Whips are just too fragile in this day and age, when a 1oz rudd can be followed next cast by a 4lb carp to give the little darlings a bit of a shock. Many dads have had cause to be grateful for the strength and longevity of a Margin Pole!

The Sideliner is Fox Match's entry level margin pole.

Long pole fishing could apply to any of the previous three sections - full depth, shallow or even margin if you get the opportunity to ship a rig into a corner or along to a vacant platform.

But most Commercial fishery anglers take the term 'long pole' to mean fishing tight to far bank reeds, either with the bait touching bottom or, on occasions, set shallow to intercept cruising fish.

On most lakes you'll need at least 13 metres of pole to get tight against the reed stems which offer sanctuary and shade to the fish. More typically it'll mean fishing with 14.5 or even 16 metres, which is a demanding task for the full duration of a session even if you've got a top quality pole like the Envoy.

It's vitally important to be sitting comfortably, with your seat box set level. There's more scope to lose fish on barbless hooks when you're shipping back with extra long poles, so you must ensure that your pole roller is perfectly positioned to avoid unwanted 'bounce'. If necessary, set a second roller further back to support the pole and reduce the risk of costly breakages.

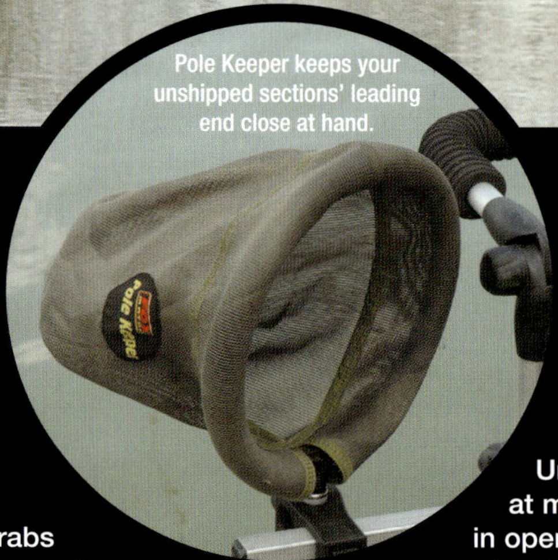

Pole Keeper keeps your unshipped sections' leading end close at hand.

A single roller is generally fine, but two are occasionally needed.

Once you've unshipped, you need some means of keeping the front end of the pole sections resting on the roller behind you close to hand. Many anglers favour plastic pole grabs or tulip grips which screw into banksticks or fit onto seat box apparatus, but Mark Pollard has been field testing the new Fox Match Pole Keeper – a circular net – and finds it far more user-friendly and less likely to damage the pole.

The same 'bounce factor' which can cause fish to come adrift if you're not very careful can also create frustrating tangles when shipping out shallow rigs on the long pole. Whenever possible, ship out you're your rig trailing in the water. This is far less likely to tangle than if it's swinging around in the air. Of course, the ability to do this depends on your chosen bait is hard enough to withstand being dragged through the water without falling off. Paste is a no-no, requiring the pole cup trick already shown.

Unless you're fishing at maximum pole range in open water, catapults are out when it comes to feeding. In a typical Snake or Canal-style lake's far bank swim, too much bait would end up overshooting into the reeds, giving the fish no reason to come out.

Accurate feeding via a Tosspot is the way to go, ensuring the feed lands right beside your rig and entices fish out from their hideaways.

Of course, fishing so close to reeds means there's always the potential for a hooked fish to dive back into the cover and snag you up. You really need your wits about you when fishing this way. Fish as short a line as possible between pole tip and float as you can get away with, without spooking the fish.

As soon as the float disappears, strike and get as much of the pole back behind you as quickly as possible. If you've got your elastic and rig right, once you get a big fish away from the snag into open water you should win far more battles than you lose.

If a fish does snag you up, try putting the pole tip over the top of the fish and slackening off. If it's not moved after two minutes then you will have to pull for a break. Ensure you do so safely, grasping the elastic under water if possible. This will cushion the float if it suddenly springs free of the reeds. On no account should you ever pull directly towards yourself, as this risks serious injury.

Above: The best way to ensure a paste-baited hook reaches the target zone intact.

Right: When shipping out to long range with shallow rigs, trail the rig through the water to reduce wrap-around tangles.

Another controversial but highly effective (where allowed) technique is The Floating Pole. As the name suggests, this involves using the water's surface to support the top end of your pole when striving to reach distant far bank features beyond the reach of normal 14.5 or 16 metre poles.

Many poles have parallel butt sections, meaning the top of the section fits into the bottom. In theory there's no limit to such a pole's length – but physical and monetary limitations tend to restrict the floating pole's maximum length to 20 or 21 metres.

Although less common than fishing to a far bank or a lily bed, the Floating Pole can also be used in open water.

> **"In theory there's no limit to such a pole's length - but maximum is usually 21 metres"**

Rig-wise, on most occasions there's just a foot or so of strong line plus a baited hook - usually a hair rigged bait or banded pellet. No float is required!

Loose feed is catapulted around the pole tip, and fish hook themselves against the weigh of the pole and the tensioned elastic. The angler then ships back and plays the fish as normal.

As already mentioned, you'll find this technique banned at many venues. It's generally off-limits down South, but seems to be allowed in certain areas of the country including a number of waters around the Yorkshire and Lincolnshire areas. Indeed, the technique first sprung to prominence when top Yorkshire match team Barnsley Blacks used it in a Super League final at Northamptonshire's Heyford Fishery.

In summary, wherever a fishery's management allow its use, The Floating Pole is a legitimate and highly effective way of building huge weights when fish are feeding up in the water. Many question its ethics, but the same has been said of the Method feeder, bait boats, and bolt rigs. As always, that's a matter for the individual to decide.

Do Not Strike!

Striking a bite on the floating pole is not necessary! The fish hook themselves against the weight of the pole and it's virtually a physical impossibility. Trying to strike can lead to pole breakages.

Anyway, with between three and six metres of pole typically resting on the water, and just a foot or so of line, reacting fast enough to actually strike would take a combination of a world class wicketkeeper's reflexes and a champion bodybuilder's physique!

Ship back steadily, resting the pole on the water until close in.

When a fish hooks itself, the pole and tip will be dragged round and the weight helps slow the fish. Your first move should be to ship several of the larger sections back behind you, still resting the top six or so sections on the water, and let the elastic take the strain. (It's always a good idea when using the Floating Pole to check that all sections are securely fixed together in the first place). Keep the movements smooth and steady, and try to avoid pointing the pole directly at the fish in case it pulls the top kit out of the pole. Keep moving the pole behind you keeping the top setions close to the water, until the top sections no longer want to float. At this point you can continue to play a fish as you normally would. If the fish is within range, simply unship as normal and play it out - using the pumping technique if required to gain back elastic prior to netting.

POLLY'S COMMENT

It's always a good idea to make sure all your sections are securely fixed together in the first place - if you want to avoid a swim or a trip out in the fishery boat!

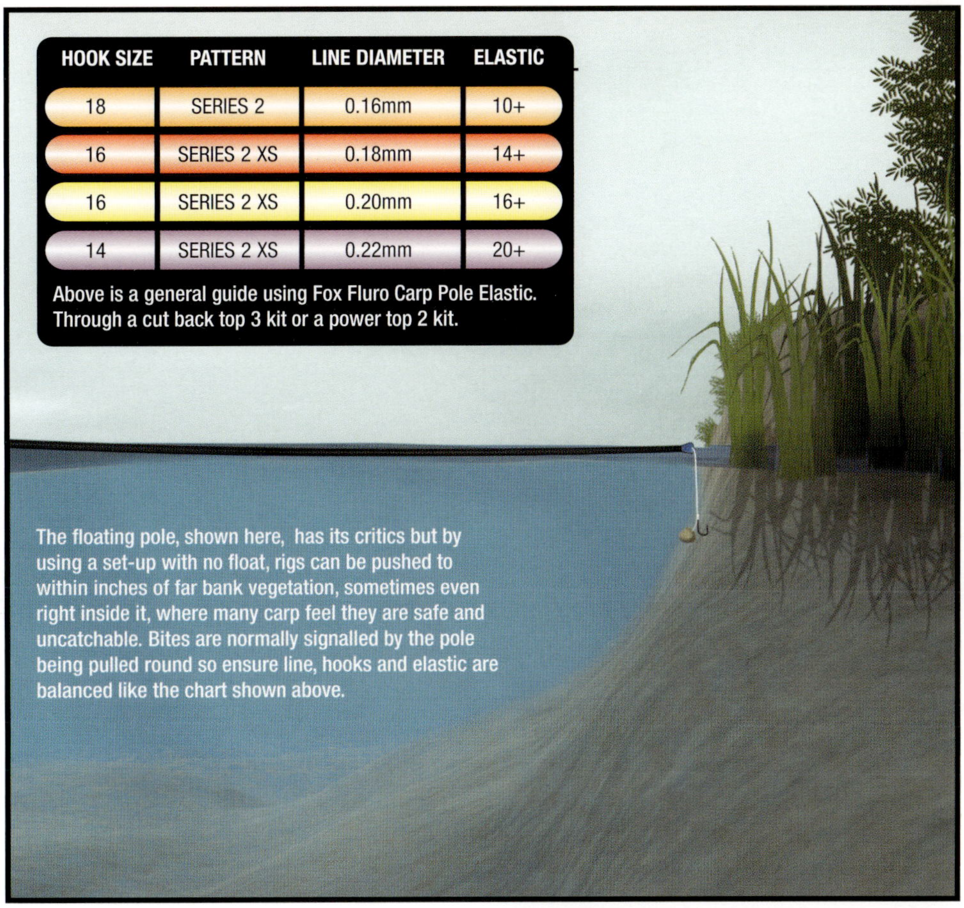

HOOK SIZE	PATTERN	LINE DIAMETER	ELASTIC
18	SERIES 2	0.16mm	10+
16	SERIES 2 XS	0.18mm	14+
16	SERIES 2 XS	0.20mm	16+
14	SERIES 2 XS	0.22mm	20+

Above is a general guide using Fox Fluro Carp Pole Elastic. Through a cut back top 3 kit or a power top 2 kit.

The floating pole, shown here, has its critics but by using a set-up with no float, rigs can be pushed to within inches of far bank vegetation, sometimes even right inside it, where many carp feel they are safe and uncatchable. Bites are normally signalled by the pole being pulled round so ensure line, hooks and elastic are balanced like the chart shown above.

Two Free Hands For Feeding

One reason why so many big weights of fish fall to the floating pole is the fact that it makes feeding so much easier.

With part of the pole resting on the water and the butt end perhaps balanced across a bump bar, as Mark Pollard likes to do, both your hands are free to load up and fire a catapult accurately and regularly.

This very fact is the backbone of the tactic's justified reputation as a great leveller. One reason why many top match anglers and fishery owners are vehemently opposed to it is that their hard-learned feeding skills on the long pole no longer give them a significant edge over less experienced rivals.

Feeding is a doddle with the water supporting much of the pole's weight.

Baits You Can And Can't Use

Top baits for the floating pole are slow-sinkers like bread, pellets and bunches of maggots. The latter two are good for catapulting out as loose feed, whereas with bread it's more a case of relying on what you have on the hook.

Floating baits are also good, where permitted. Sweetcorn, ever-versatile, is another option. But avoid anything too soft and prone to falling off the hook while shipping out, such as paste (except perhaps a hard 'conker') and cat meat.

As always, the best way to learn is to go and try a tactic yourself - preferably having first watched an expert in action. Over the next 16 pages we're giving you the next best thing - a series of actual 'live' pole fishing Scenarios as faced by Mark Pollard and Derek Willan during the production of this book. A wide variety of techniques - winter and summer - are covered, so read on...

The winter scenario is on the New Pool at Tunnel Barn Farm in Shrewley, Warwickshire. Broadly constructed around the Snake Lake principle, Mark's chosen peg – 23 - faces the end of a peninsula, with open water away to his right giving him an extra option today.

Plumbing revealed quite a steep far shelf, with the bottom leveling out at around 13 metres which is a metre short of the far bank. The same helping of bait will also go in here. Depending on response, extra pellets will be drip fed into both these swims via a Toss Pot at steady intervals.

The main targets are F1s, which Mark expects to find in the deeper water at the bottom of the near and far shelves. He'll start by cupping in a palmful of dampened micro pellets on the seven metre line where it's almost five feet deep with a nice, flat, snag-free bottom.

> **"If the going proves tough on pellet, this gives a reserve option with bloodworm."**

On the hook he'll use a 4mm Ringers expander pellet, trying both the standard and cold water varieties to see if the fish have a preference.

At 13 metres in the open water, at the two o'clock position to Mark's right, he'll cup in four satsuma-sized balls of joker in double leam. He doesn't expect to visit this swim for at least 90 minutes. If the going proves tough on pellet, this gives him a reserve option with bloodworm on the hook. He can also switch his two pellet swims over to bloodworm and joker if required.

With No.6 elastic and 0.10mm line direct to a size 20 Series 2 Fine hook, Mark is able to use the same rig and float - an MP5 in 4 x 10 capacity - on all three lines if he

POLLY'S COMMENT

I would start by cupping in a palmful of dampened Micro Pellets on the six metre line where it's almost five feet deep with a nice, flat, snag-free bottom.

chooses. That said, he'll have several spares set up and ready to use, including a lighter one on the more delicate MP6 float pattern in case scratching around on the bloodworm is required.

Although an olivette is normally only required on floats heavier than three-quarters of a gram as a general rule of thumb, Mark makes an exception for lighter rigs during the depths of winter as he's not expecting bites on the drop.

Despite a snowy day, the fish are taking pellet eagerly and Mark is able to switch between all three spots to avoid overfishing any one of them. After taking a dozen fish to 4mm pellet at seven metres, bites slow up noticeably. He refeeds the spot with around 50 pellets, and moves across to the far line where fish are also feeding.

Even a quick look with pellet over the leam on the right hand swim produces a bite, though it's much slower there. Having two different spots fishable with the same length of pole in his hand makes for faster and more efficient top-up feeds. Mark doesn't have to ship back and refill the Toss Pot provided he

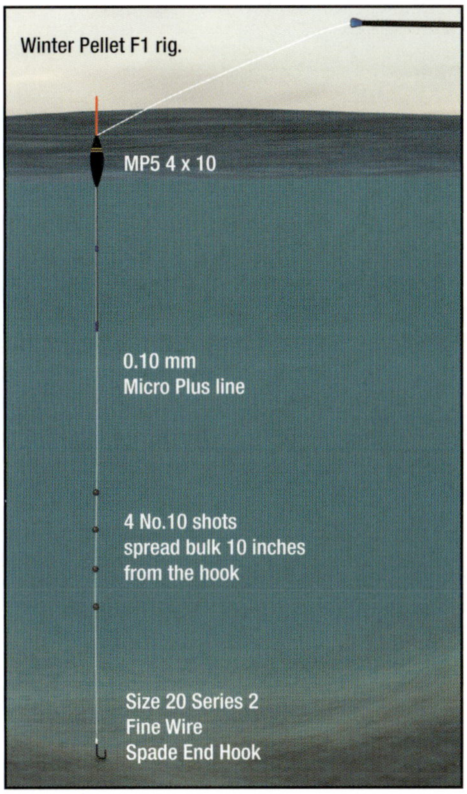

ensures there's some pellets left in it to feed the open water spot.

Snow turns to sleet and eventually rain, and the three hour session ends in still bitter conditions but with a lovely 30lb net of F1s to warm the cockles of the heart. Most came from the seven metre line and bloodworm wasn't required!

A very satisfying 30lb bag of F1s on a freezing cold, damp February day.

The end of this sunken beam is worth exploring. In match conditions the area would 'belong' to the angler on the spare platform, but in pleasure sessions use all available space!

The overhanging branches of an old hawthorn bush are the main target area in this swim. Start by feeding the edge, to tempt fish out and boost your chances of getting them out.

A shorter line along the near margin is sometimes worth setting up, especially on warmer days when carp may leave the cover and go patrolling in search of food.

Margin swims, particularly those tucked away in quiet corners, can still be productive in the depths of winter.

As already outlined, popular opinion holds with fishing the deepest part of your swim when the water is cold and lethargic fish are likely to huddle in dense shoals in the warmest part of the lake. But just as deeper water is slower to cool down, so too is shallow water quicker to warm up.

No matter how weak its rays, when the winter sun is at it peak - around noon to 2.30pm – it will have a warming effect on the shallow margins of a lake. And that vital degree or two difference in temperature could be enough to persuade a fish or two to enter the warmer shallower water for a brief feed.

Here, we join Mark Pollard on peg 21 on Tunnel Barn Farm's Bottom Lake on a raw February day. Being a longer established water than all the others on this complex, many of the fish are old, wise and have seen it all before.

Right: a very short line of just ten inches from pole tip to float for poking beneath the branches and dragging fish out fast.

Without a large head of lively F1s – eating machines even in cold weather – it takes a subtle and patient approach to try and subdue the residents of this pool in far from ideal conditions.

The swim has the advantage of being tucked back into a mini-bay, with overhanging branches and brambles along the right hand margin. Even without their summer foliage, these provide a comfortable haven for fish to sit beneath. The water tight beneath may only be two feet deep, but even double-figure carp are happy to sit here.

If every peg was used on this pool then Mark wouldn't have another option. But if

Above: Hemp with a smattering of corn is a good winter feed.

he was in a match with the peg to his right missed out, he would also explore the deepest water in front of him and further out, just off the point of the island.

Today, for the benefit of demonstrating winter margin fishing, he's only got eyes for those overhanging branches. A generous load of hemp with a few grains of sweetcorn is dumped into the main area, and that will be as far as feed goes until Mark either starts catching fish or becomes convinced that his feed has been

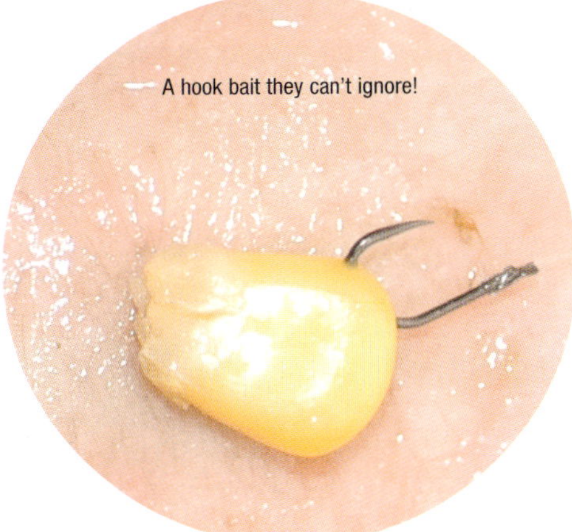

– A hook bait they can't ignore!

eaten without him actually hooking the culprits (very unlikely!). Any top-up feeds would contain around a third of the original payload.

His chosen elastic is hollow Red (grade 10+), with 0.14mm Micro Plus direct to a size 16 Series 2 standard wire barbless hook, with a 4 x 12 MXP7 float dotted right down.

Nicking on a grain of sweetcorn, Mark begins the waiting game. All the time he's watching for tiny movements on the float's tip, which is shotted to just hold in the surface film. Remember, it's buoyant enough already. Don't give shy-biting winter fish the luxury of taking a bait without you even knowing about it!

All these movements tell Mark is that there's fish in the area. It may be their fins or flanks brushing the line which causes the float to bob. But when it disappears from sight, a firm strike coupled with by a sweeping round of the pole to the left sees a fish on.

Mark immediately gets as much of the pole back behind him as the weight of the fish and angle of elastic allows. By holding on to the full length of pole, albeit just six metres, the fish would most likely be able to run deep into the snaggy cover due to the elastic not exerting enough pressure to draw it out. Of course, your tackle needs to be up to the job – as Mark's proved when extracting this handsome old mirror carp. (inset top left).

Strike, then instantly get as much pole away from the snags and back behind you as possible. Be bold or be beaten!

The term 'Silver Fish' originated on the canal circuit in the early 1980s. Certainly by 1985, when the Division One National was staged on the Oxford Canal, most match anglers understood it to mean roach, dace and skimmers – all silvery coloured as opposed to the gudgeon and ruffe which formed the mainstay of many catches.

Moving to the present, Silver Fish is now a catch-all term for non-carp in Commercials. Ignore the fact that tench are green, F1s, fantails and crucians are bronze, and orfe and goldfish are orange! In Commercial Fishery terms they're all classed as 'Silvers'.

In matches, most venues require you to use a separate keepnet for Silver Fish to avoid them being crushed by larger carp. During winter, some matches are designated 'Silver Fish Only' with carp either not counting or counting as a nominal weight such a 1lb apiece regardless of their actual size.

So if you fancy a bit of variety in your fishing, whether or not you're in a match, check out the following scenarios which detail successful summer and winter approaches for silvers. Some of the larger Commercial fisheries have one lake deliberately set aside for Silver Fish, with no carp or perhaps only a few stocked. These are ideal places to put them into practice.

SUMMER SCENARIO

Derek Willan is tackling peg 8 on Edward's Pool, a no-carp water on the massive Browning Cudmore complex at Whitmore near Stoke, Staffordshire. His targets are bream, chub, barbel, crucians, roach and rudd which average between 8oz and 1lb 8oz, and his aim is to draw them up in the water by catapulting out around 20 casters every put in. He opts to fish at 11 metres, feeling that the fish are unlikely to feed as well at closer range.

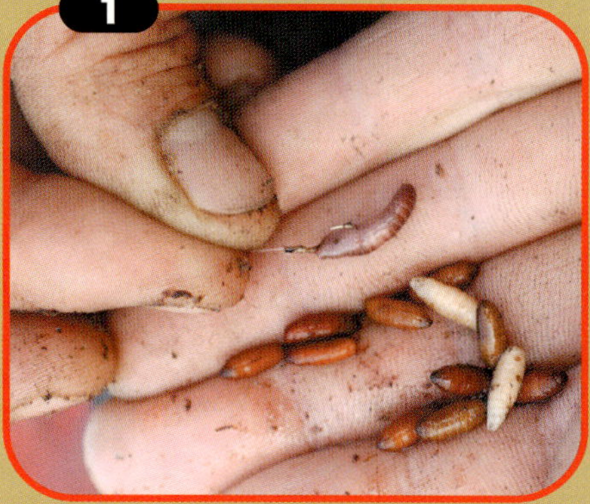

1 Hook bait is the head section of a dendrabaena worm, cut to the approximate size of his caster loose feed and nicked through the cut end. You can catch several fish on the same bait, whereas the fragile shell of casters gets smashed and requires rebaiting after every bite. Worm is far faster.

2 Using a Bump Bar to support his pole, Derek loose fed casters constantly with his catapult. By filling the 'pult' using the technique described in the shallow pole fishing section, he is able to watch his float constantly and react immediately to bites.

3 With such a shallow rig it's inevitable that most hooked fish will splash on the surface, but the disturbance doesn't affect the catch rate provided you keep raining the loose feed in on a regular little and often basis.

4 Catching skimmers and crucians like these 10oz samples very fast sometimes means an angler who opts for a silver fish approach in summer can outscore someone who opts to waits for larger carp.

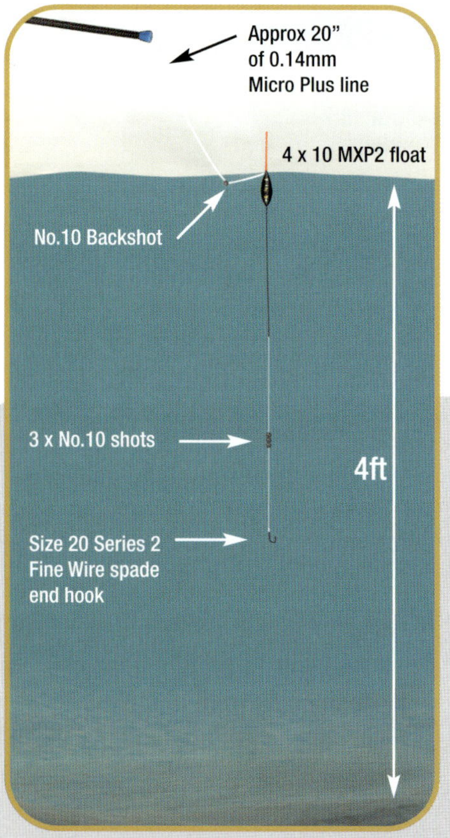

Shallow Summer Silvers Rig

Derek Willan's rig features orange Fox Fluro Carp hollow elastic, with a 4 x 10 MXP2 float set a foot deep with around 20 inches of 0.14mm Micro Plus line from pole tip to float.

Shotting pattern is a simple bulk of three No.10 shots set midway between float and a size 20 Series 2 Fine Wire spade end hook. A lighter hook is important when using smaller baits like worm head and caster, but it still needs decent strength as big fish are never far away.

If using caster on the hook, the fourth No.10 required to cock the float to perfection can be placed as a backshot in line with the float's tip. This balances the float nicely.

But with Derek's chosen hook bait today – worm head – this backshot is slid way up the line so it doesn't actually sit in the water. This is because the heavier bait weighs more or less the same as a No.10 shot.

Derek picks a nice comfortable 11 metres line to spray casters on a little and often basis on Cudmore's Edward's Pool.

A very tidy weight in less than an hour's shallow fishing, and not a carp in sight! Proof positive that Silvers can be well worth targeting in Summer for busy and highly enjoyable sport.

Bloodworm, joker and double leam.

Earlier in this pole chapter you saw Mark Pollard targeting F1s on a cold winter's day at Tunnel Barn Farm in Warwickshire. Although F1s are often classed as Silver Fish, that venue also holds some proper carp which often figure as bonus fish in match catches.

To demonstrate a Winter Silver Fish session in its truest form, we came to 22-peg Atkins Water near Cambridge.

This compact little venue is controlled by Waterbeach Angling Club. And although carp are present, including fish to double-figures, they do not count in club contests because the regulars prefer to target the mixed head of other species which includes some fine crucians to over 2lb 8oz, tench and bream to 4lb-plus.

But in the depths of winter it's roach, skimmers and perch that make up the weights.

Of these, roach are the mainstays and although samples to well over 1lb 8oz are present, these tend to shut up shop until the spring arrives. This leaves redfins in the 2oz to 10oz class as the mainstay of winter catches.

Few locals use bloodworm and joker, although the baits are not banned. Following a week of hard frosts, Mark opted to use these baits due to the fact that they fill fish up less than squatts, pinkies or maggots, and are more reliable than bread punch, a favourite for the better quality roach with some regulars.

Peg 12 at Atkins faces open water around five feet deep on the 13 metre line. It's here that Mark opts to feed and fish due to the water clarity and finicky nature of his quarry. He feels a closer line would fail to yield many bites in these tricky conditions.

He opens up by cupping in four satsuma-sized balls of joker in double leam, designed to sink straight to the bottom and begin breaking up almost instantly. These are followed by a cupful of neat joker, which will sink slowly and spread out as it goes, drawing interest from further afield.

In cold, clear water following a week of hard February frosts, Mark opts to put 13 metres of distance between himself and his quarry - the quality roach of Atkins Water.

Silver Scratching Rig

His chosen rig features grade 4 Fox elastic with a 0.10mm main line and a 0.08mm hook length with a size 22 MP1B hook, which he'll bait with single bloodworm.

Float is a 12 x 10 MP5, shotted with an olivette two and a half feet above the hook, with three No.10s plus a No.11 shot strung out evenly beneath.

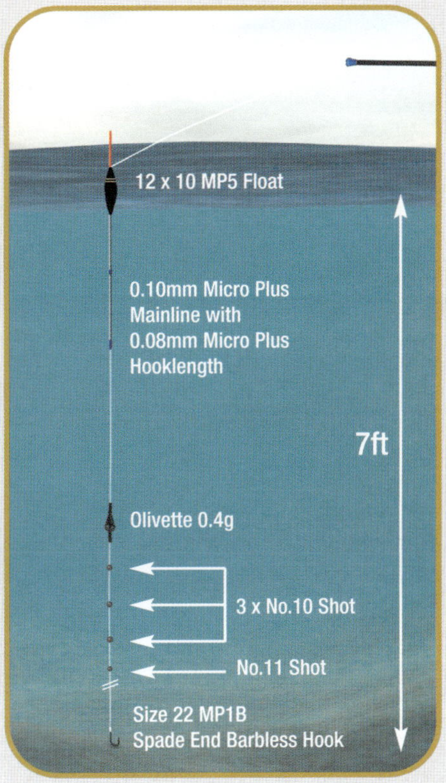

POLLY'S COMMENT

With a thin bristled float like the MXP1 or the even finer wire tipped MP5 and MP6, you can watch every single shot settle and strike at anything unusual.

The initial response, as expected, is very slow. Only four roach oblige in the first hour, but they average 4oz apiece. If the response picks up as Mark expects it to then a decent weight will still be possible.

It's important not to try and rush things in cold conditions. Putting in too much feed will reduce the chances of any fish stirring from their torpor for a brief feeding spell from taking the bait on your hook.

Cautiously, as the air temperature rises slightly despite a chilling north-easterly wind, Mark decides to add another slightly smaller ball of joker in leam. The key is to feed when bites slow right off, not when you're catching. Today this has the desired effect. Within 25 minutes of its introduction, Mark has doubled his catch and included an 8oz roach.

By the end of the three hour session, while never approaching bag-up mode, bites are coming far more regularly as the bait settles. A lone skimmer joins 17 roach – the best around 10 oz – for a pleasing 5lb bag on a very hard day.

Above left: not big and strong like summer carp, but you can't fail to admire pristine roach like this 8oz stunner.

Left: A hard-earned bag of roach plus a lone bonus skimmer during Polly's session.

Our final series of scenarios sees Mark Pollard tackling peg 17 on Pumphouse Lake at Alders Farm Fishery in a beautiful Buckinghamshire valley at Great Brickhill near Milton Keynes.

This session, on a blazing hot July day, perfectly illustrates a typical summer session on a carp-packed stillwater by combining full depth and shallow approaches on the same two lines, reacting to the level at which fish are feeding.

While there will be summer sessions where one or the other approach is better, it's far more likely that you'll have to chop and change depths in this manner.

There's carp showing everywhere on the surface as Mark tackles up, some flinging themselves clear and others cruising lazily. First job, as always, is to plumb the depth. The bottom bank of this hillside complex is the deepest anywhere on this lake with almost five feet at six metres and around six inches less at 13 metres. These are the distances Mark has in mind for an attack centred around pellets and paste.

Expecting to catch well right from the word go, he introduces around a third of a large pole cup of hard 4mm carp pellets on both lines, and is pleased to see almost immediate signs of fish showing an interest in the form of patches of bubbles hitting the surface.

Knowing that the fish in this lake average around 2lb 8oz with not many larger

POLLY'S COMMENT

Old pieces of heavier grade pole elastic are a good method of retaining hooks on pole rigs ensuring they don't become snagged in bank side vegetation.

Blackening the top few mm's of the tip with a marker pen allows lift bites to be detected, as well as the normal sail aways.

samples, Mark elects to start on a full depth paste rig featuring a 0.4gram MP3 float on 0.18mm line direct to a size 12 Series 2 Extra Strong eyed barbless hook.

Shotting comprises four No.8s spaced four inches apart, the lowest positioned two feet from the hook. This allows as natural a fall of the bait as possible. Believe it or not, you can sometimes get bites on the drop with paste. He sets the rig around an inch and a half overdepth and moulds a 50p-sized piece of paste around the hook.

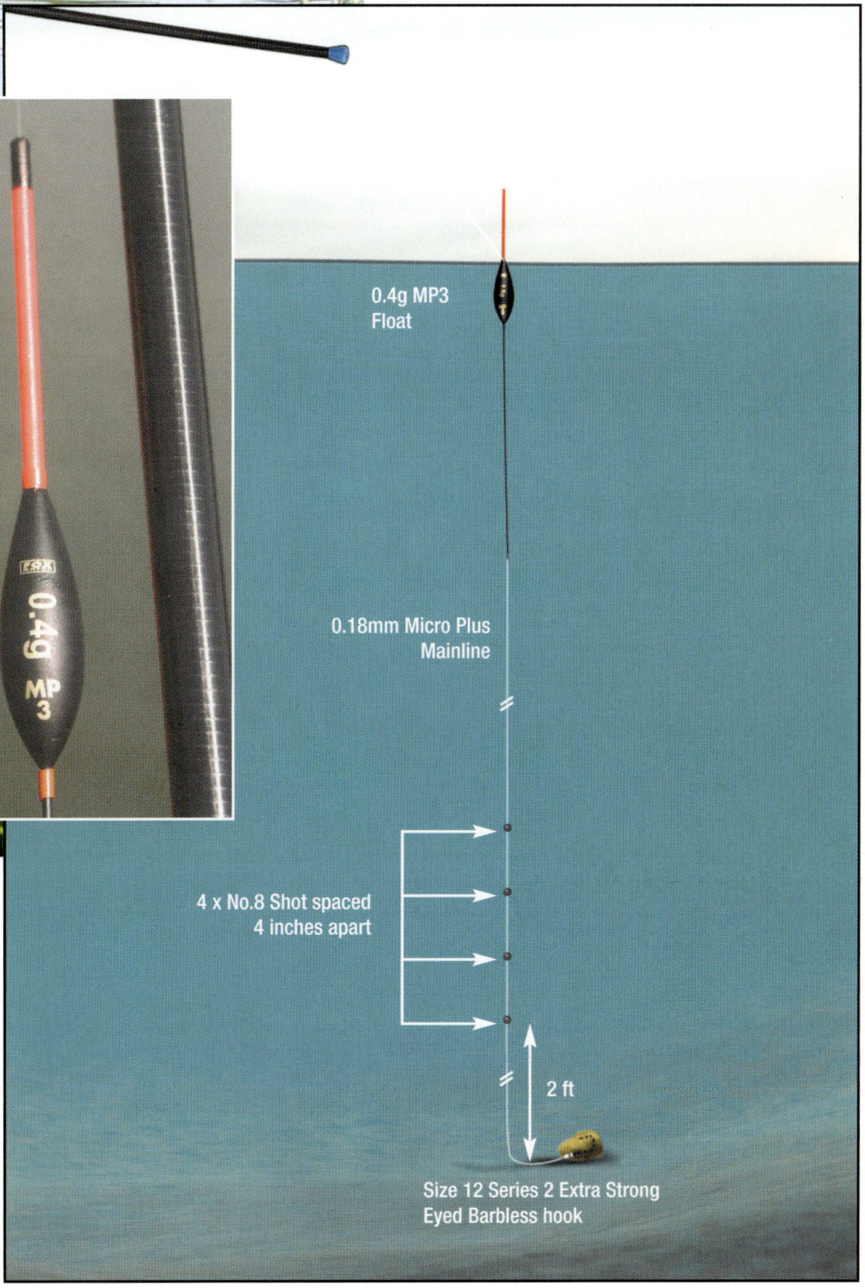

To carry the soft bait to the spot without it falling off, he slips it into an open Tosspot fixed near the top of his pole, ships out and rotates the pole 180 degrees to drop it in.

The float lays flat on the surface for a couple of seconds then gradually tips upright as the bait reaches a level where its weight is felt. Within seconds of it hitting bottom it dips quickly under, Mark raises his pole tip and a carp is on.

With hollow red elastic, rated grade 10+, Mark ships back steadily on his roller, places the tip of his third section in the Pole Keeper net and prepares to scoop out the fish. But is it always this simple? Turn the page and find out whether the session died on its butt or just kept on getting better...

PLAYING AND NETTING CARP

Whilst you may need to vary your approach to some extent with larger carp that take longer to subdue, you won't go far wrong by following this at-a-glance guide to playing and netting.

A positive strike is needed with paste due to the large size of bait and hook. You can see how the slender, long-tipped MP3 float makes a clean, minimal splash exit from the water. A bulkier bodied float would offer more resistance and potentially reduce numbers of hooked fish.

Once you've connected, let the fish run against the free-flowing elastic whilst keeping the pole low and parallel to the water's surface. Apply slight side-strain if necessary, but you must avoid any upward pressure at this point.

Keeping the pole low, feed it back steadily onto your roller until you reach the section to unship at. It's wise to leave at least one section more than the rig's actual length on to compensate for the elastic's stretch. A big fish may require two extra sections, but one is generally enough.

Manoeuvre your landing net into position whilst steadily raising your unshipped sections to see if the fish comes up to the surface for a quick netting. If it does, be ready to scoop it up but avoid fast lunges with the net which could spook the fish back into action or knock the hook out.

If not, lower the pole back to parallel with the surface and rest the net pole on your bump bar. The elastic will retract smoothly, causing the carp to stop fighting. Don't fear the hook falling out, as even barbless patterns will stay in due to the tight line caused by the fish's weight as it sits mid-depth, unsure of what's happening.

Raise the pole again in a fast but controlled manner. As the elastic re-tensions the fish will often come to the surface and be nettable. You may need to repeat this two or three times, but it's still faster than maintaining a constant pressure which could work the hook hold loose.

In the net! Ship your pole plus landing net pole back safely so the elastic retracts, unhook the fish then, still in the landing net, transfer it to a keepnet if you're in a match or back to the water if pleasure fishing. Bait up, ship back out and do it all again!

Upping The Catch Rate...

With half an hour of the session gone, Mark has landed three carp plus a couple of nuisance rudd on the full depth paste rig. But he's missed lots more bites, many of which snatched at his bait on the drop.

If a fish manages to snatch his paste off the hook, this is easily detected by the float's bristle standing further out of the water. As soon as this happens, ship back immediately and rebait.

To any experienced angler, a situation such as this indicates a golden opportunity to catch fast on a shallow rig. Today, the sheer number of fish showing at the surface in and around Mark's peg is another major clue! The question is, how best to catch them? Check out the following two pages to see his chosen approach, plus further tactical switches that led to a very satisfying final outcome…

These two twenty pounders were caught by Mark whilst pole fishing in France. The long lean nature of grass carp means they are incredibly hard fighting and are one of the hardest fish to net. By following the method shown of playing and netting fish on the pole, and by using balanced tackle, landing carp of this size becomes more achievable.

PERFECT PASTE DELIVERY

Follow this guide to getting your soft paste hook baits out to the swim you've fed and you'll spend less time with a bare hook caused by it falling off, and more time playing fish!

1

First and foremost, on hot days like this you must prevent your paste from drying out. Keeping it in a plastic bag is one option, but a bait box allows easier access. Simply rest a lid across the top, protecting the majority of the paste from the sun's rays

2

Break off a piece of paste and flatten it down, laying the hook in the centre. Better still, tie a paste coil onto a hair rig as this handy device will help the paste grip better and allow the hook to penetrate faster and more cleanly.

3

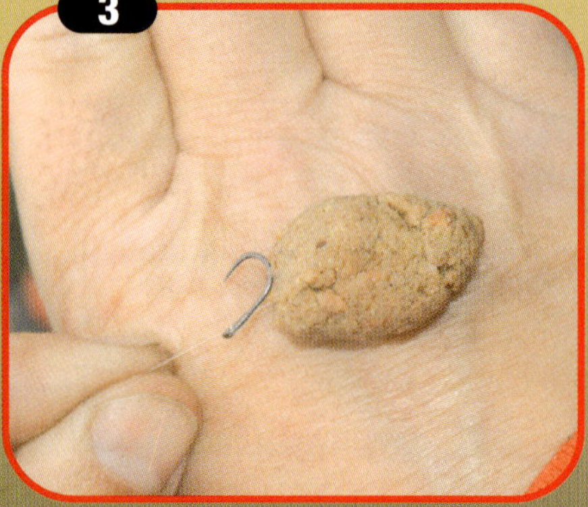

Mould the paste around the hook or coil into a roughly circular shape. Size will depend on several factors including the size of your target fish plus the voracity at which they are feeding. Today, Mark's gone for the size of a 50p coin but this is generally as large as he'll go and a 10p coin is a more typical size, especially in matches.

4

Drop the paste-baited hook into an open-topped Tosspot, which is light enough to fish with permanently attached to your top sections for the whole session.

5

Add a few pellets for extra noise and attraction if fishing shallow. For full depth paste fishing, it's better to introduce pellets in larger amounts but much less frequently, via a larger conical or Pepper Pot with the top removed, to keep fish on the deck.

6

Ship out, with your rig hanging beneath, then rotate the pole to drop the pellet freebies plus the paste-baited hook into the swim. The rig follows smoothly behind with no risk of tangles and no jerky movements which can result in the bait falling off.

Another bloomin' carp!

Just like paste fishing at full depth, a shallow paste approach can become a frustrating and time consuming approach if you don't convert an acceptable amount of bites to fish in the net!

Based on his early results plus the obvious activity, Mark reckons the odds are stacked in his favour and decides to go for it.

- A large bait such as paste is more selective than smaller pellets when it comes to ensuring the smaller species, in this case rudd, can't swallow the bait before carp do.

- The fact that he's established a swim as close as six metres allows him to begin loose feeding pellets accurately by hand, hopefully encouraging more carp to enter the fray.

- Increased competition amongst the fish should allow him to beef up his tackle even further, thereby landing fish faster and building a bigger catch.

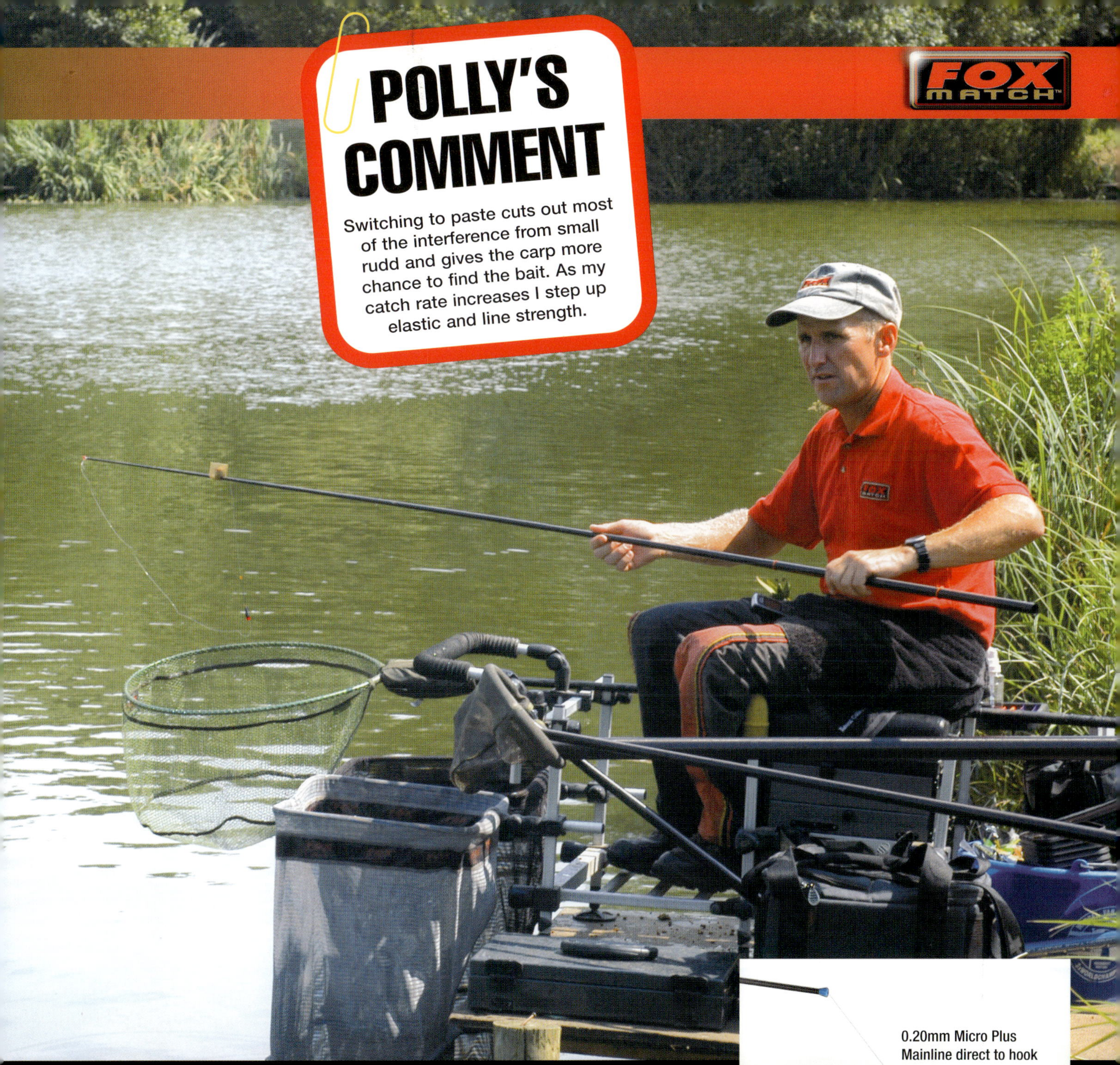

POLLY'S COMMENT

Switching to paste cuts out most of the interference from small rudd and gives the carp more chance to find the bait. As my catch rate increases I step up elastic and line strength.

To this end, Mark switches from his original top kit which you'll recall had a hollow elastic rated 10+, to a solid No.12 elastic which is set a bit tighter and will stretch less in any case.

Rig-wise, he ups the line to 0.20mm Micro Plus line but sticks with the size 12 Series 2 Extra Strong eyed barbless hook. At many Commercials a size 12 is in any case the largest permitted size. And because he'll be moulding the same sized ball of paste around it – around the diameter of a 50p piece – there's no need to go larger anyway.

In all, he has just two and a half feet of line from pole tip to hook. For fishing this shallow, a shorter float than the full depth pattern is essential to reduce the chances of fish bumping into the stem and giving false bites. It also needs to be more buoyant to support the weight of the paste ball. Mark's choice is a 8 x 10 MXP3 – a classic dome-topped balsa 'dibber' with short carbon stem.

When shotting up a dibber to fish shallow, remember the paste hookbait will take up the majority of the shotting capacity. And because it's not sitting on the bottom, only two No.10 shots are needed on the line – set a fraction apart in a mini bulk at mid-depth.

Most important of all, regardless of what depth or distance you opt to fish paste, ensure it stays on the hook while you ship out and drop your rig in. Check out the picture sequence on the left, do likewise and you shouldn't have any problems on that front.

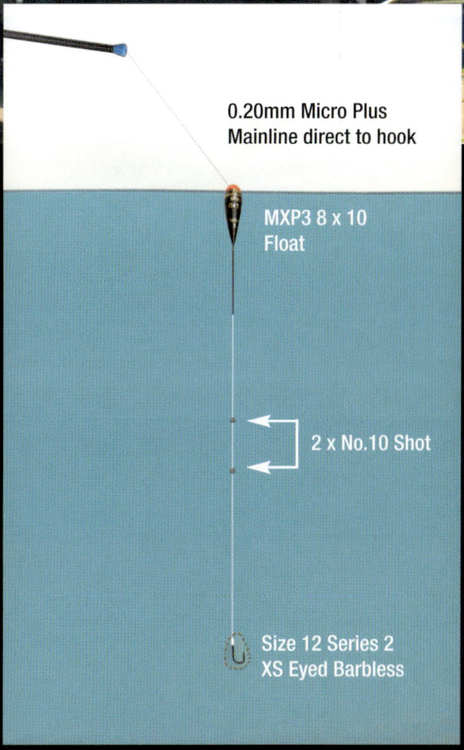

Simplicity itself - Polly's shallow paste rig.

POLLY'S COMMENT

At longer range, I prefer to fish pellet. Paste would be far too slow because missed bites would take too long to ship in, rebait then ship back out to the spot.

Sure enough, shallow paste at six metres results in Mark's catch rate increasing significantly. Over the next hour, it's noticeable how he's reacting to bites, playing and netting them much faster on the solid elastic and heavier line.

Even so, quite a few bites are missed and the occasional cheeky rudd still nips in first head of the target carp. Quite how rudd get such a big bait into their mouths is baffling, but it's proof positive of how all Commercial lake species love the pellet/paste combo.

Conscious of the fact that he's not taken a look over the 13 metre line, Mark has continued to dump the occasional large potful of pellets out there at intervals of around 20 minutes. Although it seems unlikely today, an inside line can dry up suddenly and you need somewhere else primed and ready to fish – whether in a match or just pleasure fishing. Eventually, and somewhat reluctantly, we persuade him to put down the shallow paste rig and explore that longer line.

> "An inside line can dry up suddenly and you need somewhere else primed and ready"

Knowing what he does about this lake's stocks – that there's very few bigger fish present – he explains that if this was a match he'd not contemplate such a move unless his catch rate at six metres dropped off significantly.

But we wanted him to demonstrate once again the essential art of feeding via catapult, and the 13 metre line was the perfect place to do so.

Again, Mark had assembled two rigs for this – one shallow and one deep - with the same elastics, floats, shotting patterns and line diameters as for closer in.

The only difference is hook size, a size 16 spade end Series 2 barbless. This is because he intends to fish pellet rather than paste on the hook at this longer range. Based on his findings at six metres, paste would be far too slow because missed bites would take too long to ship in, rebait then ship back out to the spot.

The long pole line which Mark fed with an initial large potful of pellets was a non-starter on a full depth rig simply because there were so many fish feeding in the upper layers.

PRIMING WITH THE PULT

Mark Pollard demonstrates how to prime a long pole swim to keep the fish competing for bait so the next drop in has a fast response.

Large payloads of pellets are essential if you're feeding a longer line whilst concentrating your attentions on a closer line, as Mark has done in this session. It's simply not possible to feed both on a little and often basis aim to keep fish on the bottom.

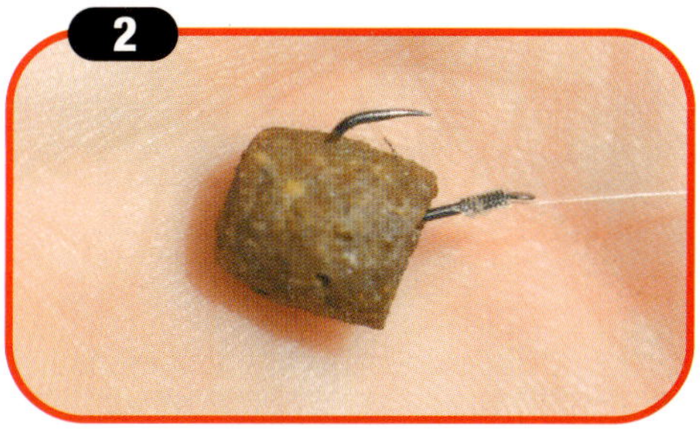

Starting his 13 metre explorations with the full depth rig and a 6mm Expander pellet on the hook, Mark is pestered by rudd on the drop. On a cooler day this may be the way to go, but he quickly abandons this idea as the time wasted in shipping back and forth is similar to how it would be on paste.

Mark switches to his shallow rig and a banded pellet, slipped through a stretch yet snug-fitting and robust Fox Match bait band which will grip the bait and resist the attentions of smaller fish while he awaits the arrival of larger carp. Banded pellets tend to stay on better than Expanders and as a result are sometimes a better option at longer ranges.

An excellent summer ploy when starting to fish shallow on a new line is to blast in several pouches of bait. Not too much – the usual ten to 15 pellets is ample as you don't want to drag fish lower down. But a quick burst of noisy freebies can draw carp in like a magnet. Rest your pole ready-assembled over your shoulder while feeding, ready to ship out fast and drop the rig into the wake of the final pouchful.

The response is usually instant, as one of the shoal of carp competing actively for the falling freebies turns and sucks in the banded pellet. The float sinks from sight, and often before there's time to lift the pole the elastic is already streaming out as a carp hooks itself and surges off.

Gain control of the fish and begin shipping back low to the water, as already described for closer ranges. Every two or three metres, load your catapult and feed the catch area again. If you haven't mastered 'pulting while holding the pole, you can even balance the pole on your Bump Bar. thigh or bankside reeds to free up both hands. Only try this if at least half of the pole is already back behind you on the roller. You can feed two or three times whilst playing a fish or preparing to ship back out again.

A FANTASTIC FINISH

After a good spell of catching carp shallow on banded pellet at 13 metres, Mark came back onto the six metre line with a shallow paste rig.

He'd continued scattering in pellets by hand on this spot as regularly as possible, usually between netting fish and shipping back out on the longer pole, and there were still plenty of signs of fish in the area – both bubbling and topping. After all, why waste valuable catching time shipping in and out at longer distances?

By the end of the session, Mark's six metre line resembled a fish farm, with numerous carp mouths breaking surface to await the next batch of pellets.

With well over 100lb in his net despite regular photo breaks over four hours, he was convinced 300lb-plus would have been on the cards today in a proper five hour session. Nearby, Derek Willan also bagged up.

Bait is almost irrelevant once you reach these competitive feeding circumstances – whatever you put on the hook will be taken.

But it's important to realise that it's how you feed the swim into such a crescendo, plus how you use reliable and balanced rigs and elastics to extract the fish quickly and safely without time-wasting tangles or breakages, that are the keys to producing really memorable summer Commercial bags.

White Acres
Country Park

Chapter 4

feeder/tip tactics

Always carry a selection of different types of swimfeeder when going to a Commercial fishery.

Having dealt with float and pole fishing it's time to focus on the art of legering - Commercial Fishery style.

Often known as Tip or Feeder fishing, the technique involves casting out either a leger bomb or a swimfeeder on a rod featuring a fine diameter top section known as a quivertip.

Immediately after the rig hits bottom, you then drop the rod onto a rest and tighten the line by reeling in the slack to place a slight bend in your quivertip in order to detect bites. These usually take the form of a rapid pull-round or drop-back of the tensioned tip. However, in winter they can manifest themselves as surprisingly gentle tweaks and nudges which demand an alert concentration.

Tip fishing is often mistakenly considered to be a lazy form of fishing. But watch any top class exponent and you'll soon see it's far removed from that preconception, and is in fact a skill every bit as demanding and ultimately rewarding as float or pole approaches.

You can of course also use electronic bite alarms and bobbin-style indicators rather than the rod tip to provide bite indication when legering on Commercial stillwaters. But because that style of fishing evolved from the specimen carp fishing scene, and is better suited to longer sessions than the average day ticket pleasure or match angler can manage, we have chosen to omit it entirely from this publication.

By mastering the many other forms of Tip fishing, we firmly believe you will catch more fish on 90 per cent of Commercials than you would by taking the twin rods and buzzers route.

Ultimately, it's up to you. But whichever approach you choose, it's important to understand the circumstances in which a Tip/Feeder approach will work better than a float or pole.

When To Fish The Tip

Deciding when to fish the Tip rather than a pole or float rig hinges on several factors, some more obvious than others when you first arrive at a fishery. In strong winds and adverse weather, Tip fishing is often the only efficient tactic. It is often impossible to present a still bait beneath a pole when repeated gusts are buffeting it around, dragging your rig out of position. Likewise, choppy waves make it hard to spot bites even with a sunken line approach on the waggler. Accurate casting and feeding is also extremely difficult in such conditions.

> **"Never forget, it's where the fish are feeding that dictates your chosen approach"**

Swimfeeders are generally much heavier than floats and are therefore easier to cast accurately. They sink faster, taking your line and rig down to sit on the bottom well away from the wave action and are unaffected by under tow. Meanwhile, your bite indicator – the rod tip – is easy to watch and react to at close quarters.

Distance is another major factor. On some Commercial Fisheries such as Snake and Canal lakes, Tip fishing is seldom required. This is because you can still reach your maximum required distance with a pole, and such waters are normally far more sheltered than wider expanses meaning decent tackle control can be achieved in all bar the worst winds. But on wider venues, the Tip is a favourite choice regardless of conditions for much of the year.

Never forget that it's where the fish are feeding which dictates your chosen approach. We've already discussed the need to fish shallow with pole or float when fish are swimming around in the upper layers of water. But when they are lower down, it stands to reason that a bait presented on the bottom stands the best chance of being taken.

Why then should a Tip approach be better than a full-depth pole or float? If the pole is ruled out due to the distance you need to cast, the main reason is that the use of a swimfeeder allows a regular introduction of free offerings in a far more accurate manner than loose feeding by catapult.

Furthermore, you can generally use heavier line and stronger rods than with float fishing. This allows you to control, play and net fish faster, boosting your catch rate and eventual total bag.

Don't confuse this with being crude, as finesse is still very important on the Tip. Over the next few pages we'll examine a host of different Tip tactics which will revolutionise your leger fishing if you grasp the concepts and put them into action. But before we do, let's take a look at the basic tackle requirements.

Rods For The Job

As with float fishing, there are a host of different rods aimed at Tip techniques. In terms of Commercial stillwaters, these range from light actioned two-piece tools such as the 11ft Fox Envoy Bomb rod through to 13ft Heavy Feeder models with solid carbon tips.

In between are a number of 11 and 12 foot rods of varying strengths. There's also the option of a 'multi feeder' such as the Envoy Carp 11/13ft model. As the name suggests, this is fishable at both 11 and 13 foot lengths, with further versatility being added through the provision of four different strength quivertips.

Glass quivertips are softer and bendier than carbon versions, although the latter may appear finer to the eye.

Carbon fibre quivertips can be produced in smaller diameters than glass versions, but have less inherent flexibility and thus will be slightly stiffer in action.

Like all good quivertips, Fox versions have their material and test curve printed on them to help you select the right one for the task in hand. In the case of the Envoy Carp Multi Feeder, the 1oz and 2oz glass models suit colder conditions and shyer biters while the 3oz and 4oz carbon tips can be brought into play when the carp are feeding more confidently or when heavier feeders are being cast further.

Although many top anglers own a separate feeder rod for almost every eventuality, it's fair to say three different types cover the vast majority of Commercial Stillwater angling.

Categorised broadly as light, medium and heavy, these would include a softer 11ft Bomb-style rod, plus 12 and 13-foot Feeder models.

If you only want one rod to cover as many styles as possible, the Envoy Multi Feeder is hard to beat as you're effectively getting an 11', 12' and 13' rod with six different strength tips which gives 18 possible combinations.

POLLY'S COMMENT

Time taken in choosing the strength of quivertip to use on any given day is seldom wasted. It takes longer to tackle down again if you get it wrong. Err of the light side in winter.

Reels For Tip Fishing

As with Commercial fishery float work, a reliable and compact fixed spool reel is required.

In tackle terms you generally get what you pay for, and this is especially true in the case of reels. A higher price reflects better quality materials used in a reel's all-important inner gearing, clutch and bale arm mechanisms.

Aside from the Bagging Waggler, Tip fishing is the most demanding area of Commercial fishery angling. If you Tip fish on a regular basis, you'll be subjecting your reel to a tremendous amount of strain. Buying cheap can represent false economy.

Bear in mind that you will normally be using a stronger breaking strain and therefore thicker diameter line for Tip fishing than for the float. For the heavier two-thirds of Tip rods, a slightly larger reel is advantageous due to its greater spool capacity and more robust gearing.

Reel sizes are sometimes expressed in terms of a 'thousands' rating. A typical float reel is rated 3000 size, while the next size up at 4000 is a more typical feeder reel. However, it's rare to require a really deep spool as 100 metres of 6 to 8lb line does not represent a great deal more capacity than the same of 4 and 5lb.

Both front and rear drag reels will do the job. Which type you choose is a matter of personal preference. As always, be sure to fill the spool right to the lip to ensure smooth casting. And re-spool with fresh line regularly as breaking strain can be dramatically reduced by the rigours of several sessions of Commercial carp hauling.

A small rear-drag fixed spool suits light Feeder and Bomb work.

Inset: Two reliable reel lines for legering work. The Illusion in particular sinks like a stone.

Most importantly of all, your reel must have a line clip situated on the spool. Use it! We'll explain why and show you how on the next page.

Which Lines To Choose?

For the majority of situations, reliable monofilaments are the chosen reel lines for Tip fishing on Commercials.

The likes of Maxima and Fox Soft Steel in 4, 5 and 6lb breaking strains are favoured by many.

However, a recent trend has been to use Fluorocarbon lines. Originally designed for carp fishing, Flurocarbons are denser than monos and therefore sink faster and better. They also have a lower refractive index of light which makes them virtually invisible in water.

Top North West angler Derek Willan, who has supplied much of the information for this chapter, uses 6lb Fox Illusion fluorocarbon for all his Commercial carp fishing and is convinced it gives him an edge over those anglers still using traditional monos.

Another type of line is braid, which has a far finer diameter for a given breaking strain than its monofilament equivalent. Highly rated by many for long distance fishing, braids do however have some drawbacks including a lack of stretch plus a tendency to tangle in win. Above all, the use of braid is banned at many fisheries due to a perceived tendency to nick scales off fish during the fight and leave the wound open to infection.

"Fluorocarbon lines are denser than mono and therefore sink faster and better"

Used sensibly, braided lines can be an asset. We'll show you how to use them in the Open-End feeder section which concludes this chapter, but remember the opportunities to use them may be limited.

Feeder/Tip casting and clipping

So you've tackled up with the right rod, reel, line and feeder for the job in hand. Your bait is at the ready and you're at your peg. What next? Cast out and start catching of course!

But wait a second. Have you got your distance sorted to perfection and placed your line in the clip to ensure accuracy? Without doing so, your subsequent catch rate will disappoint.

You may feel we are labouring this point, but it really is that important. Even vastly experienced Tip anglers who could probably cast with pinpoint accuracy 95 times out of 100 use them, simply because they ensure that ratio becomes 100 times out of 100.

Before you clip up, you need to be happy that you are casting to a spot where the fish will be happy to feed. If you're facing an island then it's a fair bet that the fish will use this as a patrol route. Casting as close as

possible to the island margin is usually the desired tactic. Drop even a foot or two short and your bite rate will decrease dramatically.

There are exceptions to this rule, such as during a prolonged spell of cold weather when fish are more likely to back off into deeper water at the bottom of the island slope. Or the slope is too steep for a feeder to hold bottom without rolling.

In open water, it's a good idea to cast around your swim with a 1oz bomb to gain an idea of depths and contours before deciding on a distance to clip up at.
An ounce bomb sinks at roughly a foot per second so depth detection is easy.

Proof of the clip's deadly efficiency.

Whatever type of swim you're in, the same rules apply. Before attaching a hook length, start by casting your feeder or bomb to the spot you're aiming for. As with float fishing, picking an immovable far bank marker such as a tree or bush will help ensure accuracy.

If it's an island margin which you're striving to get tight against, start by casting short then pay off enough extra line which you estimate will get you right to the spot, then clip up. If it still falls short or goes too far, unclip then reclip and try again until you get it spot-on.

POLLY'S COMMENT

Use black marker pen on your line so that you can clip back up at the same spot even if you need to release line to a fish which charges in the opposite direction.

BAIT BAND BUFFER LINE CLIP METHOD

If you're not comfortable with the idea of placing line in a clip for fear of it weakening, here's an alternative approach using a stretchy latex bait band w4rapped around your line then clipped up as a no-risk buffer.

1

Cast the required distance then ensure the spool sits with its line clip uppermost.

2

With the bale arm still open, place a bait band beneath the line at the required spot and pull to stretch it a few times.

3

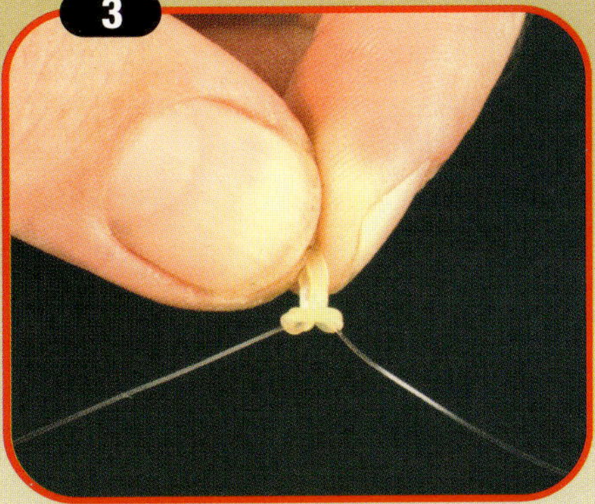

Pass the bait band's end back through on itself and steadily draw tight, adding saliva to ensure no line burn occurs.

4

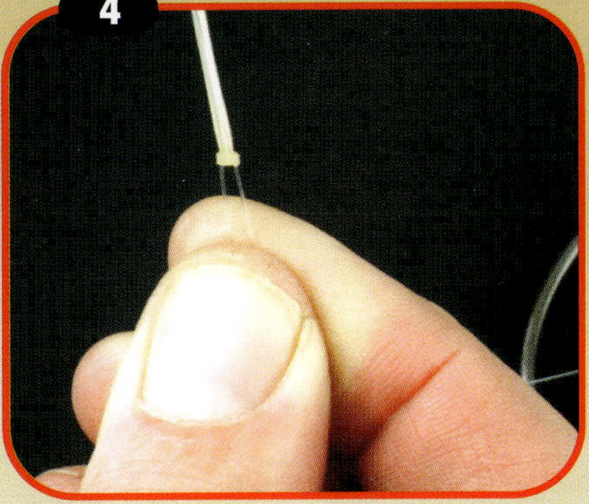

Tightened right down, the band should stay put but it can slide under pressure so it's wise at this point to colour the line either side with waterproof marker pen.

5

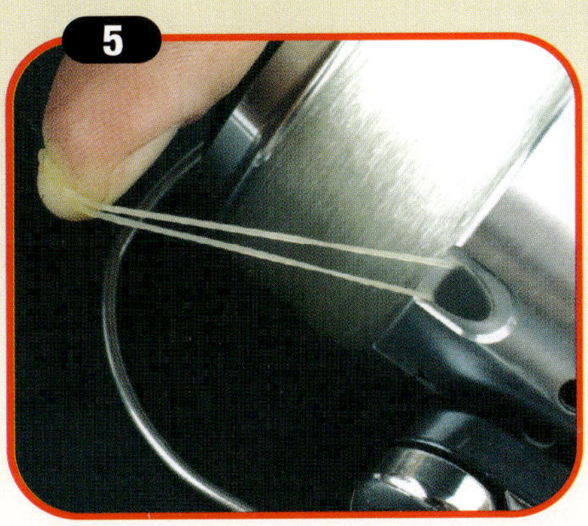

Locate the band under the reel's spool clip and test once again for strength before retrieving and recasting. If the band snaps, replace it with another.

6

On each cast, the feeder will be brought to a halt with an added cushioning effect.

CORRECT CLIP CASTING RIGHTS AND WRONGS

As with any form of fishing, there are ways of maximising your catches. When it comes to the feeder, repeated accuracy is the single most important factor. Anyone who still regards tip fishing as a 'chuck it and chance it' method is certainly missing out. While they may still catch fish, they'll catch fewer than the angler who pays attention to detail and realises that the regular delivery of bait to the exact same spot will create competitive feeding that makes the fish lose their natural caution.
One definite 'edge' is to ensure your rod is raised vertically when the cast hits the line clip. We've shown this pictorially and explained exactly why on the following pages - but check out these diagrams for an underwater view of what happens if you don't follow suit.

By lowering the rod on impact, the feeder will sink vertically and settle right beside the island.

If your rod is horizontal and there's a tight line between the tip and feeder, the feeder will be dragged in an arc away from the island.

Line Clip Lessons

So you've clipped up to perfection, added a hook length and baited the hook, replaced the bomb with a feeder and loaded it up. Your first cast will land right on the spot – but there's more to do yet before you set the rod in its rest and prepare to bag up.

You must endeavour to make sure your feeder descends to the lake bed on as near to a vertical plane as possible (requiring the rod to be upright as the line hits the clip),

rather than on a tight line arc which will swing it away from the island margin by an often critical foot or two. This is the case if your rod is still pointing out when the line hits the clip.

We've included a picture-by-picture sequence showing the angle of rod at various stages in a cast which enable Derek Willan to achieve this with monotonous frequency borne from years of practice. Check it out on the following page.

Meanwhile, it's important to ensure your line is not twisted around the tip of your rod - a fairly common but sadly unavoidable occurance known as a wrap-around - before you wind up for a cast. Unless of course you want to crack off a feeder or snap your quivertip!

Before you raise your rod behind you, get into the habit of giving the line in front of the reel's spool a couple of quick tweaks with your forefinger.

You don't even have to look up, as you should be able to feel the feeder either dance up and down - indicating the line is running freely as desired - or the tip curl round, indicating a wrap-around problem which you can sort out without embarrassment or breakage!

Below:
Right on the money! Accurate casting is no accident. Use your line clip, pick a directional marker and you can do it too!

The results of accurate clipped-up casting to island vegetation.

CASTING
RIGHTS AND WRONGS

Mastering the art of accurate casting to a line clip will be far easier if you ensure you have the correct amount of line paid out before starting your cast. Check out these pictures to know the score.

Too long. With this much line between rod tip and feeder, the cast will send the rig too high and subject the line to undue stress, risking a crack-off or a broken quivertip.

Too short. There is not enough line here to adequately compress the rod on the cast, the upshot being a cast which is sure to fall short of the target and enter the water with an almighty splash.

Perfect. Here you see a cast which is sure to land 'on the money'. With around three and a half feet of line between tip and feeder, the rod can do its job to perfection.

4

Desired Result

On many lakes including here on the Arena Pool at Browning Cudmore, baits need to be placed just inches from the central island. Heed Derek's advice and you'll soon be casting just as accurately on your local waters.

CASTING TO A CLIP - ADVANCED TECHNIQUE MASTERCLASS

Making sure the feeder falls directly down where it lands rather than arcing back towards you is a big part of the reason why some feeder anglers catch far more than others who seem to be doing everything else identically.

1

Some prefer to clip up by looping the line around the clip, others just tuck the line under. There's no right or wrong way, just personal preference.

2

Line up your cast with your chosen marker; rod directly above and behind you, bale arm released and line trapped against spool lip with fingertip.

3

Sweep the rod forward with a smooth and controlled action, releasing the line and supporting the butt of the handle with one hand to help maintain direction.

4

As the feeder begins its descent the rod should be held just above the horizontal, pointing directly at the target spot.

5

Just before the feeder splashes down, raise the rod smartly so the line hits the clip with it raised directly above and slightly behind you, the five-to-12 position in clock terms.

6

Quickly lower the rod back to the horizontal as the rig settles. By doing this you'll have created enough slack line to tighten up and get a couple of turns back onto the reel, without disturbing the feeder rig as it settled.

7

Immediately sink your line as described in the float chapter, by dipping the rod tip then striking it smartly upwards.

8

Place your rod onto the rest and tension the tip, which is essential to show drop-back bites when fishing to island margins. One good tip is to count and memorise the number of turns on your reel handle when winding back from the clip. If you suffer a line breakage you will always be able to return to the original spot. Line clips are also handy for keeping your line in place when you pack up, preventing it from springing off the spool in transit.

Some anglers have an aversion to clipping up because they fear the initial run of a hooked carp will break the line. In reality this is very rare indeed, provided you take some basic common-sense precautions.

A fish hooked against an island margin can only run left, right or back towards you – never directly away from you. Even in open water situations it's extremely rare for a hooked fish to head straight out in the opposite direction.

By following the casting advice on the previous page you will already have a couple of turns of line back on your reel spool. This is generally enough to give the fish, either by backwinding or adjusting the reel's clutch to yield under controlled pressure, before applying side strain via your rod to turn the direction of its run back towards you.

"At all stages, make your rod work for you by bringing its full fighting curve into play"

Holding the rod increases your reaction speed, helping you to hit more bites and, importantly, bump fewer fish.

As soon as the fish changes direction, wind some line back onto the spool and you'll be back in full control of the situation. Be prepared to adapt fast throughout the fight. If it runs directly away from you at any stage, point the rod straight at the fish then follow through with a steady sweep to one side or the other.

Once the fish is nearing the net you can raise your rod to apply upward pressure if necessary, but keep it low for most of the fight to minimise the risk of loosening the hook hold. By raising the rod only at the final moments you will lose fewer fish.

At all stages, make your rod work for you by bringing its full fighting curve into play.

Never allow the fish any slack. If it snaps you, step up the breaking strain of your hook length for the next cast. If it does it again, step up again!

Once netted, place the rod across your knee or to the side and draw the fish back. Be sure to keep a tight line – but not too short a line – from the rod tip to avoid tangling your line or feeder around your fishing station or in undergrowth. This makes the whole unhooking process nice and smooth, meaning you can rebait, recast and catch the next one faster.

All this talk of doing things quickly sounds a bit hurried, but it's second nature to experienced anglers. Don't try and rush things at any stage. Fast but controlled angling should not be confused with rushing!

As far as releasing the fish goes, or putting it into the keepnet if you are in a match situation, then there's no need to remove it from the landing net at any stage unless you are going to weigh and photograph it. Simply lower the net head back into the margins and let it swim off, or over your keepnet mouth then tip if you're fishing a contest. Carp are hardy creatures, but treat them with respect at all times.

SETTING YOUR QUIVERTIP

Although how much tension you put into your quivertip is partly a matter of personal preference, there are a few ground rules which some anglers swear by.

1

A tightly tensioned tip suits fishing onto island slopes, where bites will show as unmissable drop-backs as the feeder is dislodged by a taking fish.

2

Slack lining is good at close range or when fish are very active in the upper layers of the water, giving a lot of unwanted line bites.

3

Considered by many to be the prefect tension, a slight curve in your quivertip allows detection of pull round bites, drop-backs plus slight trembles and nudges.

ANGLE OF ROD

As with tips, different anglers prefer to set their leger rods at different angles to the bank.

1

Pointing almost directly out does not allow much, if any, angle to be set in the tip. This makes bite detection tricky when fish are shy, and is best suited only to slack line legering.

2

With the rod set at a very wide angle to the rig, the angler's ability to set the hook with a sweep of the rod is severely limited. On the plus side, you can follow round further if the fish runs to the line clip.

3

A perfect compromise setting sees the rod set on a rest at an angle of around 45 degrees, giving plenty of room for striking and bending into fish, or following them on the clip.

Swimfeeders come in many shapes, styles and sizes but broadly speaking there are three main varieties - open-end, block-end and Method.

Each of these has several variations, which we'll examine in turn over the following pages to explain their prime uses on Commercial Stillwaters. But for now, we'll start the ball rolling with a look at the Block-End Feeder.

Also commonly known as Maggot Feeders, Block-enders get their name from the top and base caps which prevent bait from escaping on the cast. The top cap is removable, and is usually held in place for easy replacement by a link of hinged plastic or tensioned power gum.

> **"Commonly known as Maggot Feeders, Block-Enders get their name from the top and base caps which prevent bait from escaping on the cast"**

Traditional block-enders are attached to the line via a swivel at the top end. More recently, in-line versions have found a place in many Commercial Stillwater anglers' tackle boxes.

These feature a central hollow tube, through which the line is threaded before attaching a hook length via a swivel which is pulled back to sit semi-fixed within the tube. The upshot is a feeder which sits centrally rather than hanging off the line.

Fox's finned feeders feature four aerodynamic outer vanes which aid stability, distance and direction on the cast, similar to the flights on a dart. These fins also stop the feeder rolling in a current or if there are a lot of fish present. The range includes several different types and weight options of Block-enders.

Swivel feeders have a nose weighted base with five weight options – 0.5oz, 1oz, 1.5oz, 2oz and 3oz – and come in two sizes, medium and large. They have bait release holes in the sides and on the cap, with in-line versions in the same sizes and weights.

Rotary End feeders feature sculpted, weight-down side loadings plus a unique twisting cap which allows the release rate of your chosen feed to be varied from fast to slow, according to response. There are also side holes, and four size are available – small , medium, large and extra large – with weights between 0.25oz and 2oz.

Free Flow Rotary feeders have their line attachment swivel housed within a short extension arm at the top, on the same side as the weight. This helps to act as a kind of boom, preventing tangles on the cast.

Whichever model you choose, a good rule of thumb is: choose enough weight to cast the required distance, then choose the size of feeder appropriate for the amount of loose offerings you want to introduce.

Rotary End feeder showing fully closed (left) and fully opened hole options.

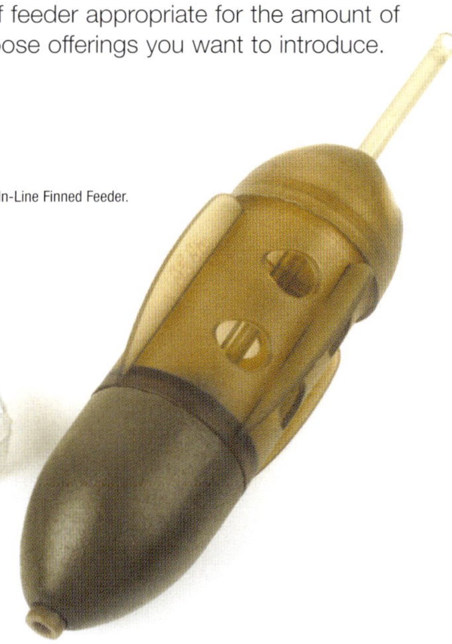

Long range In-Line Finned Feeder.

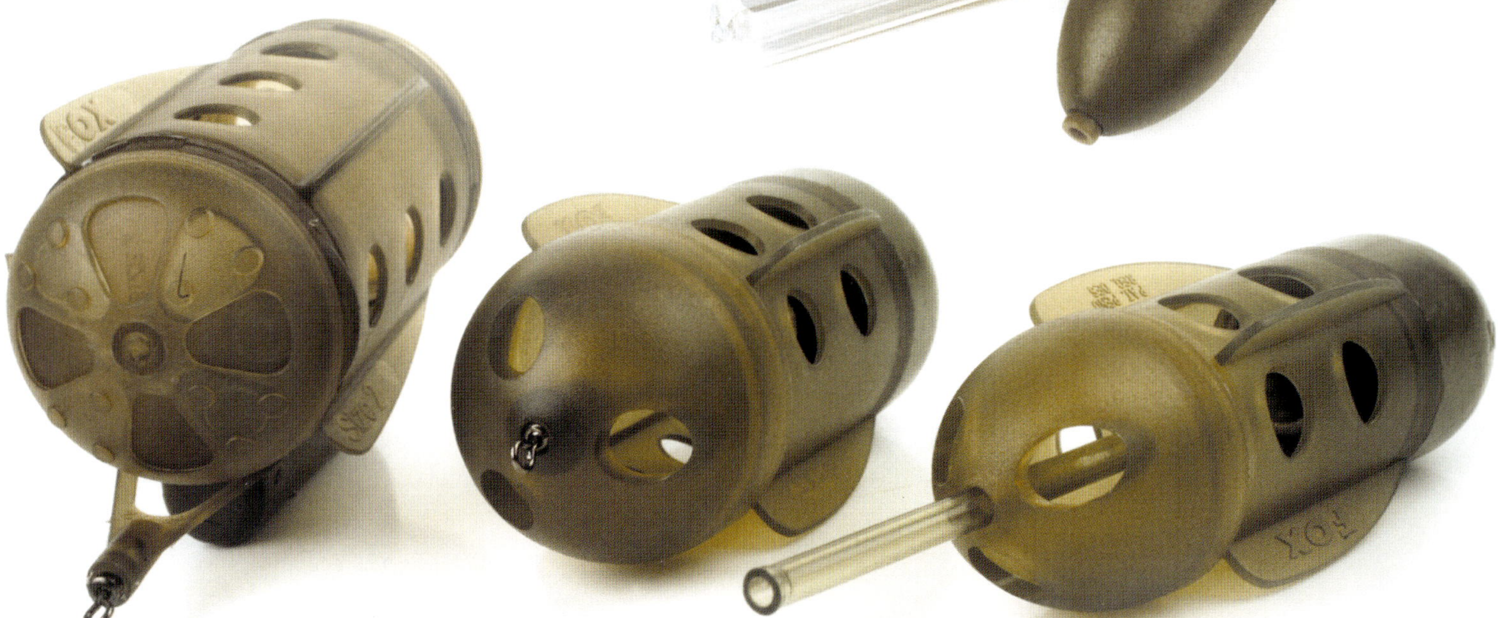

The three models of finned feeders shown above (left to right):
Rotary End feeder, Swivel Feeder and Inline Feeder.

THE INLINE FEEDER

Follow these four simple steps to rig up a safe, tangle-free and fish-friendly in-line feeder rig.

1

Thread your reel line through an in-line feeder's central tube then tie an appropriately sized swivel onto the end, using a reliable and strong knot such as the Grinner.

2

Wet the knot with some saliva then tighten down and trim back the tag end, before gently pulling the main line from above the feeder until the swivel sits within the tube with just its bottom eye showing.

3

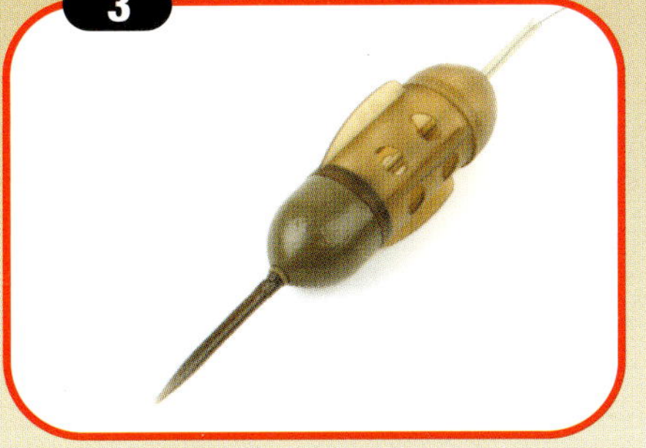

Tie your hook length then draw the end loop through a Kwik Change Sleeve before securing it to the swivel eye and pushing up the sleeve to enclose both.

4

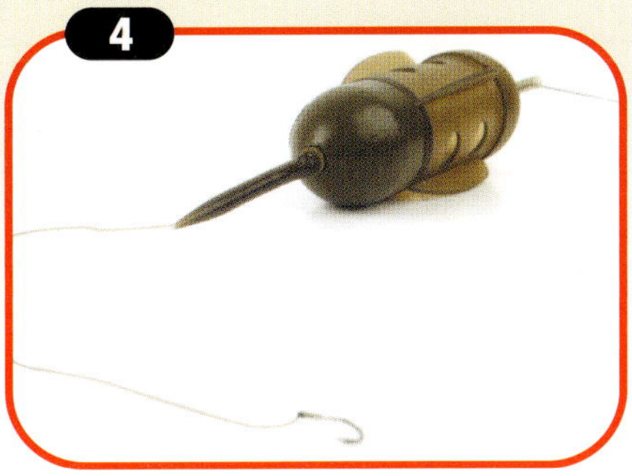

The result is a neat, safe and sound in-line end tackle arrangement which won't tangle on the cast. Bait your hook, fill the feeder with maggots or other particle-type baits and see for yourself!

Another form of feeder presentation is the Helicopter rig. Popular with the specimen carp fraternity for its ability to cast long distances without tangling, this involves trapping the hook length swivel between two semi-fixed beads immediately above the feeder. The 'helicopter' part of the name comes from the fact that the hook length rotates on the cast.

Theory and Tackle

Block-end feeders are well regarded by river anglers for species big and small, and the In-line versions are popular with specimen tench and bream hunters.
But where do they fit into the Commercial Stillwater scene?

The main answer is as an alternative to a feeder which relies on the use of groundbait to attract fish to your swim.

To qualify that statement, both of the other main types of feeder which we'll look at later – Method and Open-enders – are designed to feed groundbait.
The Block-ender isn't.

> **"Your choice of rod will depend on the distance you need to cast, the size of fish, the amount you want to feed and the time of year"**

The fact that block-enders are often termed 'Maggot Feeders' implies that their payload is live, wriggling maggots. Absolutely right in many cases – but their bait permutations certainly don't end with maggots as you'll soon see.

Quite a few Commercials impose groundbait bans or limits, and some still ban Method feeders outright. It's certainly well worth learning the various different block-end feeder approaches which we're about to show you for this reason alone.

And what's more, even where the other types are freely permitted, there are occasions when a block-ender will be the most effective of them all.

Tackle-wise, your choice of rod will depend on the distance you need to cast, the size of fish, the amount you want to feed and the time of year. It can be anything from a light bomb-type rod like the 11ft Envoy through to a beefy 13ft Carp Feeder.

Maggot feedering on Commercials is generally an autumn, winter and spring tactic, due to the fish being less active and more inclined to lay in deeper water and not move far to find their food in colder water.

But as always there are no hard and fast rules. When used with chopped worm and casters in the feeder, this method can be absolutely deadly for carp even in the height of summer.

HOOK LENGTH LOOPS

To keep your hook length pinned nice and tight to the lake bed in all aspects of feeder fishing and legering, it's wise to tie as small a loop as possible. Larger loops can cause the upper part of the hook length to arch upwards, with potentially adverse effects on bait presentation. Here's how Derek Willan achieves the perfect loop.

1

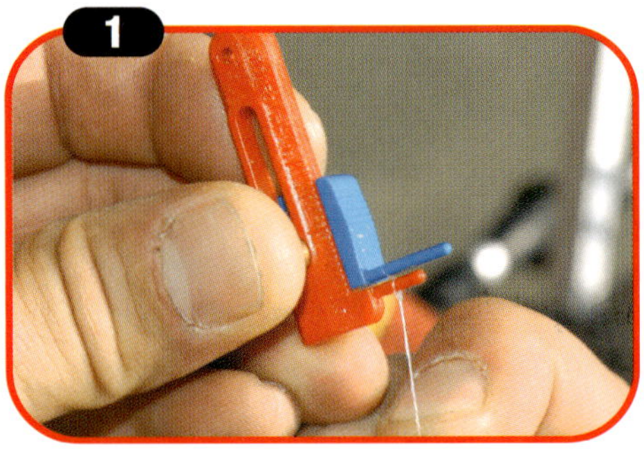

The Stonfo loop tyer has two upright pegs. The blue one slides forward to allow various loop sizes while the red one is fixed to the frame. It takes very little time to master the use of these, and it's time well spent.

2

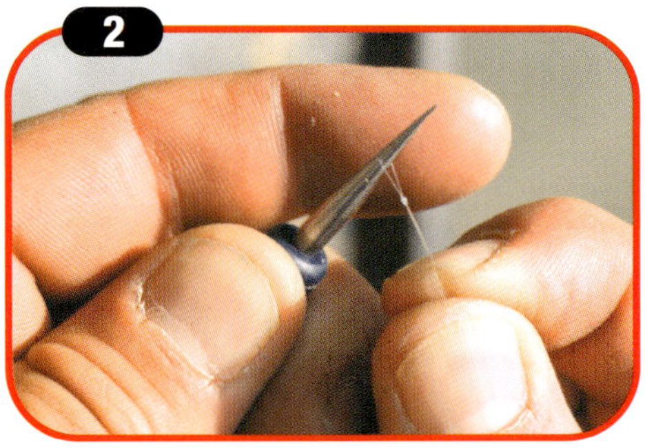

Release the formed knot from the loop tyer, wet with saliva then tighten down firmly using a knot picker's metal end to pull against.

3

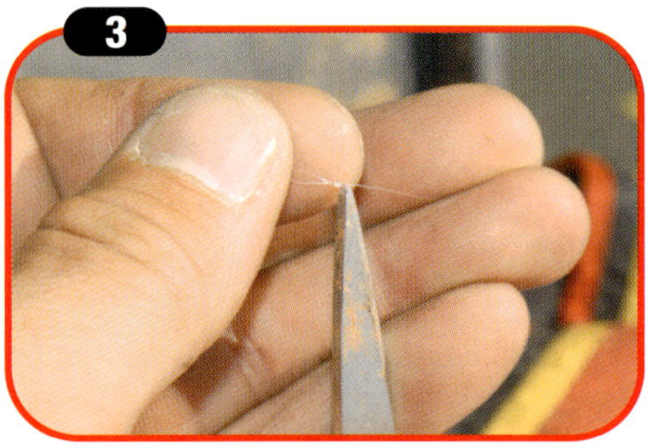

Trim the tag end down as tightly as possible using a quality pair of sharp bladed scissors. Attach loop to swivel and commence fishing in total confidence.

There are some subtle differences between using a block-end feeder to introduce 'live' baits such as maggots or pinkies to a swim, and using one to get 'inert' baits such as pellets, casters and chopped worm out there.

Using chopped worm and caster feed is one of Derek Willan's favourite ways to use a block-end feeder on Commercial Stillwaters.

Unlike bream fishing at longer ranges on natural lakes, this approach is often used at fairly close range, and seldom requires casting beyond around 20 metres. For this reason, plus the fact that it has such a forgiving action and never seems to lock up, Derek loves to use the 1 foot Fox Envoy Bomb rod.

Provided there's not too many carp in the 8lb-plus bracket, he is convinced this rod helps him catch more fish by virtue of the fact that it keeps on bending for a split second longer than stiffer models on a carp's first run.

That can buy the angler just enough time to allow them to release the line from the spool's clip, or to apply enough side strain

> **"Often used at close range and seldom requires casting more than 20 metres"**

to make the fish change direction, allowing line to be gained back onto the reel.

On the subject of reels, most match and pleasure anglers used to rely on backwinding to play their fish rather than setting the clutch to yield before break point is neared. This is mainly due to the fact that until the past few years, few affordable reels had smooth enough clutch systems to rely upon them regularly.

Although backwinding is still popular, and many who have grown up using it will never change, there's certainly been a swing towards greater use of the clutch. This is something which Derek in particular advises anglers to follow, especially if they're using light rods like the Envoy Bomb. He favours front drag reels which he feels are that often crucial bit more responsive than rear drag equivalents.

DEREK WILLAN'S CHOPPED WORM AND CASTER BLOCK-END APPROACH

Selective enough to prevent small silver fish taking the bait before larger species get a chance, the chop and caster block-ender with a worm-baited hook will catch just about everything with fins! You can experiment by adding micro pellets to the mix, which will boost your catch rate on some waters.

1

A good selection of swivels, beads and links are the feeder angler's best friend. They offer a choice of attachments for the feeder, the main line plus the hook length.

2

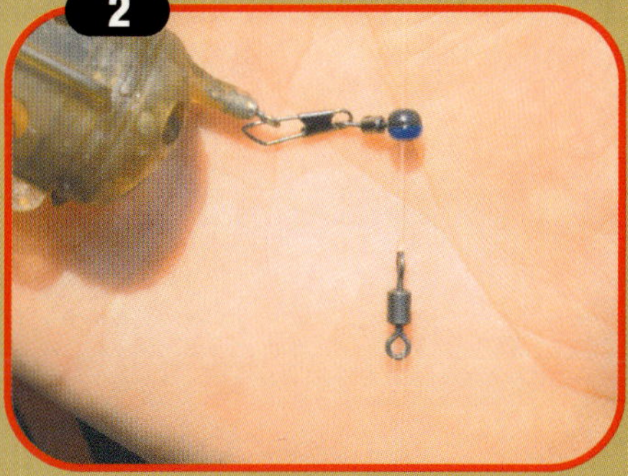

For his chopped worm feeder, Derek likes a link swivel with a smooth-running PTFE lined bead to attach his feeder to the main line. The bead acts as a buffer against the small swivel connecting main line to hook length.

3

A tucked half blood knot connects the main line to the swivel. Note that the hook length loop is left to rest against the top of the swivel's lower eye, spreading the pressure far better than by pulling it down to the bottom.

4

With chopped worm and caster being a far more inert bait than maggots, Derek likes to enlarge the release holes on one side of his Free Flow Rotary feeder by cutting a slot between them with a pair of scissors.

5

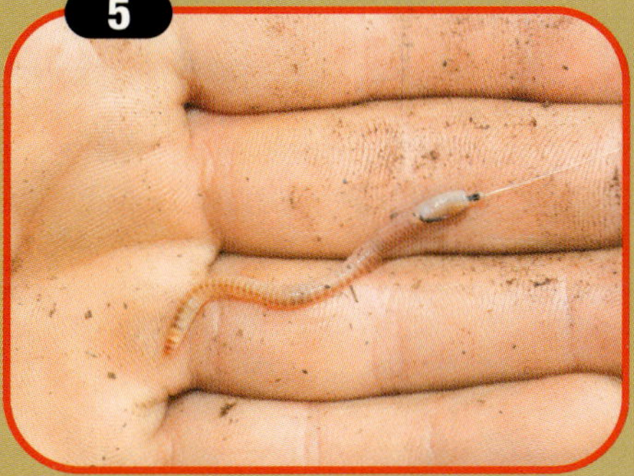

Half a dendrabaena worm on a barbless size 16 Series 2 hook to 20 inches of 0.16mm Micro Plus is the usual start bait. If Derek finds it slow going he'll drop to a size 18 and 0.14mm line. If he starts catching fast or gets broken up he'll step up the line.

6

Never pack your feeder too tightly with chopped worm and caster. A bit of space between the bait and the cap allows water to penetrate fast, forcing the feed out of the holes. With a payload like this, scoop the residue back into your bait box before closing down the feeder cap.

SETTING UP A MAGGOT FEEDER

A simple free-running set-up is both Derek Willan and Mark Pollard's favoured means of setting up a block-end feeder. Both like to use clip beads, which run smoothly on the line and help to buffer the feeder against the stop swivel connecting the main line to the hook length.

1

Attach a clip bead to the swivel in your feeder's top cap and thread the main line through. Generally speaking, you'll need lines in the 6-8lb range for summer and 3-5lb in winter.

2

Attach a small swivel to the end of the main line via a reliable knot such as the Grinner or Palomar. You can add a buffer bead for the swivel, but the bead clip is generally protective enough.

3

Loop on a hook length and you're ready to fish. For maggot feedering on Commercials, most anglers start with hook lengths of around 18 inches to two feet (rules permitting). But an ultra-short version can often score, while lengthening off to as much as five feet can sometimes tempt cautious fish.

POLLY'S COMMENT

Start on a small maggot feeder and work your way up in size if the response is good. Unlike groundbait, live maggots won't stay put on the bottom so there's no point trying to build up a bed.

There are times when you won't need to use a block-end feeder for anything more complicated than the task it was originally meant for - feeding maggots.

Maggots are a brilliant bait for carp, period. The only reason they are not used far more is the fact that many venues are choc-a-bloc with small nuisance silver fish.

Small rudd and roach in particular can render maggot feedering a no-no, simply because they pounce on a maggot-baited hook before any carp can get a look in. Even cramming three or four maggots on to the hook will not deter the greedy blighters. A pellet, however, generally will.

However, there are also waters where tiny fish are not an issue. If that's the case, you should consider using the enduring pulling power of maggots - plus the speed of hooking they bring - to your benefit.

One very important tip for maggot feedering is to never cram your feeder too full. In cold water especially, this may result in your bait not all emptying out where it's supposed to - in the area of your peg that you are casting to.

You are trying to create a relatively tight feeding zone which fish will be drawn to. But if you make this common mistake, you may well be doing the exact opposite. If the maggots do not all empty out before you wind in, the

> "Twitch your bait occasionally to induce bites by lifting the rod and turning the reel"

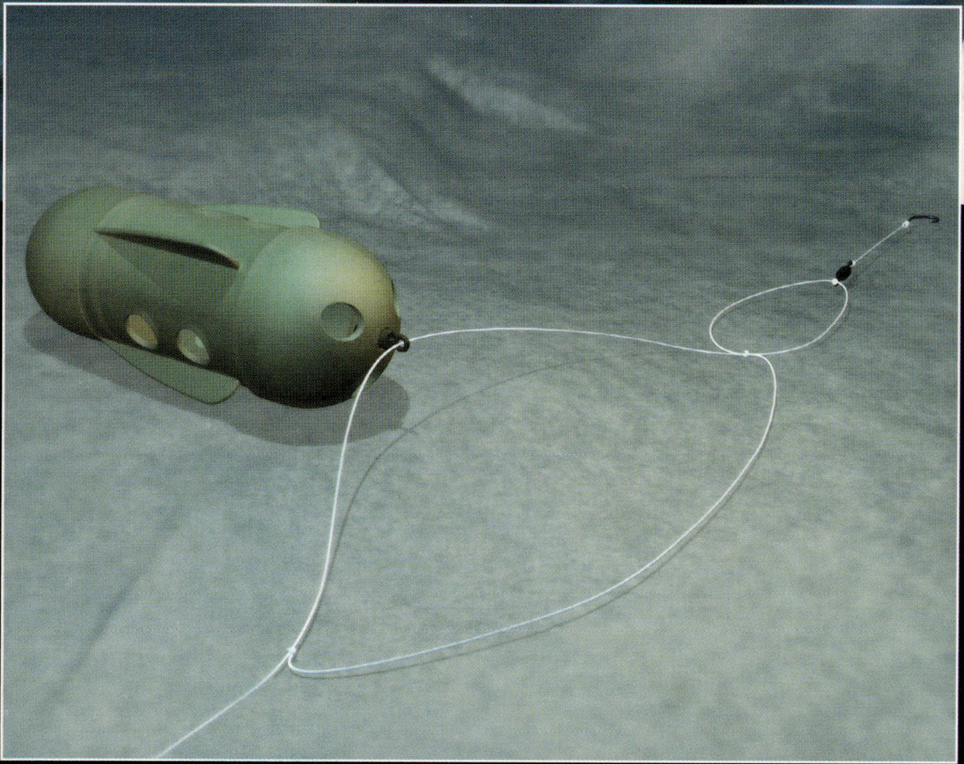

The running loop is another way to present a maggot feeder. Tangle-free and with good self-hooking properties, you should always check whether it's permitted at your venue as some consider it a fixed rig.

remaining ones are likely to be washed out in a straight line on the retrieve. This risks spreading the fish too far around the area.

In very cold water, maggots wriggle less and you may find that your feeder still isn't emptying even if you leave it out for long periods between casts. One solution is to cut longer slots between the existing holes.

Twitch your bait occasionally to induce bites by lifting the rod and turning the reel handle a couple of times.

One final tip is to try dusting your maggots with turmeric, a spicy orange powder used in Indian cooking. It de-greases the bait and helps keep it lively!

POLLY'S COMMENT

The shorter the line, the more chance there is that a carp will prick itself, as it feels resistance and bolts off whilst trying to eject the bait. And this is a big part of the Method's success.

Method feeders carry their payload of groundbait on the outside of a frame rather than inside a plastic tube or wire basket. They are generally fished with much shorter hook lengths than other types.

Put in such simple terms, the Method doesn't sound anything too special. But in reality it's hard to overstate the impact which its invention had on the fledgling Commercial Stillwater scene some 15 years ago.

The words 'revolution' or 'sensation' are often used without real justification in angling, but they are no mere hype when discussing the Method.

This tactic first emerged at Roy Marlow's Mallory Park Fisheries in Leicestershire, where carp had been stocked in the kind of numbers now considered normal (but back then a real novelty) since the early '80s. The angler who many older Mallory circuit regulars credit with its invention is Dave Hough, who is still active on the Leicestershire stillwater scene.

Certainly by the summer of 1994, when the Sky TV's first £25,000 winner-take-all Fish'O'Mania final was fished at Mallory, it was well established there. Worksop's Ian Turner used the Method to win that match, now in its 13th year and easily the most popular national Commercial Stillwater contest.

But across the rest of Britain, anglers opening the weeklies to check the result of that first Mania final were scratching their heads in unison when they saw photos of top stars netting fish with feeders still caked in groundbait!

Within weeks, that scene was being repeated at carp-stocked stillwaters across the country. The secret Method was well and truly out – and the effect was like lighting blue touch paper beside a keg of explosives.

If the floating pole created controversy, it was nothing compared to Method feeder fishing. A lot has changed between now and then, which we'll deal with in due course. But first, let's examine exactly why the Method is so effective.

Why is the Method so effective?

Early Method feeder rigs worked on two vital principles – creating a noise to announce the arrival of food to carp, then getting them to hook themselves as they engulf the baited hook.

The shorter the line, the more chance there is that a carp will prick itself as it feels resistance and bolts off whilst trying to eject the bait. And this is a big part of the Method's success.

Although there is no limit to how long a hook length you can use, it is almost always a short link of between three and six inches. And although you can let your baited hook dangle free beneath the loaded Method feeder, most anglers prefer to bury it just beneath the surface.

The Method was born out of the realisation that carp were attacking the feeders themselves much faster than the baited hook.

By shortening hook lengths and burying the hook bait inside sticky groundbait moulded around what were the only suitable feeders of the time – the Emstat frame – faster action was guaranteed. But fresh problems then arose.

Problems and solutions

Emstat feeders are shaped like a bomb, with a weight at the frame's fatter 'nose' end and a standard clip swivel for attachment to the line at the top. Rigging them to run freely on the line led to many fish not hooking themselves, or the angler striking and spooking a shoal rather than simply lifting the rod and bending into an already hooked fish.

Fixing it between two leger stops or shots led to unacceptable levels of hook length breakage on or shortly after the violent bites. A high proportion of Mallory Park's

Emstat frame feeder - Method pioneer

carp at the time were in the 4lb to 8lb range, with many already creeping into double-figures.

Enterprising anglers overcame the problem by drilling through the nose weight and passing a double-up length of pole elastic through, knotted firmly to the frame's top eye, to cushion the take then absorb a carp's lunges during the fight and netting. Instead of being rigged free-running, the swivel at the top of the feeder was now being tied directly to the end of the main line with pre-elasticated feeders being clipped on to this.

However, whilst safe and sound in expert hands, this arrangement ultimately held back the Method's development by resulting in it being branded as a fixed rig or, more emotively, a 'death rig'. Within a couple of years of the Method's first national exposure, it had been tried on most Commercial stillwaters and banned at probably 80-plus per cent of them!

Many fishery managers, with their valuable stock's welfare rightly concerning them, banned it before even seeing it. At other places, all it took was one or two inexperienced anglers who failed to balanced their reel line strength, elastic strength and hook length out properly, or who tried to cast Method feeders on woefully undergunned rods. The inevitable upshot was lines snapping above the feeder, which the fish was then left trailing around with the possible risk of the frame snagging up and tethering the fish.

Happily, awareness of the dangers has been raised. Tackle is better, knowledge more widely available. Times have changed – and so have many of the original ideas on what constitutes the perfect Method feeder and Method groundbait. Turn the page and see the modern approach.

METHOD THEORY EXPLAINED

1. The stiff groundbait mix ensures the feed is still intact when the Method feeder hits bottom.

2. The groundbait will dissolve slowly, but the fish speed up this process by attacking the groundbait. The big ball of feed drives the fish into a frenzy and they loose their natural caution.

3. In the feeding freny, the carp suck up everything, hook bait and all. The fish feels the hook and bolts. Game on!

Modern Method Tactics

As the initial hysteria and fears about the Method being a potential fish-killer have gradually subsided, more and more fisheries have removed or relaxed their bans as a result of the tremendous developments in modern tackle, rigs and feeds.

Rods and reels have improved tremendously to match the demands of regular carp hauling, with specific models designed for casting heavy method feeders.

But perhaps most important of all, it is changes at the business end of the rig which have helped to make the Method a safer and highly effective way of fishing – without any risk of accidentally teathering or harming our quarry.

> **"In-line feeders are now the most commonly used type for Method fishing"**

A typical Method hook length today, say Fox Micro Plus in 0.20mm diameter, has a breaking strain of 8lb 9oz, ample stretch and unlikely to break. It is limp enough to allow the hook to be sucked up into the mouth along with particles of groundbait.

Suitable hooks for the job were also virtually non-existent in the mid nineties. These days, purpose made ranges with wide gapes and beaked points like the Series 2 in its many guises are perfectly suited to presenting either hair-rigged or traditionally hooked baits for big hard fighting fish. They won't bend under pressure, they stay sharp and there's ample eyed or spade end barbless size and wire strength options to suit fishery rules.

All this leads us to the design of the actual feeders, plus how it's rigged...

Different feeder choices

The specimen carp scene has taught us much about the pursuit of smaller carp on Commercial stillwaters in many ways, including baits and flavours. And the fish-safety-first ethos which is all-important in the big fish world has also passed into the everyday thinking of match and pleasure anglers.

In-line feeders are now the most commonly used type for Method fishing. The term 'in-line' means the end of your reel line passes through either the centre or the base of the feeder via an integral tube.

At the upper end of all Fox In-Line models, a tapered Tail Rubber is fitted over the tube to cushion the line and prevent unwanted wobble on the cast. At the lower end, the line is tied to a swivel which is then pulled back to sit semi-fixed within an enlarged bore end section.

The hook length is tied or looped to this swivel's other eye, creating a self-hooking rig - yet one from which the fish can easily pull the swivel free should the main line break above the feeder or snag up.

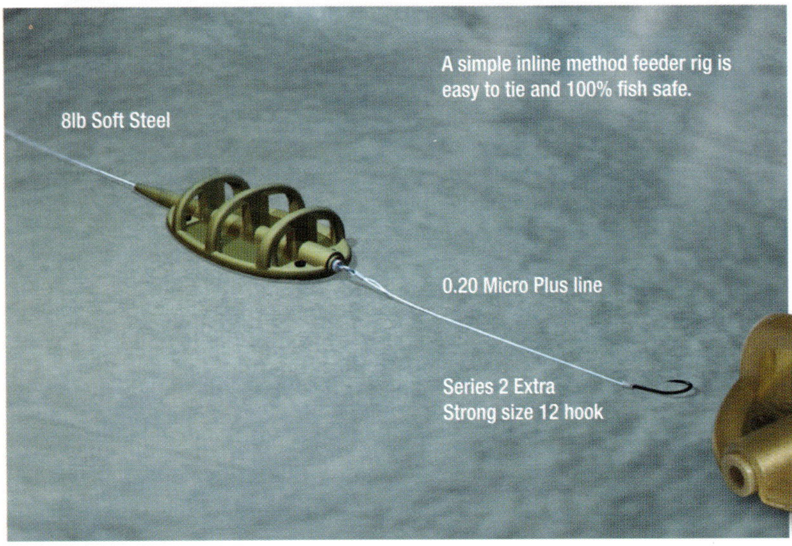

A simple inline method feeder rig is easy to tie and 100% fish safe.

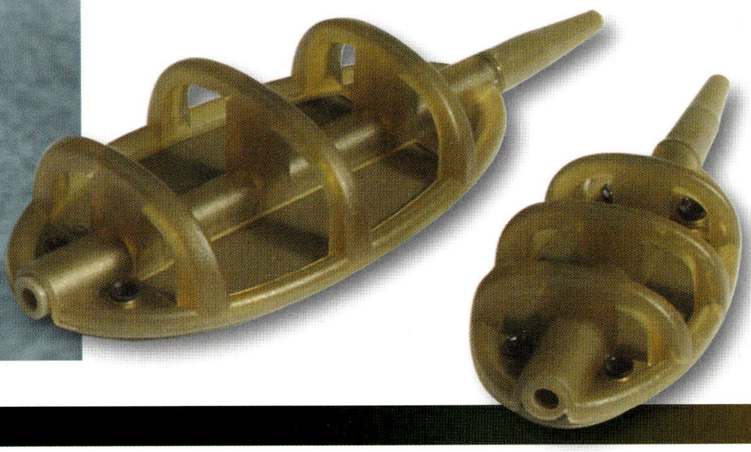

When larger amounts of feed are required, a Compact Carp Feeder is the best choice. These feature a weight surrounding the lower end of the tube within the triple-finned outer frame but are also fished in-line and are completely fish-friendly. Two fins are offset to ensure the bait always lands uppermost, when buried. They come in 1oz and 1.5oz options, with larger and heavier versions in the specimen range.

Most popular these days are in-line feeders of the Flat Bed variety. With three plastic arches to mould your groundbait over and around, they have a flat base weight that ensures they always land with your buried hook bait uppermost. Fox Match Flat Bed feeders come in two sizes – large or small – each with 20 or 28 gram base weights.

Finally, there is still a place for elasticated feeders provided they are used sensibly and within venue rules. Fox's Elasticated Flat Beds come in the same two size/weight options as in-line versions, with a length of No.12 solid elastic through a tube attached to the inner base. The hook length is tied to a base ring, while a loop in the plastic top stem lets you clip the feeder onto a swivel.

Many top anglers insist that provided a barbless hook is used, fish are easily able to shed an elasticated feeder in the event of a main line breakage above the rig. Modern tackle plus the fact that Commercial Method feedering no longer requires huge, heavy groundbait loads, makes crack-offs above the feeder a highly unlikely occurance anyway.

Groundbait then and now

In its infancy, Method groundbait earned the nicknames 'dog-muck' (that's a polite version) and 'the coconut'. A loaded 'old school' Emstat Method feeder weighed up to 4oz, with all manner of particles and hook bait freebies added to a groundbait mix designed to stay intact for long periods after each cast.

But aside from the specimen carp scene, where long waits are par for the course, this approach is the kiss of death on Commercials these days.

Now, the aim is to produce a fine, damp but never stodgy Method mix. Mixing it the evening before allows time for every single crumb to take on water. Riddling removes fish-filling lumps and puts air back in.The aim is to cast out a streamlined groundbait parcel which will dissolve into a fine yet potent pile of attraction within a minute of touching bottom.

MIXED TO PERFECTION

As well as different groundbaits, there's a variety of hook baits - from directly hooked to hair rigged within a bait band - plus presentations involving burying your hook bait within the feeder mix, or leaving it exposed outside.

1

THE GROUNDBAIT
Damp, fine groundbait - perhaps with a few larger particles in summer but riddled off for cooler weather - is squeezed around a Flat Bed feeder. Mark Pollard and Derek Willan both like Van den Eynde Method mix, which contains a few large pieces of flaked maize along with a variety of smaller particles.

2

THE CORE
How hard you squeeze depends on depth, expected catch rate and sheer experience. But bear in mind that this inner core should still dissolve on the spot rather than remain intact or form a trail back towards the angler upon retrieval.

3

THE HOOK BAIT
In winter, hair-rigged sweetcorn or dead maggots on the hook are often best. Popular summer options include hair-rigged punched meat or mini boilies, or hair rigged banded expander dry pellet (LEFT). Derek likes this latter option as it will pop-up out of the feeder as the groundbait dissolves, often causing a carp to grab at it. As the pellet takes on water it grips the band tightly and won't come off.

4

THE CAP
With a lighter squeeze than before, add a final layer of groundbait to either obscure the baited hook or – Derek Willan's favourite – trap around half the hook length so that the expander-baited hair rig pops up above it by an inch upon landing.
Cast as per usual, on a clipped up reel with a directional marker on the far bank.

Open-end feeders, also commonly known as groundbait or crumb feeders, have no end caps. They rely upon plugs of groundbait to hold their contents in during the cast and descent to the lake bed.

Free Flow Mesh Open End Finned Feeder

Free Flow Solid Finned Feeder

Free Flow Interchangeable Weights

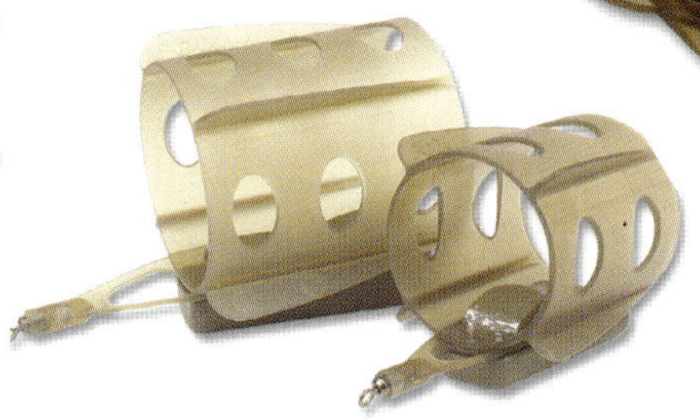

Free Flow Open End Finned Feeders

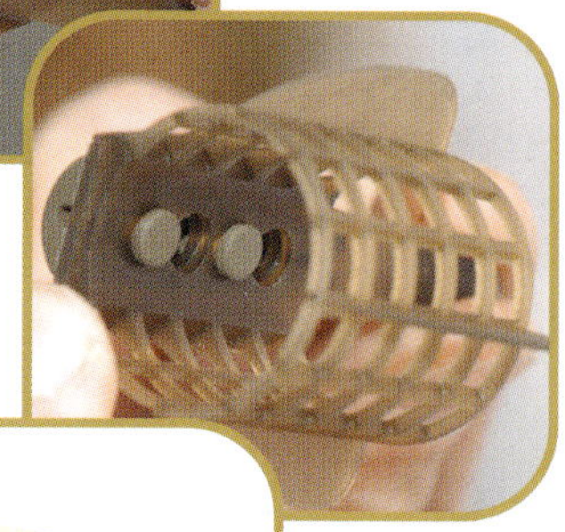

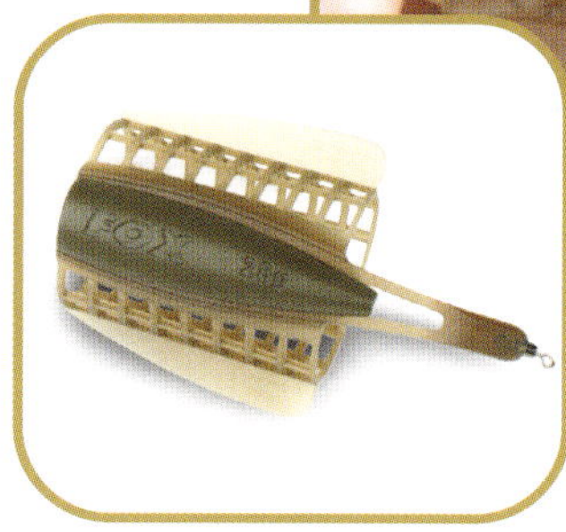

Removing and adding weights is simple thanks to Fox's key lock system

As with Block-enders, they come in many different sizes and weights, and have three main sub-categories; the basic plastic open-ender with side holes, the same without any side holes, plus the plastic or metal cage type which features a basket-like mesh.

The basic type is generally favoured in swims over six feet deep, due to its greater ability to hold the contents inside on the descent. Fox Match's free-flow open enders feature aerodynamic fins for improved casting and have a protruding plastic link housing a swivel to thread your main line through.

They come in four sizes, with weights from 0.5oz to 2oz, and are excellent in situations where you want to introduce large quantities of chopped worm and casters.

Fox's Free Flow Solid Finned Feeders are also good for deeper venues or for introducing large amounts of live, wriggling baits trapped between two end plugs of groundbait. The other big advantage of having no holes in the side is that they tend to rise faster on the retrieve, making them an excellent choice in snaggy swims.

With the same link and captivated swivels, they have excellent anti-tangle properties. And special interchangeable weights of 14, 21, 28, 42 and 56 grams are available to make the three-strong range (small, medium and large) incredibly versatile.

Fox don't produce metal cage feeders, but their Free Flow Mesh Finned Feeders are an even tougher and equally effective alternative when it comes to ensuring a very fast release of bait in shallower swims.

Also available in small, medium and large sizes, they benefit from the same interchangeable weight system as the Solid variety. These weights have a tapered weight-forward profile, and slot securely into the feeder frame's base via a pair of protruding pegs with circular discs. Simply place these discs over the larger holes in the base then push forward into the adjacent slots. They come in packs of three, four or five, depending on size.

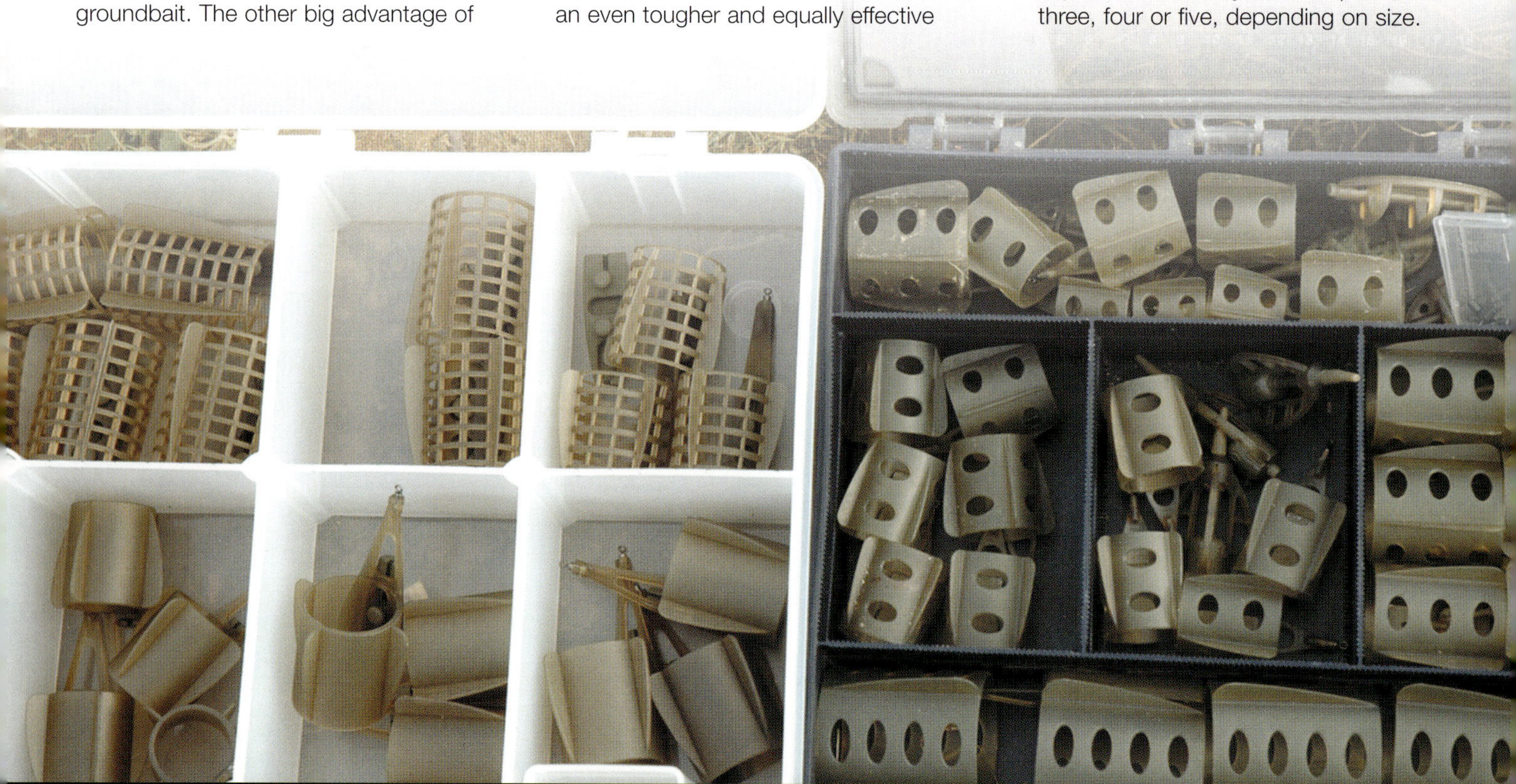

Commercial applications

On Commercial stillwaters where the use of Method feeders are permitted, open-enders have a relatively limited role.

But on venues where Method is banned or a minimum hook length rule – typically 12 inches – exists, they are essential for any groundbait approach, plus the Pellet feeder or Stickymag feeder.

The latter two are attacking summer methods, used solely with cage/mesh feeders. Preparation of both baits has already been covered, so it's simply a matter of following these procedures.

Obviously, in the case of pellets, they need to be dampened expander types rather than dry hard pellets which would fall out on the cast unless the feeder's ends are plugged with groundbait.

On Method-banned waters, carp, F1s and crucians can be targeted on a groundbait and pellet feeder combination. During summer the general rule of thumb is to use as short a hook length as the rules allow. As the water cools down with autumn's onset, lengthen your tail to around twice the length or perhaps a bit more.

Attach the feeder's swivel to a sliding link bead, and err on the side of a softer-tipped rod such as the Envoy Carp Multi Feeder in 11 foot mode, or the 11ft Envoy Bomb.

For reel line, 6lb Illusion fluorocarbon is Derek Willan's choice due to the fact that it sinks faster than standard mono and thus avoids a big bow forming in the surface drift. Even with Illusion, you'll help get

"On Method-banned waters, target carp, F1s and crucians on groundbait and pellet"

everything down nice and quickly if you strike your line under immediately after casting, as explained in the float chapter and this chapter's line clip section.

A small groundbait feeder can be the ideal way to kick-start a winter peg, but bites may not keep coming after an initial flurry of activity. If this happens, it's time to consider switching to a Bomb approach. More about that - the original form of legering - next.

OPEN END FEEDER

There's no faster or more effective way of introducing large amounts of attractor baits such as pellets, casters and hemp than with an open-end feeder plugged with a fishmeal-style carp groundbait. Ignore the method at your peril, as it can outfish even the Method on the right day.

1

The perfect size feeder for a groundbait and pellet approach in the colder months.

2

Scoop the feeder through a tub of dampened pellets.

3

Plug both ends with a bit of fine groundbait to hold the pellets in place.

4

A typical winter set up, with a 30 inch hook length and single pellet-baited size 18 Series 2 hook to 0.12mm Micro Plus.

Braid for distance

In the era before Commercials became the nation's No.1 choice for Stillwater fishing, open-end feeder fishing on lakes was largely associated with catching bream.

Much of the development of the different types of open-end feeder grew up around bream fishing, with anglers either making their own solid no-hole feeders or wrapping electrician's tape around the limited number of production models. Likewise cage feeders, which first appeared in the mid-80s and boosted catches in a big way on shallower venues.

The advent of affordable, reliable, sinking braided main lines was a huge boon to stillwater bream anglers. Being far thinner than equivalent strength monos, with far less stretch, its advantages in terms of distance casting in tricky winds plus vastly improved bite indication ensured a great leap forward.

The downside of braid was quickly apparent. That lack of stretch was prone to causing cause hook pulls when a lively bream was getting close to netting range. The solution came in the use of a monofilament shock leader to cushion the lunges of a hooked fish at close quarters.

Braided lines are banned at probably 75 per cent of Commercial fisheries. But where permitted, Tip expert Derek Willan advises you to follow his '40 yard rule'. If you need to cast beyond 40 yards, choose braid. If less, mono is a better option.

Some Commercials still contain big shoals of bream which, on the right day, can produce excellent sport to a long range groundbait feeder approach. There's also some designated 'silver fish' lakes, packed with bream, chub, barbel, tench and crucians, which will also respond to an open-end feeder approach.

In cases like this, if fishery rules permit its use then give braid a try. But be sure to include a mono shock leader of two rod lengths. To attach his shock leader, Derek simply ties a small loop in the end of his braid, then attaches the mono via a half blood knot. Ensure the tag end is trimmed as close as possible to avoid it catching on your rod rings when you cast. Being supple, the braid loop will lie nice and flat on the spool unlike mono which would tend to spring up.

Another option for attaching a leader is the Mahin knot, instructions for the tying of which are shown on the right hand page.

PATERNOSTER SET-UP

Although free running feeders are required by the rules of many commercials, a paternoster is undoubtedly a more sensitive rig for shy biting species such as bream and other silver fish. Here's how Derek Willan sets the rig up.

1

Tie a loop of approximately 6 inches long (thus requiring 12 inches of line) at the end of your main line.

2

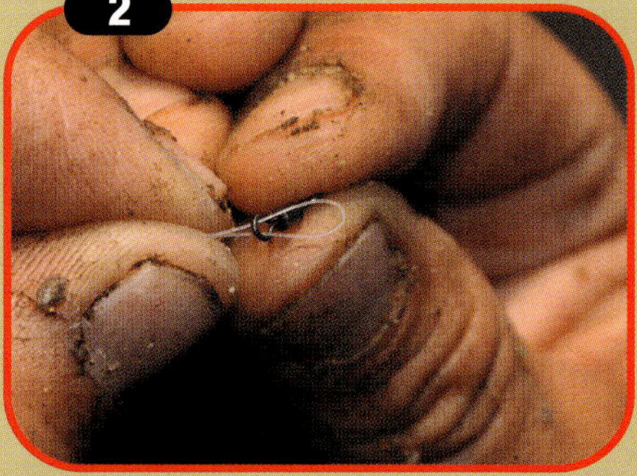

Pass the end of this loop through the snap-link swivel's eye then pass the whole snap-link swivel through this loop.

3

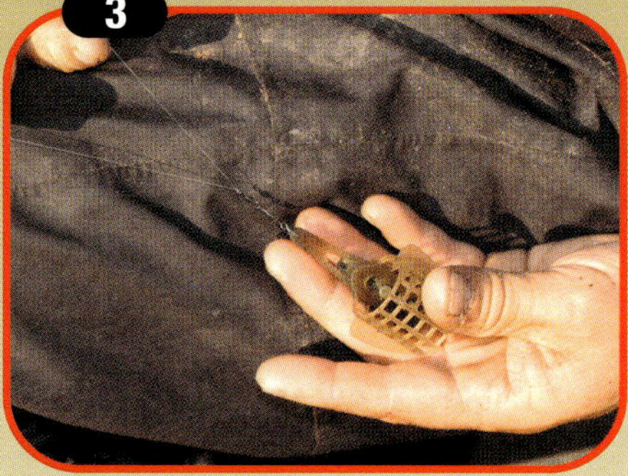

Clip your chosen feeder onto the snap-link swivel.

4

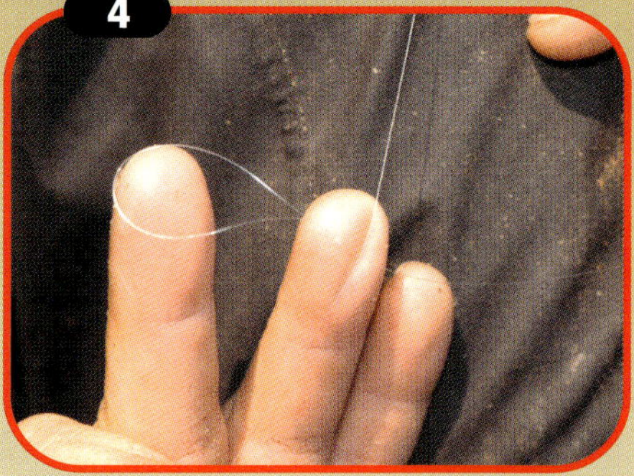

Tie a large loop at the top of your hook length and place this beneath your main line above the feeder attachment loop.

5

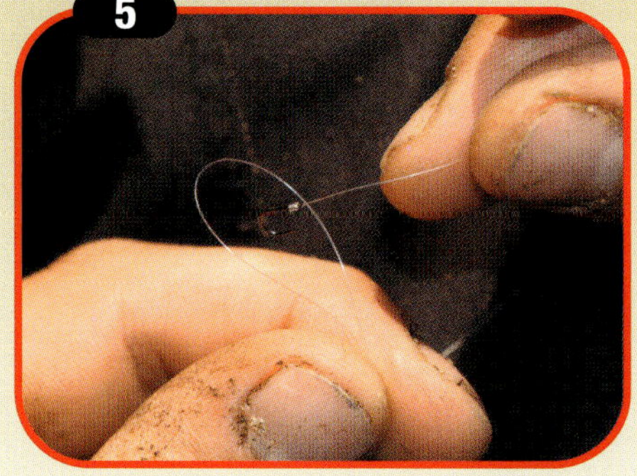

Pass your hook through this loop.

6

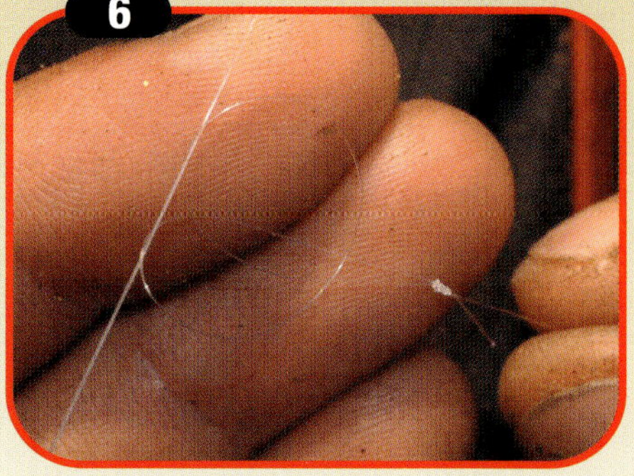

Straighten out the hook length, and the soon-to-be-completed knot should look like this.

7

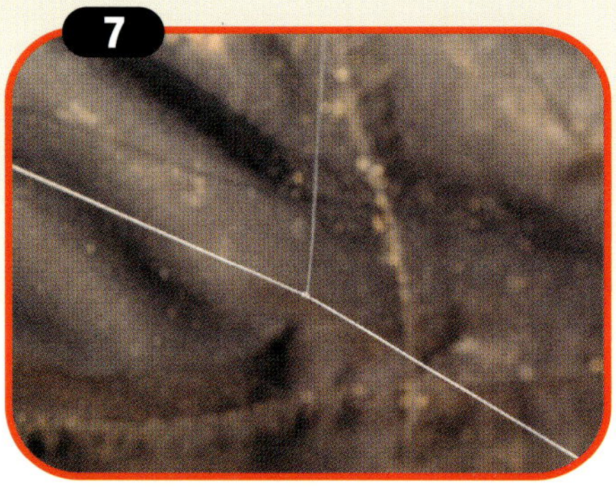

Pull tight under steady pressure then slide the knot down to butt up neatly against the top knot of the feeder loop.

8

When targeting bream and other silver fish, fine groundbaits are best. Derek Willan rates a mix of Van den Eynde Marine Green plus the old classic Supercup.

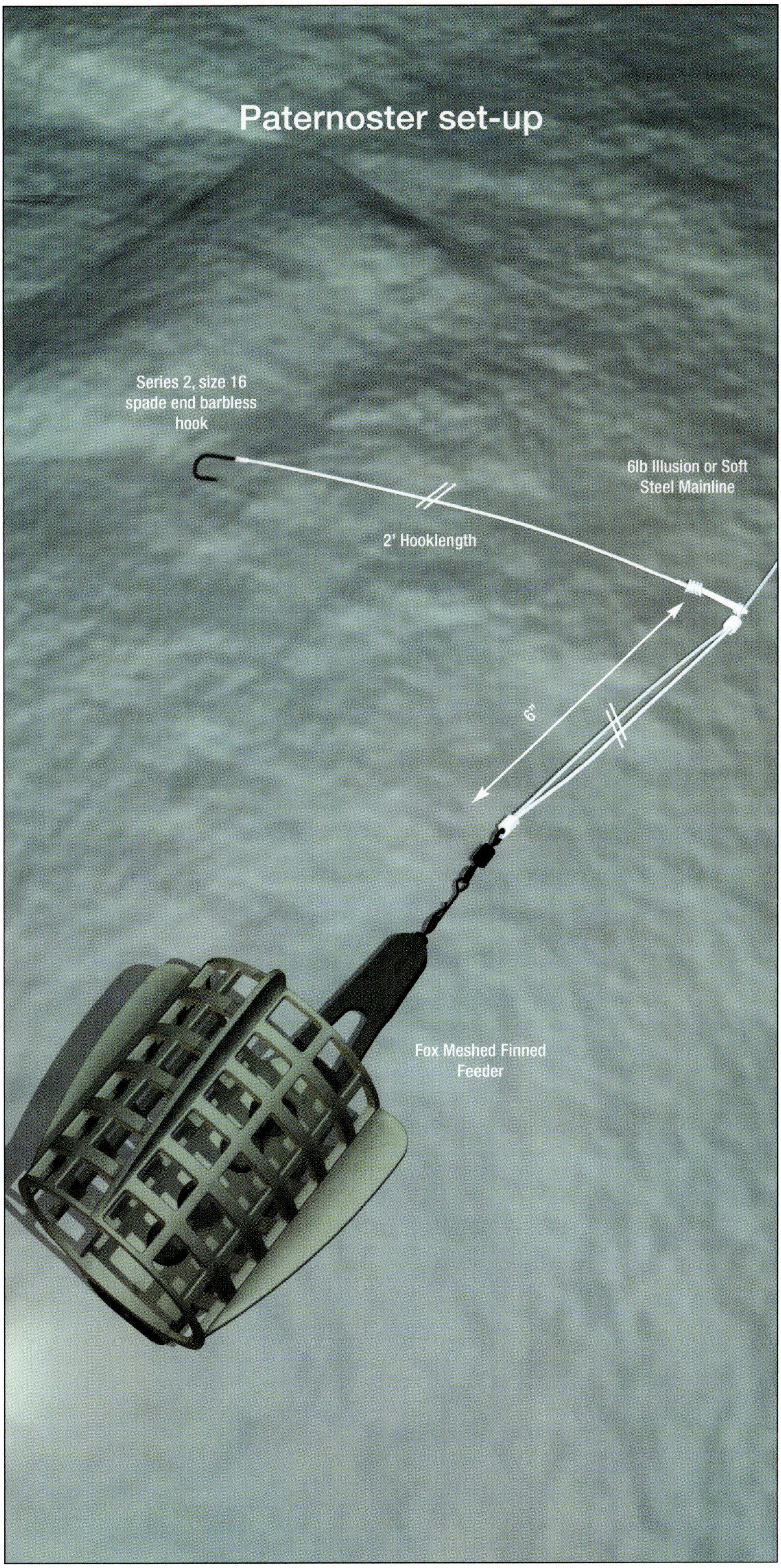

"A knot well worth learning for joining a mono leader to braided main line"

MAHIN KNOT

The Mahin Knot is an excellent knot for joining a leader to the mainline.

1

Tie a simple overhand knot in the mainline and thread the leader material through it.

2

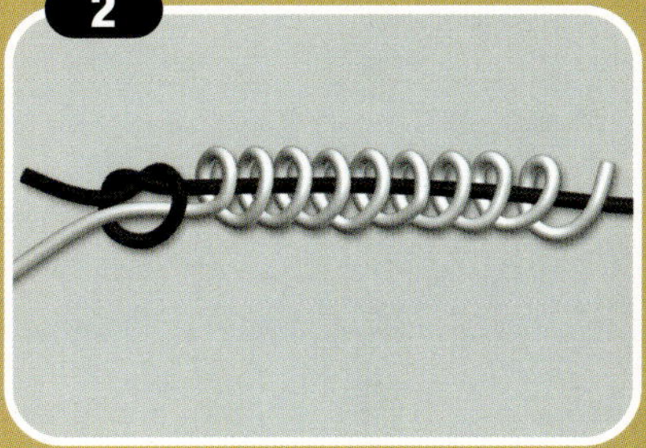

Wrap the leader around the leader 10 times working away from the overhand knot.

3

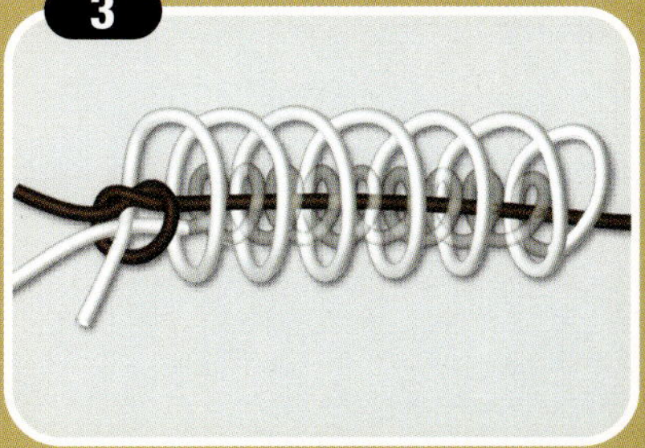

Form another eight loops over the top of the previous ones then pass the tag end back through the loop in the main line.

4

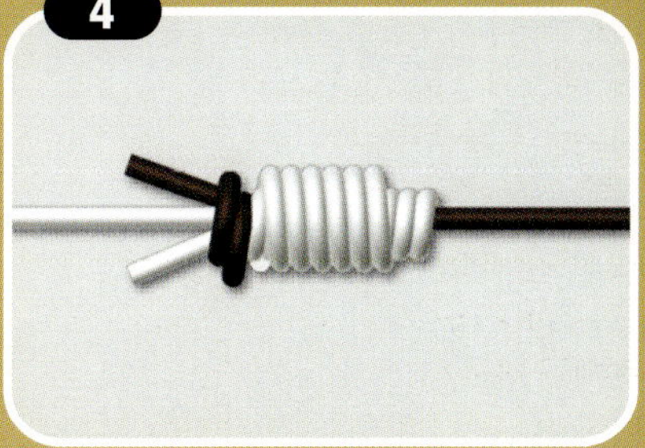

Moisten the knot with saliva as you pull it tight. The finished knot should be neat and compact.

As with its more traditional settings – rivers, canals, drains and natural stillwaters – bomb fishing on Commercials generally involves a greater degree of finesse in tackle terms than any other of the Tip approaches previously covered. But the fact that hard fighting carp and fine tackle don't normally mix successfully tends to confine bomb fishing to winter, when the fish are less inclined to expend energy on a prolonged battle. Surprisingly large carp - well in double-figures - can then be landed.

There are notable exceptions to this 'winter-only' bomb rule of thumb, such as casting out a large bread bait on a long tail and large hook to intercept cruising carp at long range in spring and summer. This tactic is especially popular at waters on the South Yorkshire circuit, where an entire slice of bread (known as a cigar) is sometimes rolled and folded up then cast out until a greedy

Fishing The Bomb

Even on fish-packed Commercial stillwaters, there are times when a legering approach using a good old fashioned bomb is superior to any kind of swimfeeder. For instance, when things are cold and you don't need want to introduce lots of feed or if you want to cast round your peg to search out feeding fish and don't want to spread lots of bait around.

In fact, during the winter, if you are unsure how many fish are going to be caught during a session it is always worth starting on the bomb to see how the fish respond, rather than introduce lots of feed via a swim feeder and over feeding the fish. Once bait has gone in, you can't take it out. However, if you start catching straight away you can unclip the bomb and switch to a feeder in a matter of seconds.

POLLY'S COMMENT

If you know you'll need to spend ages plumbing around with float or pole rigs, thread up your tip rods the previous night then take them along in Rod Sleeves with padded reel sections to save time.

carp hoovers it up and bends the tip right round.

So in this concluding part of the Tip chapter, we'll look at the undisputed No.1 way to fish the bomb on Commercials – as a winter 'scratching' method.

Don't for one minute think that 'scratching' means catching only a few small fish which won't justify the effort of leaving a warm bed to go fishing on a chilly, damp and windy day. Even a dozen fish for perhaps 20lb on light, balanced, sporting tackle can give you a session every bit as enjoyable as a summer 'ton-up'. Read on if you're not scared of a bit of cold…

To Feed Or Not?

Winter is the time when fish of all species, being cold blooded creatures whose body temperature dips along with that of the water they swim in, when you really need to think long and hard about whether you should feed them anything other than the bait on your hook!

The prime times to consider a bomb and single hook bait approach instead of even the smallest maggot feeder or mini-method cast on a 'little and seldom' basis are:

• Straight after the first frosts of the autumn or winter.

• Whenever a sudden downpour adds an influx of cold rainwater to the lake, in all but high summer.

• Any winter session where the previous night's temperatures were significantly colder than the preceding few days.

However, Commercial Stillwater fish depend upon anglers' bait to form a large percentage of their diet, so there are times even in winter when you should at least consider introducing some feed either via a small feeder or catapult. Such as:

• When the air and water temperature has been stable for a period of several days, even if nights have regularly been sub-zero. Fish adjust to conditions and will need to eat at some point.

• When winter sun has been shining for a few hours, consider feeding a bit of bait into the shallowest part of your swim as this is the place that will warm up quickest.

• By introducing a small bed of bait via a couple of casts with a feeder into one tight area of your swim, thus giving yourself an alternative option to cast over from time to time.

Carry a variety of leger weights. Flattened sides help them stay put on steep underwater bars and slopes.

Mark's hair-rigged corn set-up used with a straight lead.

Winter Bomb Scenario

The pleasure of playing a decent sized fish on light yet adequate winter bomb tackle has to be experienced to be appreciated.

That said, for match anglers it's not just about enjoying the fight. The desire to win means the most effective tackle and tactics must be chosen, and make no mistake: the bomb can be a match-winner in the right circumstances.

To demonstrate the technique, we'll go 'in session' with Mark Pollard on a cold, bright January day at Browning Tingrith's Fringe Pool.

Although this water contains plenty of carp which run well into double-figures, Mark knows they are unlikely to feed in such conditions. There's been an erratic run of night frosts - some very sharp indeed - interspersed with bright clear days and a mixture of north-westerly and easterly winds over the past week. However, the past two days have seen night temperatures just above freezing and there's no ice on the lake. Encouraging conditions in Mark's opinion.

Fringe Pool also holds a large head of silver fish – mainly roach and rudd – but targeting these on pole tackle with maggot baits is more likely to bring a run of 2oz stamp fish instead of the 4 to 12oz sample needed to build a decent weight.

Instead, Mark has in his sights the pool's large head of brown goldfish and crucians – similar to F1 crucian/common hybrids in their general willingness to feed in cold weather. With these fish averaging between 1-2lb, it won't take too many to build a satisfying weight.

Select the finest tip you can when fishing the bomb.

Fishing a peg midway along the M1 motorway bank, Mark intends to cast around 20 metres into 5/6ft of water, and knows from experience that there's a soft layer of silt above a hard clay bottom. Even in winter, tell-tale bubbles often surface as fish nose around for food.

Normally, Mark would opt to use an 11 Envoy Bomb Rod for the winter bomb. But the signs of activity suggest he may catch fast enough to justify swapping to an open-end feeder and putting down some groundbait later in the session, so he opts for an Envoy Multi Feeder in its shortest 11ft mode, with the 22 inch glass tip – the second finest of the six available - fitted.

Reel is a rear drag Fox prototype loaded with reliable sinking 4lb mono. A beaded

Play bomb-hooked fish slow and steady, keeping the rod low to the water.

POLLY'S COMMENT

Be careful when positioning your bomb rod. Look out for overhanging trees and bushes that may impede casting or the rod once placed in the rest.

Concentrate hard and react fast to bites. Note the very stable Pole Rest which cradles the bomb rod butt.

A colourful 20lb-plus bag of goldfish and crucians such as this will brighten up any winter's day when larger carp may not have fed.

link swivel is fitted to take a 1/4 oz Fox Ledger Weight. These flat sided bombs have an enclosed swivel with top eye attachment, plus twin flattened sides to prevent rolling on sloping lake beds.

Of the nine weights available (1/8oz to 2oz), Mark's chosen the second smallest. This is because he's not casting far, plus he's chosen a fine quivertip that will adopt a nice bend without dislodging the bomb.

The reel line terminates in a swivel with a rubber buffer bead. A 2ft hook length of 0.10mm (2lb 9oz) Micro Plus with a size 20 Series 2 Fine Wire barbless spade end hook completes the rig. He can now chop and change between corn, double and single maggot and even pellet hook baits. If the response is slow he'll change down to a size 22 hook.

But if it's more positive than expected, a change up to 0.12mm (3lb 6oz) hook length will allow him to play fish in a bit faster. If pellet or corn is the going bait, a size 18 may even be required.

As the session unfolds, Mark soon realises no drastic changes will be needed. Bites are few and far between, but when they come they are positive pulls on the quivertip. Not the big wrap-arounds that summer carp give, but still hittable bites in most cases. However, you need to concentrate hard and try to keep your hand poised either on or just above the reel fixings for a fast strike.

As with bigger fare, he plays the crucians with his rod low, winding them back slow and steady. Never try to rush when you're on a small hook, as this is nearly always self defeating.

On the day, hair-rigged corn takes most fish but a couple fall to soft pellet and, later in the session, single red maggot brings three fish in four casts. Double maggot went untouched.

All this shows the need to ring the changes with a winter bomb approach – and the eventual 20lb-plus bag proves the value of the tactic!

Acknowledgements

Fox Match would like to thank the following for their kind permission and co-operation in allowing access for photography during the compilation of this book.

Alders Farm, Great Brickhill, Bucks.
Tel: **01525 261713** or visit **www.aldersfarm.com**

Brookside Fishery, Stretton, nr Warrington, Cheshire.
Tel: Mike Timmis on **01925 730893.**

Browning Cudmore Supreme Angling Centre, Whitmore, Staffs.
Tel: 01782 680919 or **07756 857137**
or visit **www.browningcudmorefisheries.com**

Browning Tingrith Fishery, Bedfordshire.
Tel: Ann Freeman on **01527 714012**
or visit **www.tingrithfishery.co.uk**

Chestnut Pool, Langford, Bedfordshire.
Tel: Pete and Jane Wilson on **01462 701865**
or visit **www.chestnutpool.co.uk**

Tunnel Barn Farm, Shrewley, Warks.
Tel: Mike Hamlington on **01926 842975** or Pete Rice and Graham Young in the on-site tackle shop on **01926 842188.**

Waterbeach AC (Atkins Water and Magpie Lake), Cambs.
Tel: 01223 861978.

Index

L

M

N

O

P